Web Stalkers
Protect yourself from Internet Criminals & Psychopaths

911 Series

Stephen Andert
Donald K. Burleson

RAMPANT
TECHPRESS

This book is dedicated to my wife Deanna whose love and support made this book possible.

-Stephen Andert

My portion of this book is dedicated to my wife Janet for her loving support and understanding.

-Donald K Burleson

Web Stalkers
Protect yourself from Internet Criminals & Psychopaths

By Stephen Andert and Donald K. Burleson

Copyright © 2004 by Rampant TechPress. All rights reserved.

Printed in the United States of America.

Published in Kittrell, North Carolina, USA.

911 Series: Book 1

Series Editor: Don Burleson

Production Editor: Teri Wade

Editors: Cindy Cairns and Robin Haden

Cover Design: Bryan Hoff

Printing History:

February 2005 for First Edition

ISBN: 0-9745993-9-5

Library of Congress Control Number: 2004115996

Table of Contents

Acknowledgements

This type of reference book requires the dedicated efforts of many people. After each chapter is delivered, several experts carefully review and correct the technical content. After the technical review, experienced copy editors polish the grammar and syntax. The finished work is then reviewed as page proofs and turned over to the production manager, who manages the cover art, printing distribution, and warehousing.

In short, the authors play a small role in the development of this book, and we need to thank and acknowledge everyone who helped bring this book to fruition:

- Linda Webb for the production management, including the coordination of the cover art, page proofing, printing, and distribution.

- Mike Reed for his wonderful illustrations.

- Teri Wade, for her help in the production of the page proofs.

- Cindy Cairns and Robin Haden for their careful tedious editing.

- Bryan Hoff, for his exceptional cover design and graphics.

- Janet Burleson, for her assistance with the web site, and for creating the online shopping cart for this book.

With our sincerest thanks,

Stephen Andert
Donald K. Burleson

Preface

In the beginning, the Web was created as a vehicle for the sharing of information among respected academics and scientists. The Internet is now available to all manner of unsavory characters and the natural anonymity of the web has provided a breeding-ground for a whole new generation of criminals.

Just as we use the web to improve our efficiency; crooks, creeps and sundry weirdo's use the web to further their illicit goals.

The intent of this book is to create a safety handbook so that everyone could understand the pitfalls and perils of this wonderful and exciting, yet perilous new means of communication.

We hope that you enjoy this book and that you will find some useful information to help you stay safe in the 21st Century.

The Illusion of Anonymity

Privacy on the Web?

Today's society is rich in information. With the emergence and growth of the Internet, a wide array of data is globally available as long as an individual has access to electricity, a telephone line and an Internet service provider. Indeed, the Internet overflows with information on just about any topic one could name. But what does all this mean when it comes to personal privacy?

Many people live under the assumption that their personal lives are relatively private. With information just a click away, this couldn't be farther from the truth. Items that most people would consider private such as credit ratings, mortgages, details of divorce and even interactions with the law are all safety tucked away in a secure database.

For example, in the state of Florida it is possible to request a public records check and see the complete criminal records for anyone, for any reason. There is a modest fee associated with this process, and the response is immediate via the Internet. Florida is hardly unique in this respect. In fact, there are many companies that offer this type of search nationwide.

They, who would give up an essential liberty for temporary security, deserve neither liberty nor security.

Benjamin Franklin

In addition to providing access to useful information for the conduct of business, the Internet has generated an entirely new avenue for recreation and leisure time. Chat rooms, blogs and online multi-player games are popular ways to spend time and interact with others. The majority of Internet users are unaware that these venues keep a file or record of the information exchanged within the confines of that area, sometimes saving information automatically to an archive for future reference.

Anyone using the Internet today must be aware that anything stored by a computer is likely to have a much longer lifespan than fragments of casual conversation shared between friends. As a result of computer storage capabilities, words written and forgotten long ago can resurface many years later.

The reality of life is that with a few minutes and a few dollars, information can be obtained on almost anyone. This chapter will explain why these data sources are available and what, if anything, can be done to keep personal information private.

Background Investigations

Previously, pre-employment background investigations were performed only when job candidates applied for positions that would place them in close proximity to sensitive information or large sums of money. Indeed, it would seem reckless for a company to hire someone who would have access to significant financial or intellectual resources without first administering a thorough background inquiry. Clearly, in cases like this, the inquiry is not only appropriate, but vital. Recently, this has become a much more prevalent practice as companies try to select candidates with as few skeletons in their closet as possible.

Growing Internet usage and an increasing demand has created an increase in the number of online companies that provide background checks. Some of these companies produce accurate information and comply with the legal requirements for information verification. Others may not take the same precautions and may not be able to provide the same level of accuracy.

Jordana Beebe is the Communications Director at the Privacy Rights Clearinghouse. According to Ms. Beebe, one way to ensure a background search is performed properly and legally and that it produces accurate results is for an employer to use a recognized background investigation or employment screening company. This is important for a couple of reasons. First, working with a reputable company will help ensure the search complies with the law. Secondly, some Internet information brokerage firms and programs may turn up illegal or incorrect information. This could put an organization in hot water if the reason for not hiring an otherwise ideal candidate is based on inaccurate information.

Ms. Beebe also relates that any background investigation should follow the guidelines set forth in the Fair Credit Reporting Act. One of these guidelines includes the right for the subject of a background investigation to obtain a copy of the report if the information it contains was used in making the decision not to extend a job offer.

Some employers will also conduct a credit history check, especially when the job involves access to liquid assets. Credit checks are readily available through online services such as Equifax, Experian, and TransUnion. While a company may not be able to legally discriminate against a candidate for irresponsible financial dealings, it may be able to obtain the following information:

Poor payment history - If the candidate has a history of late payments, it might relate to their personal integrity and commitment to obligations.

Defaulting on payments - Failure to meet financial obligations to creditors is considered immoral by some employers.

Bankruptcy - A lending institution may not hold a bankruptcy filing against someone beyond the statute of limitations, which is seven years.

It is important for the savvy job applicant to know their rights. Some laws may prohibit a company from considering this information when evaluating a candidate for employment. It is important that anyone seeking such information acquire proper notification and authorization when conducting a background investigation. Federal and State laws provide guidelines mandating explicit permission from the subject *before* conducting a background investigation.

Real-world case: The Shaeffer Murder

In 1986, the television show *My Sister Sam* introduced the public to an up-and-coming young actress named Rebecca Shaeffer. Though relatively unknown before landing the role, the success of the show seemed certain to launch Rebecca into a promising career as a television star.

Her ambitions, however, were cut short when on July 18, 1989, Robert John Bardo showed up at the front door of Rebecca's home and shot her. He'd been stalking the young actress. After failing to get any information from Rebecca's agent, he paid a private investigator $250 for her address. Unfortunately, it was that simple.

The ease at which anyone can obtain a private address is staggering. In California, the local DMV office will provide a private home address for only one dollar! All that is required is a short form with the requestor's name, the subject's name, and a reason for requesting the information.

The next section delves deeper into the issues surrounding data disclosure.

Disclosure of Private Information

The protection of personal privacy is necessary for anyone with a web accessible database. It is the responsibility of the Information Technology department to ensure information is not improperly disclosed to third parties. However, web hackers are increasingly successful at breaking into web databases for personal gain including finding "dirt" on an ex-friend or previous boss, or using their access to a system for extortion or harassment.

Disclosure by Proxy

Many companies may also disclose private information in discrete and subtle ways. For example, some companies sell aggregated information under the premise that it does not reveal individual personal details. This idea could easily backfire when personal details are revealed by process of elimination.

The following are a few examples of queries that any private investigator could use to find a person's identity:

- All female veterinarians in Nome, Alaska who have been diagnosed with a venereal disease.

- All Native American piano tuners in Stuttgart, Germany with a felony record.

- All kangaroo breeders in Burbank, California with charitable donations in excess of one million dollars.

Unfortunately, there are those who would capitalize on mistakes in a websites data disclosure; therefore, aggregate disclosure must be carefully screened. More importantly, website owners are now being held directly accountable for breeches in their web data security.

Web Site Responsibility for Data Privacy

In a typical website, data access occurs at many levels:

- at the end user presentation layer;

- at the middle tier;

- at the application server layer;

- at the web server layer;

- at the standalone application screens; and finally,

- at the database level directly.

Dealing with confidential data on the web

Responsible websites, with confidential medical or financial information, are required by law to have strict auditing systems and be able to provide a report on anyone and everyone who has viewed specific data.

Many Federal laws such as the Health Insurance Portability and Accountability Act of 1996 (HIPAA), the Sarbanes Oxley Act (SOX) and the Gramm Leach Bliley Act (GLBA) changed the way that databases are secured and audited. Some of these federal regulations impose severe criminal penalties for non-compliance and malfeasance with protected data.

For example, HIPAA laws provides that an intentional leak of information calls for a fine of up to $250,000 per incident and may result in the imprisonment of the executive in charge for a period up to 10 years. The severity of the penalty and the personification of responsibility is enough to make the executives of many organizations take this law and the issue of privacy and information protection very seriously. Non-compliance with these regulations can also expose companies to multi-million dollar civil lawsuits from customers if their private information has been improperly disclosed.

Regardless of the database architecture or specific product, all data audits must capture the following information:

Who – A full identification of the person viewing or modifying the data.

Where – A log showing the specific application procedure and method used to access the data.

When – A reliable date-time-stamp, globalized to Greenwich Mean Time (GMT).

What – A full listing of all data entities that were viewed or modified.

Why – Context-based information describing how the data was disclosed.

These web-based database systems have extremely complex and complete auditing mechanisms, but they remain vulnerable to outside hacker attacks.

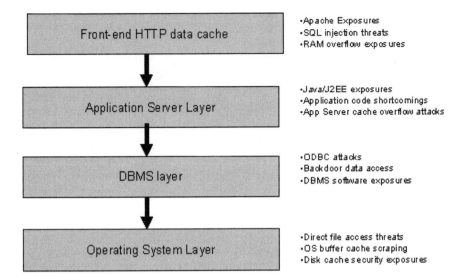

Figure 1.1 – *An example of a data access structure and its vulnerable points*

As shown in Figure 1.1, there are many ways that web hackers can obtain confidential information. In addition, internal disclosure of private information is also a potential problem. This is especially important for online health care databases. Successful web companies apply sophisticated filters to the audit trails at data capture time to spot suspicious trends and patterns in data access, as in Figure 1.2.

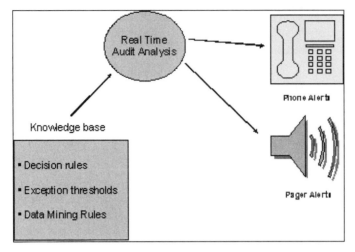

Figure 1.2 – *Real time audit analysis*

Many websites that contain confidential financial or personal data have built-in alarms that sound when there is an attempted breech or an unauthorized data access. This will immediately alert the Webmaster or Security Administrator to the attempted intrusions.

In today's litigious society, almost every breech of privacy and security is followed by expensive litigation. On the issue of medical records privacy, the situation is even more fluid and prone to severe security lapses. HIPAA addresses this problem by mandating the audit requirements of these records and strictly enforcing the requirements by placing stiff penalties for non-compliance.

In cases where personal information has been improperly disclosed, the courts have become very severe. Litigation against Internet domain owners with ineffective, "home-grown" auditing solutions can be devastating. In almost every court case, the security and auditing code is found wanting, and the victims often win huge cash judgments.

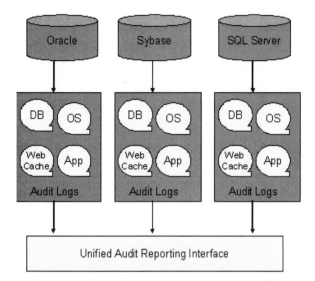

Figure 1.3 – *Unified Audit Reporting Interface*

Using the Unified Audit Reporting Interface displayed in Figure 1.3, every line of code is put under a magnifying glass and security experts from around the world are called in to judge the quality of the data privacy solution.

One does not need to look far to see public cases of computer security violations and the liability suffered by the custodian of the data. With millions of dollars at stake, there are many resourceful hackers waiting for a website custodian to make a mistake and expose confidential information.

The following sections explore specific ways that companies lose control of information.

Real-world Case: The Hotel Database Fiasco

In a widely publicized court case from the 1990's, a major hotel chain collected detailed information about their weekday guests' use of their hotels. They employed a data warehouse analyst who created a target marketing campaign, offering special coupons to those guests who frequently used the hotel on weekdays.

This marketing campaign was a mass-mailing that targeted weekday-stay guests with coupons sent to the home addresses of the guests. The results were disastrous. More than a dozen people were clued into their spouse's infidelity as a direct result of this coupon campaign and more than six divorces resulted from the company's actions.

While this action was not in violation of the privacy laws per se, the result of the campaign was the disclosure of private information that was damaging to a third party. A more suitable approach in this case would have been to mail the coupons to the guests' work addresses.

Next, ways the web can be used to violate personal privacy will be explored.

Finding Criminal History

Many people are surprised that their entire history is available in public records. For just a few dollars, reliable background checks can reveal times in a person's life when they have been charged with a crime and whether they were convicted of that crime.

These reports are commonly used to pre-screen employees and can be obtained without a person's knowledge or consent. This is especially onerous because a potential employer is free to disqualify a candidate, even if they are bound by law not to consider charges that were dismissed. On most job applications, there is an area provided for an authorizing signature. Applicants should be aware that by providing a signature, they may be consenting to a background check.

One might think that a DUI (Driving Under the Influence) or a DWI (Driving While Impaired) arrest should not matter to an employer since the job they are applying for entails crunching numbers or preparing meals. An employer might agree, or if they feel the person's record is an indicator of future job performance, they might decide to hire someone else. The following is a mock-up of a criminal background check. Note the high level of detail, with complete dates, charges and outcomes.

Subject	ROBERT SCUMBAG
Race	White
Sex	Male
Date of Birth	**/**/1966
Height	74 INCHES
Weight	310 POUNDS
Hair Color	BROWN
Eye Color	BLUE
Address	LIZARD LICK NC 27531

Case 1 Details

Case Number	01928VF 027253
Jurisdiction	NC
County	RALEIGH
Charge Class	Felony
Offense	POSSESS HEROIN
Statute	90-95(D)(1)
Sentence	6 MONTHS COUNTY JAIL
Fine Amount	40,000.00
Disposition Date	08/06/1989
Disposition	PROSECUTION COMPLETED

Amended Charge Class	N/A
Amended Charge Description	POSSESS HEROIN

Case 2 Details	
Case Number	01FF3BF 027253
Jurisdiction	NC
County	CHARLOTTE
Charge Class	Felony
Offense	POSSESS MARIJUANA UP TO 5 LBS
Statute	90-95(D)(4)
Sentence	2 YEARS PRISON
Fine Amount	N/A
Disposition Date	08/06/1991
Disposition	DEFERRED PROSECUTION

Case 3 Details	
Case Number	6354242F j35342d
Jurisdiction	NC
County	RALEIGH
Charge Class	Felony
Offense	POSSESS STOLEN PROPERTY
Statute	440-462(Z)(1)

Sentence	TWO YEARS CHAIN GANG
Fine Amount	N/A
Disposition Date	08/06/1994
Disposition	PROSECUTION COMPLETE

Case 4 Details	
Case Number	6354242F j35342d
Jurisdiction	NC
County	RALEIGH
Charge Class	Felony
Offense	ASSAULT W DEADLY WEAPON
Statute	230-23(D)(41)
Sentence	DISMISSED
Fine Amount	N/A
Disposition Date	02/17/1998
Disposition	DEFERRED PROSECUTION

In addition to immediate access to criminal history, one can also obtain instant access to pubic records of civil litigation. Civil court investigations involve all matters of public record including divorces, real estate transactions and civil lawsuits. These public records reveal information about a person's personality and predilection to enter a lawsuit, which is very important if trying to minimize liability. However, an employer should remember to check with an attorney before using this information to reject a candidate.

Some hiring managers become concerned when a candidate has a history of suing a previous employer for problems at the workplace, such as sexual harassment or unfair treatment. In addition, when a company hires a candidate, that employee will have some level of access to company assets. Therefore, it is important for the company to decide whether the candidate is suited to the type of work available. In today's litigious society, employers know that the choices they make today could be fodder for a lawsuit tomorrow. Imagine the following scenario in a courtroom:

```
"Mr. Smith, you are the Human Resources manager for XYZ Corporation,
is that correct?"

"Yes, I am"

"And you were in fact the person who approved Mr. Doe's application
for employment?"

"Yes I am"

"What position did he apply for?"

"Delivery truck driver."

"Did you do a background check?"

"No, we verified his driving record here in our state for the past
18 months."

"So you didn't check his record where he lived two years ago and
therefore didn't know about the accident he caused killing a family
of four?"

"No, we only checked this state."

"So the deaths that he caused could have been prevented if you had
only checked his driving record a little further back!"
```

A situation that flows along the lines of this fictional dialogue is the fear of every person responsible for hiring employees. Concern for liability and protecting safety for all is an important reason for making criminal records publicly accessible.

In the above scenario, an applicant was hired when a limited background check policy did not reveal previous driving related issues. The opposite scenario might be a situation where a person is turned down because of a minor infraction on their record that has little or nothing to do with the position for which they have applied. It is possible that an error was made on the report and the negative data is incorrect. In any instance in which negative action is taken based on the results of a background check, the candidate should be informed regarding the specifics used to make the decision. This will allow the applicant to respond appropriately and attempt to correct the record, if needed.

Whether criminal records should be available to the public is a matter for debate, but for all practical purposes, they already are. Most states have information on registered sex offenders available online. The following web page, http://searchenginez.com/sex_offenders_usa.html, contains links to every state with a known sex offender registry and allows the user to access information specific to their area.

In addition to publicly available information, many companies may, for a fee, perform the search and present the results to an applicant in a report. Unfortunately, a few unscrupulous employers may still conduct a background investigation without proper authorization from the applicant or without legal precedent.

A Wealth of Civil Information

Non-criminal lawsuits, marriage licenses, drivers' licenses, real estate transactions, and tax liens are all examples of civil transactions that may be public record depending on a person's geographic location. A tax lien is one method that local and state governments can use to collect unpaid taxes. Filing a tax lien requires a public notice. This means there is no secret list of tax liens. In fact, many places have a web-based search that will allow anyone to search public record announcements. Figure 1.4 shows an example of a typical search screen that can return a listing of public records.

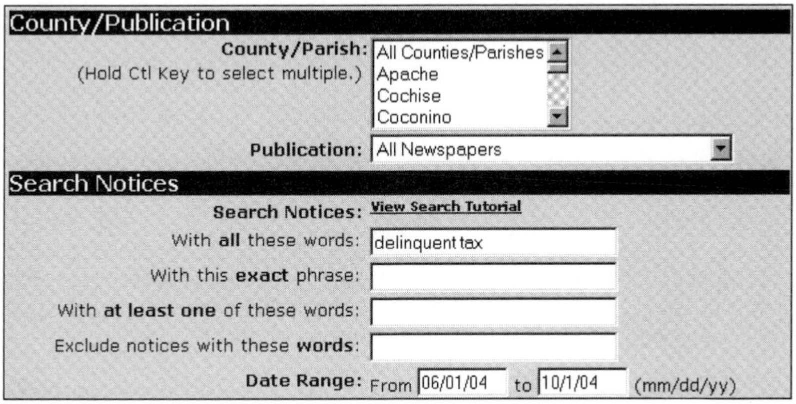

Figure 1.4 - *A typical web page to search for delinquent tax notices*

Although current privacy laws make this less likely now, many of the transactions, which are part of the public record, including divorce proceedings and bankruptcies, have included social security numbers and personal address information. All this, of course, is information that should stay private.

Sources of Personal Information

Voter registration records are an excellent source of information and often contain unlisted phone numbers, birth dates, social security numbers and physical addresses. Since voter registration information is a matter of public record, it is often available upon written request. A person need only write the voters registration office of the county of interest and request it. It should be noted that the rules governing the dispensing of this information are subject to frequent changes, and there is usually a small fee for the information.

Many people have been asked to sign a petition for one thing or another. This is an area where one must be careful about what personal information is provided. If a petition form includes a space for entering a social security number, choosing not to enter it may be the wisest course of action. If the information is lost or stolen, it could be misused. Including a social security number should be optional and should not affect whether the signature is counted in support of the petition.

A social security number is a vital piece of personal information. It is used by the IRS, employers, banks and insurance companies. Unauthorized access to a social security number can lead to numerous problems, some of which may be serious.

In Section 7 of the Overview of the Privacy Act of 1974, 2004 Edition, found at 5 U.S.C. § 552a Disclosure of Social Security Number, provides that:

"It shall be unlawful for any Federal, State or Local government agency to deny to any individual any right, benefit, or privilege provided by law because of such individual's refusal to disclose his social security account number." Sec. 7(a)(1).

However, there are exceptions to this rule. Most notably, any other federal statute requiring disclosure of the social security number supersedes this statute. In spite of this, the act makes it clear that social security numbers are intended for specialized purposes related to government services and are not to be given out lightly.

Genealogy Websites

Another location for personal information is web sites designed to help would-be researchers piece together family histories. Whatever the reason for researching ancestors, there are many tools available that make the task easier than it has been in the past. Many local and regional government agencies make various public records available on the Internet. Some charge a fee and others are free. Genealogy.com and ancestry.com are two web-based services that operate as information clearinghouses. These information clearinghouses easily extend a search over a wider area than would be possible by manually going to each state or county website and performing searches separately.

The Social Security Death Index, or SSDI, offers a way to search for deceased persons that participated in the Social Security program. The results include social security numbers. This provides an easy way for a deceased individual's social security information being used for fraudulent purposes. Indeed, a deceased person's social security number was used by a criminal to register voters for a presidential election.

As the next chapter will demonstrate, criminals can use social security numbers to engage in many types of destructive and illegal activity, including identity theft.

All about Anyone: Just a Mouse-Click Away

Many people know that Google.com is a popular and effective search engine. It is so popular in fact, that Google has become a verb. The verb *Google* is frequently used as a synonym for search. For example, instead of asking someone if they searched for the address of a restaurant on the Internet, one might ask, *"Did you google that restaurant?"*

Using a search engine like Google.com is a good way to discover how much personal information is readily available on the Internet. Simply use a web browser like Internet Explorer or Netscape, surf to www.google.com, and type a name in the search box. If an individual participates in online communities like UseNet or e-mail discussion lists with public archives, their name will most likely be listed many times.

Other search engines specialize in locating phone numbers and physical addresses. One widely used web site of this type is Directory Assistance Plus (www.daplus.us). With just a person's name and the state in which they reside, it is possible to retrieve not only their phone number and address, but also more speculative information. Personal data available with these types of searches may include the estimated value of a person's home, how long they have lived there and their salary. It goes without saying that easy access to this and other types of personal information can become dangerous.

Finding Private Medical Information

Medical records are a source of valuable information for those invested in the healthcare industry. Trying to predict market demands for medical services in the future is no easy task. A great deal of data must be accumulated and analyzed. The more information that goes into formulating these projections means the greater the odds of producing an accurate forecast.

Health and wellness statistics for the U.S. population are available to anyone who cares to investigate. These records do not violate personal privacy, since all data applies only to demographic groups. The problem occurs when individual privacy is overlooked, and personal healthcare information is used by intrusive companies hungry for data to fuel their next business decision.

When the Health Insurance Portability and Accountability Act of 1996 (HIPAA) was passed into law, one goal was to reduce the unauthorized sharing of private patient information. The penalties for unauthorized disclosure of what the act calls "individually identifiable information" are severe. An individual can be punished by fines of up to $250,000 US Dollars and up to 10 years in prison.

The Medical Information Bureau Group, Inc. is a medical information clearinghouse. MIB is an association of over 500 U.S. and Canadian life insurance companies that provide information and database management services to the financial services industry. MIB was created to help ensure the accuracy of the information provided to the underwriters of life, health, disability and long term care policies.

MIB will also make an individual's personal information available for a small fee. There is no charge if the information has already been released to an insurance company and has resulted in adverse action, such as declining to write an insurance policy or a rate increase. When a person requests a copy of their records, MIB will provide the following information:

- Nature and substance of information compiled.

- Name of member companies that provided information.

- Name of member companies that received information in the previous 12 months.

More information about MIB can be found at the following web site, www.mib.com/html/consumer.html.

Programs such as NetDetective offer to provide information about tens of millions of people from the United States and Canada. These services may provide detailed information regarding military service, driving records, vehicle histories, and medical records. While these types of information services provide a legitimate product to many reputable companies, there are questions about the proper use of this personal information. The law is clear regarding how this information can be used, what can be considered in what circumstance, and so on. However, the law does not guarantee compliance and the potential for abuse or at least misuse is very high.

There is a wealth of personal information readily available for anyone interested. But for those who seek very specific and sensitive information, a more direct method is used. Often they just ask for it. Through elaborate tricks and scams, thousands have been persuaded to surrender valuable information and suffered the consequences. The next section will explore ways to keep from becoming a victim.

Tracing E-mail

Most people have received an e-mail message from senders they did not know. Maybe it was a car dealer inviting them to test drive a new vehicle, the publisher of the magazine they subscribe to reminding them that their renewal is due, or someone explaining how they can order medicine over the Internet. The majority of people recognize the e-mail addresses of their friends. However, when they receive a message from cotw@qwest.com, they may not realize that it is from Crossroads of the West, the Western re-enactment society they joined a few months ago.

If they are receiving messages that are of harassing, libelous, or of otherwise unwanted nature, they may want to know the real person's name associated with those messages. These messages are not classified as *spam* (unsolicited marketing), rather they are e-mails that may threaten physical violence, death or may simply be harmless. Regardless, more information on the sender may be desired. So how does an individual find out who is behind a given e-mail address? Two ways to do this are through WHOIS and FINGER.

Using WHOIS & FINGER

Before explaining these terms, a little history of the Internet is required. Most people are familiar with "browsing the web" or "surfing the Internet" using a program called a *browser*. The more common browsers are Netscape Navigator and Internet Explorer, but there are many others such as Mozilla, Opera, Lynx, and Mosaic. These browsers use directions given to them by *name servers* to locate the web pages a person is searching for.

Logging onto the Internet and going to a favorite website seems like a quick and easy operation, and it is, but there is a lot going on behind the scenes. The Internet is a large and complex network, and navigating it requires computers to perform extremely quick operations, locating pieces of information all over the world and delivering them to the requesting browser.

Web browsers accomplish this impressive feat by using large computer servers as a sort of post office. Just as a piece of mail is delivered first to the correct state, and then to the proper zip code before finding its way to a street address, so a server directs computer browsers to increasingly precise locations until the information they seek is located. It will ask its name servers for a digital address that tells it where it can find a location such as yahoo.com. That digital address is called an IP address and it looks similar to this: 204.12.14.200.

Technical details on how name resolution or any other part of the Internet works can be found at www.ask.com. This is the web page of Ask Jeeves, which is very tolerant of English language searches and will provide good links with a simple query along the lines of "how does the Internet work."

The name servers get their information based on who "owns" a particular domain. Master name servers provide this information to other name servers. These master name servers are the official source of information about which domain is owned by whom as well as where that web page can be found.

Some programs have been around since the early days of the Internet explosion, WHOIS qualifies in this category. WHOIS can be extremely helpful for finding information about a domain. WHOIS can be accessed using a web page such as the one operated by Network Solutions at www.networksolutions.com/en_US/whois/index.jhtm. This reports information provided at the time the domain was registered. It is in the domain owner's interest to keep that information current since this is how an owner is contacted when the domain registration is set to expire. Failure to renew the domain could result the registration of the domain by a person other than the original owner. This action is known as *pagejacking* and is described in a later chapter.

Usenet Searches

The Usenet is another type of network used for gathering and disseminating information. The main function of a Usenet is to facilitate discussion between people of like interests. Groups within the Usenet network are broken down into newsgroups, which are named and categorized by subject. Messages can be posted to these newsgroups by members of the group and everyone currently subscribing to that particular newsgroup will receive the post. This means that two or two hundred people can have a conversation and share news and tips about a topic they all enjoy.

The messages that are part of the Usenet can usually be searched for a very long time after being posted. This can be very useful if seeking information about an old computer system. It is important to be aware that any information provided to a newsgroup on the Usenet will likely be around for longer than one would expect.

Government Tools to Reveal Personal Details

The government has tools of its own that are extremely effective in gathering information. The threat of terrorism has added significant weight to the arguments of those who lobby for more powerful means to gather information. The fear of some is that once the data is accumulated, no matter how legitimate the reason, it might be misused.

The government's tool of choice is a collection of three programs known as the DragonWare Suite. The programs that comprise the DragonWare Suite are known as Carnivore, Packeteer and Coolminer. No information on these programs has been officially released; however, it is believed that together, these applications allow the Federal Bureau of Investigation (FBI) to collect packets of data from the Internet, assemble them to recreate copies of the original e-mail messages or files being transferred, and analyze the recreated items to identify specific patterns of behavior.

While a collection of utilities like DragonWare could be used to identify terrorists planning an attack, it could also be used to identify citizens legally expressing a point of view that is contrary to a given group such as a political organization. It is also important to realize that the collected data could be vulnerable to hackers and others who might desire to use this information for criminal purposes.

Another government tool called MOSAIC Threat Assessment Systems is a product that screens threats against public figures. Instead of using the resource-exhausting method of chasing down every threat, this system helps officials to evaluate the seriousness of a given threat.

Corporate Anti-Privacy Tools

Besides the tools that the government may use, many companies also provide tools that can be utilized by businesses and home users alike to monitor and track computer and Internet usage. Spector Pro, a computer surveillance program, is one such product that is made by SPECTORSOFT. The latest version of this tool allows a person to track e-mail usage, instant messaging traffic, websites visited and programs used. This surveillance program is a great asset for accumulating data. In the business world, management has a responsibility to ensure that business secrets are not leaked from the company. In the home environment, parents have the responsibility to monitor children to make certain that their use of computers does not put them at risk of becoming the victim of a sexual predator, for example.

Coming to grips with the reality that much personal information has become all too readily available is the first step in protecting one's self from prying eyes. The following section will explore further measures that can be taken to keep personal information just that, personal.

This section has provided an overview of the illusion of anonymity on the web. Next, some tools and techniques to minimize exposure will be explored.

Protecting Web Privacy

By this point, most readers should be beginning to realize the dangers involved in the loss of privacy and are wondering what can be done to protect themselves. *"An ounce of prevention is worth a pound of cure,"* the old saying goes, and that is especially true when it comes to guarding privacy. Every time a person signs up for a mailing list, posts a blog, or adds their name to a guest book on a web page, they should consider privacy issues and act accordingly.

A good first step is to make use of privacy protection software. These programs are designed to help establish some level of anonymity for the web surfer by preventing unnecessary information from being shared.

Another old saying, *"an apple a day keeps the doctor away,"* is a good idea for healthy living. Likewise, the following *"apple"* contains good ideas for assessing one's privacy status. While it is not necessary to check security daily, periodic evaluations are very helpful. Figure 1.5 shown below illustrates four areas that should be considered to help ensure better privacy protection.

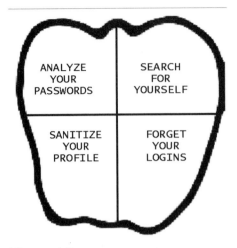

Figure 1.5 - *The apple of security*

The sections that follow will focus on the four elements of the apple of security.

Sanitizing an Online Profile

Volunteering as little information as possible is one of the best ways to protect privacy. One of the main ways that people give away information about themselves is filling out user profiles. Most e-mail accounts, chat rooms and newsgroups allow users and members to complete a rather detailed personal profile. The idea behind this is to allow members of an online community to get to know each other better.

While the idea seems innocent enough, it flies in the face of all sound security practices. Internet users cannot afford the luxury of ignorance or apathy. Awareness is the best defense against invasion of private information. Volunteering date of birth, place of employment, real name, address or phone number, especially together in one location is like a feast on a silver platter for an identity thief. It simply should not be done.

A favorite sports team, vacation spot, or preferred type of automobile may sound like harmless pieces of personal trivia, and in most cases that is just what they are, but keep in mind that information is power, and the more someone knows about a person the more vulnerable that person is. Before revealing anything, one should ask, "*Who needs to know?*" In most cases, the answer is "*Not you*," so don't share.

The Search for Self

How secure is personal information? As part of a privacy self-assessment, it is helpful for an Internet user to perform a couple of Internet searches using their own name as the text to locate. Most people are surprised at the volume of information they find.

Unfortunately, once personal information is out there, there is no getting it back. The record cannot be expunged. The only recourse is to change the information so that what is available is no longer accurate. For example, get a new phone number, keep it unlisted and do not give it out. Start using a new e-mail address. Internet service providers are very good at setting up new addresses; it is simple, does not take a lot of time and it is free. Choose an address that is non-descriptive, includes nothing traceable such as a real name and does not invite unwanted attention.

Analyze Passwords

The easiest way for a hacker to gain unauthorized access to an account is to figure out the password. Therefore, choosing a password that provides a high level of security is of the utmost importance. .

There are many things to consider when making passwords more secure. A person should choose a password that is not easily associated with something readily identified with them. For example, avoid family member's names, pet names, favorite sports or activity, hometown, etc. Choose a word that is not in the dictionary. There are hacker utilities available that will run through every word in the dictionary, trying all of them systematically in an attempt to gain access to an account. Adding numbers is another common way people change passwords. Someone might use "January10" for their password because that was the date they created it, and when the account requires a password change, they may very well simply change the password to "January11" to make remembering it easier. Hackers will frequently move from a dictionary attack to a modified attack in which they add numbers to the end of each word in the dictionary. This slows down the process due to the large number of attempts required. However, hackers will sometimes modify this to use the dictionary words in order of popularity. There are lists of commonly used passwords, which hackers use to make their attack faster.

Selecting a password that is not a dictionary word and includes numbers does not necessarily guarantee safety. The next tool that hackers can use is a brute-force attack. This attack tries every combination of letters and numbers until it finds a valid combination. This means that if this attack is used, "my1dog" is just as likely to be hacked as "password." The best defense against a brute-force attack is password length and alphabet selection. A four-character password will take less time to hack than one that is eight-characters long. A password involving only lower-case letters is less secure than one using lower-case letters and numbers.

Figure 1.6 shows the maximum time needed to complete a brute-force attack. Notice that simply going from a six to a seven-character password using only lower-case letters increases the time from less than one hour to nearly one day. Adding numbers to the password increases the time to nine days.

	Number of possible characters in password		
Length of Password	26 (single case letters only)	36 (single case letters & numbers)	52 (upper & lower case letters only)
4	0	0	1 minute
5	0	10 minutes	1 hour
6	50 minutes	6 hours	2.2 days
7	22 hours	9 days	4 months
8	24 days	10.5 months	17 years
9	21 months	32.6 years	881 years
10	45 years	1,159 years	45,838 years

The password search time with respect to length of the password & number of possible characters used. The search speed is assumed to be 100,000 passwords/second

Figure 1.6 - *The longer the password, the safer it is from brute-force attacks*

The downside to having longer passwords with more different characters is that they are more difficult to remember. A password that is not easily remembered will probably be written down and stored near the computer. A hacker then only needs to snoop around the workstation to find the note, and eureka, they have access.

The keys to selecting safe passwords are as follows:

- Use letters and numbers.

- Use at least seven or eight characters.

- Do not use a dictionary word or combination word.

- Never write them down!

- Change them regularly.

Forget Logins

Most on-line account log-in routines will provide the user with the option of having the system remember their password. This results in the user not having to enter their password the next time they log into the account. As illustrated below, these password memory features can be configured to user preferences.

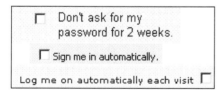

Figure 1.7 - *Most people should avoid using password memory features*

While these websites are performing a well-intentioned service by attempting to make things easier for their users, the increased risk of unauthorized access more than offsets any benefit realized by saving a few key strokes. These options should almost never be used due to the security risk. Therefore, remember the two most important rules about saving passwords:

- Never "*remember*" passwords on a shared computer.

- All computers are shared.

Having covered the four elements represented in the apple of security, attention can now be turned toward dealing safely with vendors and other online sellers.

Safely Purchasing Online

"Don't get robbed via the Internet."
(graphic courtesy of J.P. Gonzalez)

As the Internet has evolved and developed, e-commerce has experienced an absolute explosion and on-line purchasing has taken its place as one of the most popular activities for many Internet users. As such, learning to navigate the world of on-line purchasing is extremely important. Adhering to the guidelines that follow will benefit those seeking to interact safely with vendors and others in the world of on-line shopping.

Taking the time to read and follow guidelines, which are available at online buying services like E-bay, Yahoo! and others is time well spent. These guidelines can be summarized to the Latin phrase *"caveat emptor"* or *"let the buyer beware."* The single most important way to stay safe while dealing with vendors and other online sellers is to use common sense. A person's gut feeling is one of their best safety devices. If a person comes across a deal that sounds too good to be true, it probably is. Although this is not always the case, the interested party should proceed with caution.

Computer scams can originate from seemingly nice people.

For example, a laptop computer listed for $100 might be a scam, or it is possible that the person selling it recently purchased a new one and just wants to get rid of the old one. Most online shopping forums have seller ratings based on previous purchaser feedback. Review the information closely. A brand new seller with an unbelievable deal should call for more caution and the use of an escrow service. If the seller has been active for several years with little to no negative feedback, and after contacting them they appear legitimate; one might decide to proceed with the purchase.

In the course of reading e-mail or browsing the web, a person is likely to see product advertisements that include links to websites where the product may be purchased. If a shopper wishes to learn more about the product or offer, it is advisable to open a second browser and use the search engine to go directly to the webpage of the item, rather than link to the page from the advertisement itself, because some links are fraudulent. While appearing to take the shopper to a trusted location, E-Bay for example, they may in fact link to a look-a-like web page where scammers ply their trade.

Regardless of how a person arrives at any online shopping or retailer website, the challenge remains; how can the site be evaluated for trustworthiness? One way *not* to evaluate a website is by its appearance. A neat and professional looking website is not extraordinarily difficult to create, and it is well worth the effort for criminals if it means bigger returns.

To assist in the evaluation of sources such as web pages, Alastair Smith has compiled a list of links. This list is available at www.vuw.ac.nz/staff/alastair_smith/evaln/evaln.htm.

Use the following criteria when evaluating web pages:

Accuracy - After an initial review, is there anything on the web page that is not accurate? If the company recently changed their phone number and did not update their web page with the new information, will the web page be updated when product availability or a price change occurs?

Authority - If the web page proposes a solution to a problem, verify that the author is qualified to make that suggestion. Receiving advice on motorcycle maintenance from a cooking expert will undoubtedly ensure the motorcycle will never be the same again.

Objectivity - When looking at the web page for a news media outlet (newspaper, television, radio), many people expect unbiased reporting. Consider the source of the information and make sure to determine opinions from facts.

Freshness - Look for the last updated date and for the most recent additions. A corporate website might have a special section for newsworthy events. If there is nothing new, it could mean the company has vanished.

Completeness - Is everything offered on the site available? Do all of their links work? Is any information missing such as return and exchange policies?

Privacy Policy - Is it displayed prominently? How will they use purchaser information? Will they share it with others or use it for marketing purposes?

For many browsers, one clue regarding the security of a web page is the picture of a padlock at the bottom of the window. If the lock is closed, then the site is using security. Otherwise, if the lock is open, the site is unsecured. Another indicator of a secured site is that the address starts with https instead of the usual http.

Always look for the clues the Internet browser reveals regarding the security level of the current web page. If filling out a form that includes personal or financial information, make sure that the lock icon is locked or that the site address starts with https instead of http.

When using an unsecured web page, it is important to remember anything that is typed is visible to anyone who may be looking. There is no encryption, so make sure nothing is entered that needs to remain private.

If the web page is encrypted, then the information transmitted should be safe from most prying eyes. Because the work required to decipher the encryption is difficult and time-consuming, it removes most criminal motivation for routine transactions. Realize, however, encryption only reveals the security between a person's own computer and the server they are using. The data for most websites and shopping sites is stored in databases. These databases contain any personal information customers provide including addresses and credit card numbers. Since employees have complete access to the information contained therein, the database may not be as secure at the transaction being used.

Whether shopping online for products or services, it is critical to use common sense. Although this section refers to shopping online, the same warnings and guidelines also apply to online credit applications.

Note - it is extremely important to evaluate any web page before applying for credit. Every person should make certain that it is clear with whom they are dealing when providing personal information requested for a credit application.

Comparison Shopping

When making a significant purchase, it pays to shop around. This can be done easier online than personally driving all over town. To make comparison-shopping even easier, there are online shopping services that act as personal assistants for the consumer. These services use programs that search the Internet; gathering information on the desired item, at which sites that item is available, and at what cost. Because these programs use different methods to collect information, there are often some variances in the return results. Therefore, it is in the best interest of the consumer to try more than one. Rather than simply going to a few e-commerce or e-tailers sites, a wider Internet search usually results in a better price.

Figure 1.8 shows the results of a search for a particular digital camera. Notice that the item is sorted by total price, which includes tax and shipping charges. The lowest price without these charges is from a different e-tailer; but for this search, shipping to this particular California zip code would make it only the second best choice.

The top two choices have over 2,000 customer reviews. All four e-tailers listed have a rating of 4 out of 5 or better. Although the price difference is small, this example illustrates the methodology of the search.

PRICE COMPARISONS	Bottom Line Price calculated for zip code 90210 (Change)						Sorted by BottomLinePrice
	Seller	Base Price	+ Tax	+ Shipping	= BottomLinePrice	Availability	Seller Rating
See it at	butterfly by photo Featured Merchant Merchant Info	$296.00	No Tax	$9.95	Your Best Price $305.95	Yes	★★★★☆ 2195 Reviews
See it at	ElectricSam 888-767-7726 Merchant Info	$289.18	No Tax	$18.18	$307.36	Yes	★★★★☆ 2183 Reviews
See it at	Blue Switch Digital Merchant Info	$308.95	No Tax	Free	$308.95	Yes	★★★★☆ 164 Reviews
See it at	Harmony COMPUTERS Merchant Info	$309.00	No Tax	Free	$309.00	Yes	★★★★☆ 437 Reviews

Figure 1.8 - *Comparison shopping example*

Consumer Reports is an independent, nonprofit organization that rates products, consumer organizations, etc. They tested a number of shopping sites and awarded top marks to BizRate.com and Shopping.com. Still other well-known shopping websites to try include mySimon.com, PriceGrabber.com and PriceSCAN.com. These sites also provide a list of e-tailers that offer the product a consumer may be looking for. From there, it is up to the consumer to determine what level of trust to place in a particular company.

Whether surfing the web or conducting online shopping, a user visits many sites and consequently creates a pattern of habits. The next section will explain how this pattern is tracked.

All about Cookies

Despite its name, in the computer world, a cookie is not a snack. Cookie is the name given to files that a web page leaves on the hard drive of personal computers. Cookies help websites learn usage patterns, frequency of return visitors, and other pertinent information. They can also store private information. A cookie might be used when shopping online to keep track of items placed in the consumer's shopping cart. After paying, the consumer's credit card number is placed in a cookie on the hard drive of their computer so that the next time they shop at that site, the *"Use the same credit card as last time"* option is available.

Clearly, this is a potential security risk. If one website could read another website's cookies, criminals could gain access to any credit card a user has ever used online. This is not normally possible, but there are security vulnerabilities that could allow this to happen. Another problem with cookies is that they identify, to anyone viewing them, which sites were visited. If someone is looking into the job market and their manager views the cookies, he could see the names of the popular job search sites.

Most web browsers give the user the ability to either prevent all cookies or delete them upon request. Preventing all cookies would significantly hinder many activities that people undertake on the Internet. A better solution is to regularly delete cookies manually. This means that any Internet-related password or account information that has been stored on the user's computer will be erased. The next time a web-based e-mail or online shopping site is visited, the user will need to type their user id and password again. Figure 1.9 shows a typical screen that is used to delete cookies.

Figure 1.9 - *Deleting cookies is a good idea for security*

Deleting cookies manually may be a bit of a pain. However, if it saves the user from having to deal with financial fraud or identity theft, it is worth the extra effort.

If the computer is one that is shared, when the user is finished with their task, they should delete all cookies before leaving their workstation. If the computer is a laptop or portable computer, then erasing cookies is even more important because if stolen, the thieves could go on a shopping spree using the credit card information left in cookie form.

There are companies that sell programs called cookie managers. These programs allow the user to control which cookies they want to keep and which ones they want to delete. One of the best features of this type of program is its ability to alert the user every time a cookie is left on their computer. It is very insightful to realize just how often this happens.

Privacy Enhancements

Most people are unaware that it is not necessary for them to manually enter personal information in order for another computer to extract that information. Some commonly used web browsers maintain a user profile of the person running the browser as well as information about the computer on which it is running. If another computer on the network requests information in the proper format, the browser may provide the data requested behind the scenes. The user will not be asked to authorize the data transfer, and in fact, will probably not be aware it is happening.

Vulnerability Analysis

Until a person realizes just how vulnerable their personal information actually is, they may lack the motivation necessary to take the steps to protect themselves. There are a couple of websites designed to help a person realize just that. Privacy.Net (www.privacy.net/analyze) and Anonymizer (www.anonymizer.com/privacytest) provide free evaluations that determine just how much a user's information might be available to websites visited.

Much of the information that can be gathered is often technical. This includes things such as the IP address, the browser version and the operating system being used. This may seem unimportant to most people, but a hacker

---

can look at that information and find a security flaw that has not been patched, which can then lead to a compromised system.

Methods to Maintain Privacy

This section introduces products that help maintain privacy. There is no right answer for everyone, so security conscious people need to evaluate the various programs available to find the options that best suit their needs.

Riverdeep Interactive Learning is one company that produces products designed to help users heighten their security posture. Among Riverdeep's offerings is Identity Theft Protector™, sold under the Broderbund brand name. This program features a user-friendly interface that makes it a good choice for less experienced computer users. As an added bonus, the cost of the program is very reasonable.

Another company with products along the same lines is Anonymizer Inc. While Riverdeep offers products in many areas, Anonymizer specializes in privacy software. Anonymizer allows a user to navigate the Internet privately and securely, keep the user's IP address hidden, encrypts all Internet communication and removes unwanted spam e-mail.

Lance Cottrell of Anonymizer, Inc explains in layman's terms how their privacy service works:

"It takes all of the traffic you have going to the Internet, web browsing, e-mail and rather than have your computer send it directly to the Internet, goes to the Anonymizer network where it is mixed with the traffic of 2 million other active users and hidden behind other domain names that are changed.

This prevents web sites that you go to from knowing who you are or geographically where you are in the world, or even that you are using Anonymizer".

These are just a few of the companies who sell products for privacy maintenance. There are many others, so do some research and find what works best. In addition, The Electronic Privacy Information Center (EPIC) has a list of tools that are available to enhance Internet privacy at www.epic.org/privacy/tools.html.

Dumping a Computer

Nearly every form of consumer electronics on the market today has become disposable. It is doubtful that there are any new DVD repair shops in the neighborhood. The rapid pace of technological advancement has made the lifespan of many new products shorter than one could have imagined just a brief time ago, and computers are no exception.

A study by Carnegie Mellon University puts the number of computers that will be in landfills by 2005 at 150 million. According to a recent study by the National Safety Council, more than 63 million personal computers will likely be retired in 2005.

Some of these retired machines will end up in the storage sheds of well-intentioned techies, who plan on fixing them up one day or using them for parts. Others may be donated to charitable organizations that can still make use of older equipment.

 In some areas like California and Massachusetts, disposing of computer equipment in the garbage is illegal and can subject a person to fines.

However a person chooses to retire their machine, it is vital to ensure that all sensitive data has been completely removed. Even if equipment is destined for the landfill, provided that is a legal method for disposal, precautions must be taken. The information contained on the hard drive of most computers is a gold mine for anyone who knows how to retrieve it. A machine used for on-line banking, or to conduct e-commerce will be loaded with sensitive data. It is not necessary for a computer to be operational in order to uncover information. Any moderately tech-savvy crook can remove the hard drive from a discarded machine and get access to everything on it. Before throwing away an old computer, remove the hard drive and destroy it. This is the only way to ensure the hard drive is never read again.

If a computer is to be passed on to another user, perform the following steps. This will help ensure a smooth transition.

- Configure all programs to require a password or PIN *every time* it is accessed.

- Delete or uninstall all programs with any personal information, including e-mail and financial programs.

- Delete all files with personal information, including spreadsheets and documents.

- Use a program to overwrite all deleted files so they cannot be recovered.

- Format the hard drive. This should be done *after* all of the preceding steps have been performed.

- Format the hard drive again. It cannot hurt. In fact, the State of North Carolina requires their government agencies to format hard drives as many as 25 times prior to sending a computer to surplus.

- For extra protection, install another operating system to overwrite data again.

- With a bootable floppy disk, use the FDISK utility to render permanently any remaining information useless.

There are companies that specialize in reclaiming useful parts from discarded computers. Some operations will make use of system components like memory (RAM) or processors (CPU) to build refurbished systems. Others will melt down the main circuit boards to obtain the precious metals used in their construction for resale.

If making use of a company to dispose of a retired machine, be sure to research exactly how it will be done. Investigate the security and privacy policies in place. Be sure to learn how the company safeguards information that may continue to reside on the system when they receive it, and how the machine is destroyed. Keep in mind that the disposal of certain computer components involves the handling of hazardous materials and must be done in a precise fashion in order to comply with current safety regulations. It may also be helpful to consult with local computer technicians and retailers to learn how they handle the disposal of old machines.

Many non-profit organizations benefit from donations of computers. Often, they prefer working machines with a minimum system requirement available upon request. Links found at www.justgive.org/html/ways/ways7.html#2 may be helpful. Be sure to do research before donating equipment to any organization.

While most people's activities are legitimate, the above story serves to highlight the seriousness of removing personal information before disposing of any computer equipment.

Conclusion

To many, the Internet gives the illusion of anonymity. This chapter has offered information in an effort to demonstrate that this anonymity is very limited. Anyone with the right program, a little time, and basic skills can, in many cases, uncover a person's secrets.

E-mail messages that are long forgotten by the recipient can continue to exist on mail servers well after the messages were sent. Postings to Internet forums or web-logs ('blogs) many times written with very little thought, can remain for years.

This could very well impact the results of background investigations conducted for a variety of reasons; business, employment or personal. The various types of information at risk are:

- Criminal records (arrest records).

- Civil records (bankruptcy, divorce).

- Medical records (from medical and insurance providers).

- Personal information (SSN, address, unlisted phone number).

- Internet information (e-mail address, IP address).

This chapter also reviewed many risks brought upon by lack of Internet privacy, and presented ways to protect privacy in the future.

Some believe that to worry about trying to be anonymous or invisible on the Internet is neither possible nor necessary. They argue that the loss of privacy results in a better Internet experience and makes online commerce more productive. And at the opposite end of the spectrum, many worry that privacy may be nearly impossible to maintain and thus work aggressively to ensure as much privacy as possible.

Nevertheless, criminals are using the internet to conduct crime at an ever-increasing rate. In addition to this, and yet another concern to many users, is the risk associated with the government having too much information.

There may be times when triple-encrypting and anonymously re-mailing an invitation to a family reunion may be too much security. Yet, conducting an important business negotiation without any consideration to security would be foolish. Security measures employed should be tailored to the need.

Understanding Web Personalities

Introduction

The web is especially dangerous because of the magnetic attraction the Internet holds for those with personality disorders and mental illness. Therefore, more stable Internet users must start by understanding the fundamental nature of web interaction and explore a framework for understanding personalities on the web.

Chapter 3 will focus on the psyche of the web stalker while this chapter focuses on common mental deviants on the web, reviewing problems in text-only communications and exploring assessment techniques for various personality types. The first step in the process is to explore the hindrances of remote communication on the Internet

The Problem of Text-Only Communication

Surprisingly, psychologists have noted that only 7% of face-to-face communications is verbal while the other 93% is non-verbal. In other words, people use body language cues as a main source of communication. According to psychological studies, it is more challenging for men to accurately predict non-verbal or body language cues than women, who seem to be far more attuned in this area of communication.

"I didn't even know that she was upset until she hit me with the rolling pin."

Would it then stand to reason that since women are better at evaluating face-to-face body language, that men are better at evaluating the written word? This would be an interesting study to be sure. Whatever the case, the internet's text-only communication gives everyone, regardless of gender, the opportunity to evaluate text based on the punctuation, syntax, and grammar of the written word. This allows an individual to form their own opinion of said text.

Safety in a Text-only World

Without the subtle nuances of the spoken word, detecting humor, sarcasm and anger can be very difficult. Writers have always relished the ambiguity of the written medium and have used a host of word tools designed to introduce double entendres and hidden clues into their text.

On the web, the inherent lack of non-verbal communications leads to many misunderstandings.

- A simple typographical error in a sentence might change the meaning of the thought that the writer intended to convey.

- A word with multiple meanings might be read with a different meaning than what was originally intended.

Even the choice of font can be the source of consternation for some. The following is an example from a UseNet newsgroup:

```
btw... a**hole, why don't you type in a normal font.

The bold mono-spaced font is difficult to read. If you don't know
how to change fonts read the book that came with your browser!
```

The next response is even scarier and demonstrates how even the tiniest matter can enrage some individuals:

```
Well, D***head... I type in the fonts I happen to like.  I didn't
realise you'd been apointed head of the Font Police.
I suppose lying, dishonest SOBs like you get to pontificate on
anything, though, don't they?  Anyway: I can recommend a good
optometrist if you find it difficult to read.

Incidentally, "Arial" is not a mono-spaced font, but I'm sure you
won't want facts to get in the way of your "argument".

Look [poo]-for-brains most folks, except blowhards like you, don't
use BOLD and ITALIC except for emphasis. I guess you didn't learn
that in school.
```

So, how does one communicate effectively in a text-only world? Users need some method to communicate emotion.

The World's First Emoticon

The founding fathers of the Internet decided to use special characters to indicate simple emotions. For Internet history buffs, the following is the very first bulletin board message that proposes the use of symbols to indicate jokes in 1982:

```
19-Sep-82 11:44    Scott E  Fahlman            :-)
From: Scott E  Fahlman <Fahlman at Cmu-20c>
```

```
I propose that the following character sequence for joke markers:

:-)

Read it sideways.  Actually, it is probably more economical to mark
things that are NOT jokes, given current trends.  For this, use

:-(
```

The "reading sideways" of these symbols allows the expression of facial
emotion without being face-to-face. Once users adapt to turning their heads
90 degrees, the symbols make a lot of sense and add emotion to text
statements, helping to fill the non-verbal void in text communications:

```
:-)     Joke
;-)     Wink
:-(     Sad
:-|     Straight face
:-o     shock or surprise

(:-)    messages dealing with bicycle helmets
@=      messages dealing with nuclear war
<:-)    for dumb questions
o>-<|   messages of interest to women
~=      a candle, to annotate flaming messages
```

While primitive, these icons helped immensely to remove the ambiguity of
text-only communications.

Anger does not always translate into words

Even when using a medium that does not support emoticons, one can still
portray a statement that they think is funny with a <funny> or <grin>

---

comment. This will at least let the reader know that the sender thought it was funny.

As the web evolved in the mid 1990's people started to use *emoticons*. The word emoticon is an internet-created word that comes from joining the words emotion and icon. These emoticons are icons that can be inserted into some e-mail programs, instant messaging programs, and web sites to help clarify the non-verbal intent of messages.

Emoticons	
Code	**Image**
:mellow:	
:huh:	
^_^	
:o	
:)	
:P	
:D	
:lol:	
B)	
:rolleyes:	
-_-	
<_<	
:)	
:wub:	
:angry:	
:(	
:unsure:	
:wacko:	
:blink:	
:ph34r:	

Source: Invision Power Services

If a user is making a potentially inflammatory statement and knows it, a little smiley face with horns would help to clarify that intention. If a user thinks that a particular comment means they are the coolest person around, the sunglasses smiley would be appropriate.

This only a sample of the many variations on these *"smiley's."* Instant Messenger (IM) tools have an even greater range of emoticons, allowing users to express all ranges of emotions.

With that introduction to the challenge of text-only communications, the next step is to start with an easy diagnosis of the education level of the user on the other end of the dialogue. While not always correlated to intelligence, it is relatively easy to detect one's level of education when entering text messages.

Intelligence and Formal Education

Criminals utilizing the World Wide Web possess various levels of intelligence and some of the most dangerous criminals in history have been extremely intelligent. Users cannot let a high IQ fool them into a false sense of security.

Nevertheless, evaluating a person's IQ is one way to establish clues to character and purpose. If one accepts the statistics in the revolutionary book, *The Bell Curve*, it is apparent that people vary widely in intelligence with the USA national average IQ being heavily skewed by a number of factors. Why does one need to assess intelligence on the web?

The answer is that users have very few clues about the person behind the keyboard and must rely on whatever clues are readily available. These techniques are especially useful for identifying "posers" who pretend to be more intellectual than they are in actuality.

The greatest skew in intelligence is found in an evaluation of IQ averages by level of formal education level:

- Basic illiteracy - 85

- High School Graduate – 105

- College Student – 120

- Graduate Student – 128

- Medical Doctor – 135

So, how can Internet users gain an advantage by learning techniques for quickly pre-judging people with little or no detailed information about them.

Assessing IQ on the Web

Assessing IQ comes in handy in many instances. One such instance would be if one were approached by a con artist posing as a "professional." Many of these posers will deliberately introduce big words or famous quotes into a conversation in an effort to impress others with their high-level of knowledge. They can be very adept at using Google to find synonymous words, but terrible at fashioning a coherent sentence. This type of criminal should immediately be considered dangerous because they are deliberately attempting to mislead.

Willful deception is always a major red flag, and users should always be very wary of anyone who is *posing* as someone or something that they are not.

The first step here is a non-scientific foray into web IQ assessment that consists of looking at some actual examples. Some readers may remember Carroll O'Connor, the brilliant actor who played Archie Bunker in the hit 1970's sitcom *All in the Family*. Prior to his acting career, O'Connor was a High School English teacher and was often amazed at his students' inappropriate use of the English language. He would later incorporate some of these memorable sayings into his character's dialogue.

- "We need a basinoon for the baby"

- "That's just female intermission. They know what we're thinking"

- "You need to go see the groinocologist"

- "My job ain't got nothing to do with thinking, and I'm very good at it"

- "They were making suppository remarks about my intelligence"

- "Sticks and stones may break my bones, but you are one dumb Polock"

Many people enjoy the creative use of the English language, and subtleties can reveal volumes about the education and intelligence of a person on the web. Here are some actual examples taken from Internet message boards and forums.

From someone posing as a medical doctor:

```
I am uphawled at the way your doctor treated you.

If you were really starel then the Clomiphene treatment would make
you ferdal.
```

From someone posing as a college professor:

```
I don't no if this makes a difference, but it's soley my opinion.
```

Here's one from an alleged Electrical Engineer:

```
I think that my clame stand for itself and I never said I was a no
it all.
```

Legitimate misspellings can be forgiven; however, fundamental errors in word usage, sentence structure and grammar are always dead giveaways. With these few basic tools for identifying phony experts, the next step is to gain information on how to categorizing people in cyberspace.

Assessing Personality on the Web

The Minnesota Multiphasic Personality Inventory (MMPI) has been a recognized tool for evaluating personalities for decades and the 500 true/false questions employed in the tool provide incredible insights into personality. Unfortunately this tool is not readily available online, so users must learn to make broad generalizations about character on the Internet.

To properly understand the motives and mind-set of any individual, it is useful to classify the end user into personality types. By quickly identifying the type of person, one can anticipate their motives and desires, and devise a strategy to deal with them effectively.

This approach may sound Machiavellian, but it works very well especially for those who already have some experience with electronic media. In addition, most people tend to have very specific personality characteristics, and can generally be categorized into one of the following types:

- The Wannabe

- The Rottweiler

- The Baby

- The Luddite

- The Scientist

- The Charger

- The Empath

- The Zealot

These characteristics are deliberately exaggerated for the sake of illustration and are designed to help the internet user notice similarities with people they have interacted with in cyberspace. The caricatures for these personalities are from Mike Reed's Flame Warriors collection.

The Wannabe

The Wannabe is extremely self-absorbed and naive, and will try very hard to appear educated. They can present a real danger and therefore should be treated with extreme caution.

Because the Wannabe harbors a deep resentment for "real" professionals, they love to go on the web and pose as such, making false, ridiculous and damaging statements. Personalities in this category often suffer from very low self-esteem and delusions of grandeur.

Hallmarks of the Wannabe include:

A huge imagination – The Wannabe loves fantasy, and has a very vivid imagination. Their desire to be other than what they are shows a clear case for low self-confidence. They are constant dreamers and sometimes make outrageous claims, sometimes even staunchly believing their own lies.

The Bragger - The Wannabes tend to "toot their own horn." They will often brag about their experiences, degrees and knowledge. And because of their overactive imagination, will create outlandish tales that are not even true, most of which are easy to spot. The Wannabe can be very intelligent and it is not always easy to tell the truths from the falsehoods.

Believes everything they read – Deep down, the Wannabe knows that they really don't understand what's going-on inside a computer and cover-up their ignorance by believing that anything displayed on their monitor is the Gospel Truth.

The Wannabe often considers his job mundane, usually a "pencil pusher" or position where they do not get the respect they deserve. They also have plenty of time to dream and surf the web where they can live out their inner most desires.

The Wannabe is especially vulnerable to anything having to do with technology and there are entire tabloid markets devoted to educating the

Wannabe. They are also voracious readers and love anything that has to do with the creative world; art, fiction, movies, etc.

Aliens are Developing New Operating Systems

By Pierre A. Noyd

An anonymous source within the CIA has just confirmed an alien conspiracy to take over the Internet with a new operating system. Sources confirm that the "open source" Linux operating system is more open than anyone imaged, and is being developed by extraterrestrials.

Taking-on semi-human form and using cryptic names such as Linus Torvalds, scientists speculate that the aliens are introducing Linux as a precursor to a full-scale alien invasion.

"Once they seize the Internet they can cripple our infrastructure" notes Dr. Max Diphthong of Macrosoft Corporation. "We are taking this threat very seriously and we encourage all loyal earthlings to avoid Linux at all costs. Using a proven environment such as Windows is the best defense".

The Rottweiler

The Rottweiler is the most aggressive and annoying of the web stalkers. Stubborn and prone to exaggeration, the Rottweiler is fierce and vocal, and relishes tearing into the unsuspecting netizen. The Rottweiler will remind one of a television evangelist at the apex of their sermon.

The Rottweiler is especially difficult because they continue to vent, even after an issue had been addressed. The Rottweiler is usually male, and is the type of end user who loves the thrill of battle, carefully planning their assault for the best advantage.

Hallmarks of the Rottweiler include:

Exaggerates everything – The Rottweiler immediately assumes the worst and is quick to turn every minor inconvenience into a major disaster. To the Rottweiler, everything is an emergency.

Multi-tasking – The Rottweiler loves to multi-task and enjoys surfing the Web while at work. They are extremely productive, yet still manage to spend much of their day on eBay or posting obscenities on Internet message boards.

Confrontational – The Rottweiler is at their best when engaged in an argument, and no amount of fact is going to diminish their zeal.

Some Rottweiler's are deeply insecure about their gender roles and overcompensate by being super-macho males or super-feminist females.

The Baby

The Baby is one of the most common types of web weirdoes. Prone to temper tantrums, the Baby is characterized by a deep fear of computers and contempt for the meanies on the web.

Deeply insecure, the Baby is most dangerous when they manage to enrage a nearby Rottweiler. The Baby loves to whip the Rottweiler into a frenzy and then sits back to watch the fireworks. Often the Baby is well aware of their shortcomings and will use these outbursts as a tool to get what they want.

Hallmarks of the Baby include:

Self-centered – The Baby will become emotional over every Internet problem. The Baby is very sensitive, and takes it as a personal affront when they cannot get their computer to do what they want. The Baby will assume that every web slowdown is directed at them exclusively,

---

usually by a deliberate attempt by an anonymous web stalker. A Baby can often be identified because they complain *"Why are you doing this to ME?"*

Blames others – A Baby is never responsible for their own actions and believes that all web problems stem from the evil people on the Internet.

Lacks comprehension – A Baby cannot bear to hear technical explanations. Babies hate acronyms, and see real technical people as deliberately showing-off by using incomprehensible computer words like "connectivity" and "URL." Babies will ask lame questions like what does "Microsoft," "Browser" and "Java" stand-for, as if this knowledge will give them deep insight into the fundamental nature of the Internet.

Because a Baby's outburst is often entertaining, some web weirdoes relish the idea of watching the Baby throw a tantrum. For example, if one uses X-Windows, it is great fun to get the IP address of a Baby and display fake error messages on their screen. The following are a couple of fun messages that get Baby going:

YOU HAVE JUST ACTIVATED THE KUDZU VIRUS. YOU ARE NOW SENDING AN INFECTED E-MAIL TITLED "ME NUDE" TO EVERYONE IN THE COMPANY DIRECTORY.

HAVE A NICE DAY.

PER YOUR REQUEST, DELETING ENTIRE PERSONNEL MASTER FILE YOUR USER-ID HAS BEEN LOGGED FOR AUDITING PURPOSES.

The Luddite

Luddites are characterized by a profound fear and distrust of technology. Scared to death of change, the Luddite reacts violently to any changes to their favorite web sites. Talking with a Luddite can remind one of the time they tried to teach their grandma how to use e-mail and she thought the mouse was a foot pedal, like the one on her sewing machine.

Closed-minded and rigid, the Luddite will fight every Internet enhancement, especially those that make their lives easier and will steadfastly refuse to allow cookies, or java servlets.

Hallmarks of the Luddite include:

Distain for electronics – PDAs are unknown to the Luddite, and they rarely own a cell phone, VCR, or any device that might require programming. They may display an abacus in their office and are usually proficient with a slide rule.

No concept of feasibility – The Luddite believes that computers are much more sophisticated than they really are, and believes that HAL 2000 computer in the movie *2001 - A Space Odyssey* was real. This distorted belief system fuels their fears that the web will someday rule the earth.

Back-to-basics mentality – The Luddite longs for the days when life was simple, and their hobbies, such as candle making, sewing, woodworking and reenactments, reflect that desire.

Control Freaks – The Luddite is the type of person who will become greatly upset to learn that their data resides in the same database as data from other people. Not caring to understand web security, the Luddite will often insist that their data is not contaminated with other data.

Here is a typical Luddite response in regards to a floppy disk complaint:

"I followed the instruction to the letter! " The directions said to remove the floppy from the sleeve and then insert the floppy. It wasn't easy; I had to use a pair of scissors to get the thing out."

The Scientist

The scientist is brilliant and sometimes shy, hates disorder, chaos and conundrums, and greatly enjoys diving into the internals of the Internet.

The scientist tends to have a love of music, and gravitates towards degrees in pure majors such as History, English, Math, or Physics. Scientists always keep their home page neat and orderly, with everything in its proper place. Their motto is *"Prove it,"* and they love to try out new hypotheses on anyone who will listen.

Common indicators of the Scientist may include:

Attention to detail — Scientists like order in every area of their lives and their website is no exception. They miss nothing, and pride themselves on attention to detail.

High professional standards — The Scientist believes that everything can be described with mathematical equations and every assertion about behavior can be proven with experimentation. They sometimes require people to "prove" their assertions, and they hate "rules-of-thumb."

Highly reliable — Scientists spend their days in chat rooms, posing hypotheses and cranking out "proofs" of their theories to anyone who will listen.

Extremely eloquent — Some Scientists can be identified by their pretentious prose. These people love to use obscure words and complex verbal syntax, and normally keep an Oxford English Dictionary (OED) close at-hand. They love puns and double entendres, and enjoy using obsolete words that have not been popular since the early 1800s.

The Scientist sometimes loves to degrade others who fail to understand their words. This is often done to bait the respondent and to show-off their superior skills. Here is an actual example from a Usenet newsgroup:

```
...my characterisation of you as a "fake, phony, and a fraud" also
stands! I'll add LIAR to that also!

You really don't understand the English language very well, do you
Jack, otherwise you'd know what "tautology" means.

Oh yeah, I forgot COWARD fits well too.
```

The Charger

The Charger personality is generally characterized by a "can-do" attitude. They are always bright and outgoing, and seem to be in a hurry. They tend to be impatient, especially with stupid questions, and they never "suffer fools gladly."

The Charger's home page is in complete chaos with icons and notes posted everywhere in a seemingly random fashion. The Charger is often a pragmatist and prefers experiential learning to theory.

The Charger gravitates toward degrees in real-world majors such as Computer Science, Engineering, or Business Administration. Their personality is competitive and they may love sports, especially one-on-one competitive engagements such as golf or tennis. Their motto is, *"Anything worth doing is worth doing to excess."*

Characteristics of the Charger personality may include:

Highly creative — The Charger personality likes to think "outside the box," and often develops novel approaches to solving problems. The Charger personality loves new web features and sites, and likely has a history of causing their PC to crash as they investigate the latest Korean website. If left to their own devices, they will spend all day scouring the web for new tools and techniques.

Highly dedicated — Charger people always excel at their jobs, often taking every technical certification exam that has ever been offered. Their job is the most important aspect of their lives, and they are first to volunteer to work on Thanksgiving and Christmas.

Strategic orientation — The Charger is more concerned with long-term results than operational details. The Charger relies more on rules-of-thumb than experimentation, and does not like to "waste time" experimenting with changes before actually trying them.

Highly productive — If one is on a deadline and has a problem requiring a Herculean effort, the Charger personality can be counted upon to get the job done on-time and under budget.

The Charger personality likes stimulants, may drink volumes of coffee, keep lots of candy and sweets on the desk, and may be a chain smoker.

The Empath

The Empathetic personality is outgoing, friendly, and brings to mind a beloved Aunt or Uncle. Being people-oriented, the Empath is more concerned with the social aspects of the Internet and loves to participate in group activities such as chat rooms and interactive message boards.

Empaths are sometimes lacking in technical skills, but they make great managers, and are highly skilled at team building and very tolerant of coworkers' shortcomings. Empaths tend to gravitate toward people-oriented majors such as Psychology, Sociology, or Education.

Their hobbies may include working with animals or volunteering with civic organizations. They like sports that include team activities such as soccer, but avoid one-on-one sports. Their motto is *"No one ever wrote on their tombstone, I wish I had spent more time at the office."*

Characteristics of the Empath might include:

Charming — People cannot help but like the Empath. They are generally extroverted and always sensitive to the feelings of others. Empathetic people make great bosses because they care more about ensuring that their workers spend quality time with their families than getting a project completed on time.

Technically stable — Empaths have no great interest in new web features or the latest Internet technology and are content to keep their systems stable. They excel in situations for which 24 x 7 availability is required, and they will never change anything on their PC unless they have a compelling reason.

Modest — The Empaths may be highly licensed and certified in processional careers, but they will never talk abut them because they are concerned other people might think they are being pretentious. Even if they win prestigious awards, they appear almost embarrassed about any public recognition.

Above all, the Empath places family above work in importance. They sometimes refuse to work evenings or weekends, and cannot understand why anyone would devote their whole life to their career.

The Zealot

The zealot is a dangerous personality type that is firm and unyielding in their belief system. Whether it is religion, sports or hobbies, the old saying applies, *"You can always tell a Zealot, but you can't tell him much"*.

The religious Zealots are super-easy to recognize because of their need to bless or save everyone. Some Zealots are especially dangerous because their dogma is inviolate and they believe they have a moral obligation to break laws and attack people, all in "The Name of the Almighty".

The Zealot has one sole purpose in life, to convert others to their way of thinking. Sports Zealots are completely immersed in their teams, hobby Zealots completely immersed in their activities at the expense of everything else. On the web, many religious Zealots become web stalkers. They relish in offending others with their dogma, willfully challenging anyone who might disagree and then threatening them with dire consequences.

Psychologically, a Zealot usually has some form of Obsessive Compulsive personality disorder and may have deeply rooted security issues. Incapable of free thought, the Zealot works hard to fit everything in the world around them into their belief structure.

They are suckers for any technology products with a religious spin and they are especially susceptible to products that appeal to their fear of damnation.

Satan is Invading Computers!

In a startling revelation, Christian experts have announced that increasing numbers of home computers are being possessed by Lucifer. While demonic possession has been well-documented for thousands of years, it has only been recently that Lucifer and his evil minions have started to possess home computers.

"The problem is becoming epidemic", says Father Paddy O'Chaire of the

Satanic Studies Commission. "Christians everywhere must be vigilant to know the signs that their PC has become possessed". Fr. O'Chaire offers several signs:

•Your computer requires you to press a button named "Start" when you want to shut it down.

•Idolatrous symbols appear without warning on your desktop, taking the form of animated paperclips or common house pets.

While Satan's evil motives remain clouded in mystery, some suggest that the Beast is planning to take over the Internet. To circumvent a worldwide disaster, prominent Exorcists have teamed

with renowned software engineers to create **The Exorciser®**, a special package designed to cleanse your PC from demonic possession.

According to Father O'Chaire, "This software can save your soul. Satan walks among us and we must always be wary of Lucifer's power".

This software can save your soul
Father Paddy O'Chaire

For a limited time, **The Exorciser®** is being offered at the special introductory price of only $99.95. **The Exorciser®**

is also available for UNIX and Linux.

But Wait! There's More.

If you order today you get a free sample of **Wholly Water!®**, an all purpose blessing device for every occasion. Direct from the sacred waters of the Sea of Galilee, **Wholly Water®** is triple-blessed and comes in a convenient aerosol spray.

The Zealot is very confident in their beliefs and relishes challenging anyone who might not share their devotion.

Just like the Spanish Inquisition, the religious Zealot will either save one's soul, or label that person as satanic if they fail to embrace their rhetoric. In most cases, the Zealot will remind others that the Bible insists on the death penalty for unbelievers and those who dare to challenge them.

For example, the following is an excerpt from a book written by a licensed medical doctor, detailing the evils of astrology and encouraging fellow believers to do the will of God and help with their *"earthly death"*:

"It is clear in this [Bible] verse that God is planning an "eternal death penalty" in hell for astrologers.

However God also commanded an earthly death penalty for all false prophets, whether they prophesy on behalf of the arrangement of stars in space (as do astrologers), they prophesy on behalf of "other gods".

> "Therefore, according to the Bible, astrology and "channeling" are sins against God which should also be crimes against the state, and should still carry the maximum sentence of death."

Real-world case: The naughty Nuns

The *Associated Press* reported that several Catholics nuns used their Biblical beliefs to commit acts against the U.S. Military:

```
Three nuns facing prison time for vandalizing a missile silo asked a
judge Tuesday to acquit them on all charges, declare a mistrial or
order a new trial. Ardeth Platte, 66, Jackie Hudson, 68, and Carol
Gilbert, 55, were convicted by a federal jury April 7 of interfering
with the nation's defense and causing property damage of more than
$1,000.
```

With that introduction to some broad general categories of online personality types, the next step is to delve into the details of how to acquire more information about other Internet users by studying online interactions.

Personality Conflicts on the Web

The fun begins when websites display more than one personality type. As one might expect, conflict often arises, and it can be great fun listening to each personality type complain about the shortcomings of the others. The following is a synopsis of the complaints that are commonly heard from varying personality types on the web:

Complaints from the Scientist —The Scientist personality tolerates and likes the Empath, but has a real problem with the Charger personality. The Scientist feels that the Charger is a "loose cannon" and cannot understand their impatience and disregard for detail. Secretly, the Scientist thinks that the Charger personality is dangerous, and cringes at their propensity to rush into every new web tool without complete supporting justification.

Complaints from the Charger — The Charger personality sees Empath as being lax and slow and also faults them for having highly misplaced priorities because they put family before work. However, they have a much bigger problem with the Scientist, whom they see as rigid and overly cautious. Secretly, the Charger thinks that the Scientist personality should "get a life" and stop wasting time proving theories.

Complaints from Empaths — Privately, the Empath does not understand the high level of dedication of the Scientist and Charger, but they would never say that aloud because it might hurt someone's feelings.

Conclusion

This chapter has been an introduction of the nature of Internet communication and the many different personalities one interacts with on the web.

Many issues concerning text-only communication have been presented. They can be summarized as follows:

- The Problem with Text-Only Communication – Without the ability to hear a person speak and assess their body language, evaluating intent becomes a matter of grammar, syntax and word usage. Emoticons are now a popular way to emphasize meaning.

- Assessing Intelligence – Through the use of spelling, grammar, style and sentence structure, Internet users can evaluate another user's general intelligence level.

- Assessing Personality - To assist in the classification of the mindset of an individual, information on the various personality disorders most commonly found on the Internet, thus allowing a user to quickly identify and deal with particular personalities.

- Personality Conflicts – Learning which types of personalities align and conflict will ultimately give the Internet user an edge when interacting with others.

The next chapter is more serious. It delves into the darker side of the Internet in order to help users understand those Internet users with serious mental health issues as well as those dangerous individuals with malicious intent.

Web Weirdos

With the Internet, what one doesn't see is what one gets.

Introduction

While many people on the Internet would be considered "normal," the absence of face-to-face contact makes the web a haven for all manner of "fruits and nuts."

The anonymity of the web makes it an ideal haven for all sorts of people with diagnosable mental health issues, from the mildly neurotic to the certifiably insane. The challenge is being able to recognize the signs of those with a dangerous mental condition. This chapter will briefly introduce the specific types of web weirdoes, how to spot them and what dangers they present to the general public.

The Land of Fruits and Nuts

Volumes have been written about the root causes and treatments of mental conditions, and dozens of famous psychologists from Sigmund Freud to Carl Rogers express opinions on the nature of neurosis and mental defects.

Whether subscribing to the Freudian notion that repressed desires are the root of neurotic behaviors or believing the Rogerian theses that the causal origins of deviant behavior are of little consequence; everyone agrees that it is in one's best interest to learn how to reliably spot those with personality disorders, which might be threatening. Without degenerating into psychobabble, there is a need for some type of roadmap to the world wide web of weirdos so that people can navigate the electronic world in relative safety.

Many people have a moment of epiphany when they first recognized that friends and neighbors were a whole lot more screwed-up than they could have imagined. If one prefers not to pre-judge people, the upcoming sections will not be particularly enjoyable; however, it is still important to understand that people found on the Internet may not be remotely like what they may seem. It is built into animal genes to judge the safety of any situation, and the lack of visual and verbal clues available while communicating through the Internet makes it especially challenging.

There are websites, which cater to paranoid schizophrenics, with something like the Aluminum Foil Deflector Beanie (AFDB), designed to protect the psychotic from harmful mind-reading control carriers.

An Aluminum Foil Deflector Beanie (AFDB) is a type of headwear that can shield the brain from most electromagnetic psychotronic mind control carriers. According to www.zapatopi.net/afdb.html:

> "AFDBs are inexpensive (even free if you don't mind scrounging for thrown-out aluminium foil) and can be constructed by anyone with at least the dexterity of a chimp (maybe bonobo). This cheap and unobtrusive form of mind control protection offers real security to the masses.
>
> Not only do they protect against incoming signals, but they also block most forms of brain scanning and mind reading, keeping the secrets in your head truly secret. AFDBs are safe and operate automatically. All you do is make it and wear it and you're good to go! Plus, AFDBs are stylish and comfortable."

Software manufacturers are also catering to the needs of the web psycho. The MindGuard ® software is an excellent example.

According to the website, "MindGuard is a program for Amiga and Linux computers that protects a user's mind by actively jamming and/or scrambling psychotronic mind-control signals and removing harmful engrammic pollutants from the brain."

All versions of MindGuard have the following features:

- Biorhythmic synchronization

- Birth name based numerological functions

- Logging

- Support for all known psychotronic carriers

- Modular carrier system for easy upgrades

- DePsych mind deprogrammer removes post-psychotronic empagrams

- Automatic signal deciphering

- Dishevel-Bippsie, PsyDET, LZI, and LZII algorithms

Source: zapatopi.net/mindguard.html

The following section presents information on the most harmless of all web weirdos, the socially inept and will reveal details about the more dangerous web deviants.

Social Incompetents and Neurotics

While the planet is filled with socially inept people, the web has a greater than average share of people without basic social skills. Ever since the 1950's, people with a desire to avoid human interaction have been drawn to the solitude of computers, a safe place where they can interact without fear of persecution.

On the web, socially inept people are usually seeking a partner, a set of friends or an intimate relationship. The socially inept user is like the kid who always was picked-on at the playground, and their clumsy advances toward people on the web can be frightening.

For example, he simply does not understand that if a woman tells him she cannot go out with him because she is washing her hair; she probably is not washing her hair, but is actually letting him know she is not interested. He figures that the answer will be 'yes' if his timing is better, so he asks her out repeatedly.

Fortunately, the socially incompetent person frequently can be convinced to stop their pursuit; especially when threatened with public exposure such as a stalking complaint.

The Pseudo Stalker

There are many borderline wackos on the web who will challenge others' patience and give-off scary signals. Termed "inappropriate affect" by psychologists, inappropriate responses are a sure tip-off. This inappropriate response might come-off as merely unpleasant, but it should always be taken as a warning signal.

As noted earlier, the safety of the web emboldens otherwise introverted or withdrawn personalities, especially those picked-on types who have a deep-seated fear of confrontation stemming from years of taunting and ridicule. Their repressed anger comes out in savage, inappropriate attacks, similar to those in old WWII Nazi movies.

The age-old adage, "Never trust anyone who feels compelled to remind you that they are honest" applies, but with a different spin. The following are some common categories of inappropriate affect:

Inappropriate Aggression – Those who respond to non-offensive communications with inflammatory comments are more often than not suffering from a diagnosable condition. Their outbursts help them to offset their feelings of low self-esteem, and just as a Masochist enjoys inflicting bodily pain, this borderline psycho derives pleasure from demeaning others. Here is an example:

```
As ever, Jack, you reveal yourself to be an utter idiot.  Because
you can't be bothered to search Deja News, you resort to personal
attacks, and claims of "Liar! Liar!".

Do yourself (and us) a favor, Jack: go away.
```

Inappropriate Insults – Those with a need to degrade and demean others often have a serious personality disorder related to self-concept issues. They hurl inappropriate insults at others with carefree abandon, knowing that they are insulated by the web from real-word repercussions. Here is an example from a UseNet newsgroup:

```
Yawn.  If my parents failed to teach me common decency, Lord alone
knows how yours spent their time...
```

This personality disorder is also characterized by an, *"I'm more erudite than you"* attitude and the insults are often combined with inappropriate aggression:

```
Robert, there is just no point trying to have a debate with you.

Your understanding of English words seems totally at variance with
mine.

And you are disingenuous in your use of analogy.
```

Intimidation – Veiled threats, carefully worded to skirt the "credible threat" threshold, are often used by web stalkers to intimidate other users. These types of web stalking threats indicate that the stalker has the presence of mind to calculate the attack, and they should always be taken very seriously. Here is an example:

```
He won't be back, Jean.  The modest abuse you saw him receive
publicly here yesterday is nothing compared to the threats and
abuse he has received privately.  Nothing.

Com'on Howie, fess up, you're a punk. Punks like you usually get
the crap kicked out of them. Stand up and be a man Howie, don't
hide like a little fairy.
```

```
Tell me you are sorry, and ask me to forgive you! I just might do
it! I might let you off the hook! Then again I might not! One
never knows till one tries!!!!
```

Not all of the difficult people that seem to be in such abundance on the internet will be as nasty as those discussed thus far. As is the case with all societies, the cyber-society that has evolved around us has its share of those who do not know how to behave appropriately. The severity of their transgressions will run the gamut from mild to malicious.

On the mild side, there exists the type of person that likes to post inflammatory statements to an e-mail list or a blog, and then sit back and watch the sparks fly. Others want to be confrontational and start fights with members of a group, while complaining to the moderator and anyone else who will listen about how poorly they are treated. It only takes one or two troublemakers to ruin a great group and send the quality members packing, looking for a more enlightened arena in which to engage in discussions.

There have even been cases of individuals getting into altercations online and attempting to file legal action against another party. How the legal intricacies of the web develop and what constitutes solid grounds for litigation is for the courts to decide. A later chapter will explore the internet and the laws in more detail, but for the purposes of this section, suffice it to say, it is always advisable to take the high road when dealing with difficult people online.

One cannot be responsible, if one does the right thing, as hard as that may be from time to time. As for determining when someone has crossed the line and if legal action has become appropriate, exercise restraint and reserve this option for only the most grievous offenses. Note here, that threats of violence against another person violate the law in any forum and can result in prosecution.

Remember, that while web stalkers may begin communicating in an irritating manner, many will progress to direct threats. Never dismiss any disturbing or frightening comments as "probably nothing" or "probably harmless." Words often lead to actions and all threats, even veiled threats, should be taken extremely seriously.

Types of Web Weirdos

While the web is indeed a bastion for flakes of all sorts, it is important to note that there is a strong genetic and external component. According to a respected psychologist, many of these disorders can be brought on or aggravated by external factors such as illnesses, alcohol, prescription drugs, or illegal drugs. Some of these disorders; schizophrenia and compulsive tendencies, in addition to those factors, can exacerbate stalking behaviors. Also, central nervous system disorders (CNS) including some forms of schizophrenia may also have an impact on an individual's behavior. There is ongoing research into treatments for organically-caused stalking disorders, but many experts believe that brain dysfunction is a major factor in the aggravating web stalker's behavior.

Certain personality disorders may make a stalker more dangerous. Without the benefit of scientific research, a brief synopsis is presented for the more common types of web weirdoes.

The Narcissist

Narcissists love themselves excessively and feel that everybody should love them as well. When they attempt to initiate a relationship and are spurned or rejected, they take it personally. Sometimes a narcissist is borderline psychotic, which increases the danger they pose to the public.

Often "a legend in their own mind", the narcissist will fanaticize about being a famous person such as a Rock Star or a politician and they sometimes cross the line into delusional grandiosity, believing themselves to be omnipotent.

The Doper

The web is a wonderful place for those with substance abuse issues, and many of these netizens can pose a serious threat to children. Dopers band-together and justify their need for the substance and once convinced that their behavior is "normal," they reach-out to naïve people and push their wares.

The Delusional

Some personality disorders and schizophrenics have delusions of grandiosity, and the web is a perfect haven for them. Unlike the stereotypical nut who truly believes that they are Napoleon, paranoid grandiosity can range from a very mild feeling of innate superiority to a full-blown psychotic delusions.

Common web occupations of the delusional personality include psychics and animal communicators where these special people use their special powers to clean-out the wallets of trusting souls.

The Bi-Polar

The bi-polar individual tends to have mood swings from a state of depression to a manic, highly energized mood. In the manic phase, they become insistent on getting their way and become very persistent. When combined with psychotic features, the bi-polar can be especially dangerous.

Deviants on the Web

Following that introduction to the less harmful netizens, this section will provide information on the real threats on the web, those deviants who use the Internet to prey on innocent victims.

> "*We* are deeply ashamed of what *we* did"
>
> - A New Jersey defendant claiming to have a multiple personality disorder at their sentencing.

True mental diseases can range from a mild neurosis such as fear of flying to full-blown clinical psychoses. For instance, the web is a great haven for those with inappropriate sexual preferences, and these sexual obsessions can drive some web deviants to prowl and prey upon unsuspecting people. The first attraction of the web for deviants is the false acceptance they get for their condition.

The Internet is a safe dwelling place for all forms of sexual deviants, from the annoying exhibitionists who e-mail naked photos of themselves, to psychotic sexual deviants such as necrophiliacs who enjoy sex with dead animals. The anonymity of the web lends an air of legitimacy and makes the web stalker feel justified in satisfying their demented desires.

Because of the seemingly safe environment of the Internet, many deviants gather together and decree that their deviance is acceptable and natural. Once confident that they are not deviant after all, they feel free to prey upon the general public.

There are many bizarre deviants on the web, and each of the following groups can unfortunately find friendship and conspirators:

Child Molesters – Pedophiles gather on the web in order to share contact information and justify their repulsive desires. Consider this statement found online:

```
"When will people understand that children have sexual desires and
there is nothing wrong with helping them find pleasure in their
sexual desires?"
```

Law enforcement officials across the globe agree that the urge to molest is incurable, and this precipitated the formation of sex offender tracking systems. Unfortunately, these evil people will use the web to seek opportunities to prey on children.

Bestiality – Many animal molesters find solace that there are others who enjoy getting it on with Fido or Mr. Ed, and they band together to share tips and tricks.

Necrophiliacs – This bizarre group of weirdos enjoys sex with deceased things. Since human corpses are hard-to-find, many of these sick people will kill pets in order to have relations with them.

Mutilators – Deeply disturbed teenagers often practice "cutting," otherwise known as the practice of inflicting pain for pleasure. This type of masochism is a well-known clinical disorder, but groups of sick kids use the web to justify their actions and find acceptance from fellow sufferers. Here is a published sample on the web from a self-mutilator and anorexic:

```
I cut myself as a teenager but was never hard-core about it. For
me, it went hand in hand with anorexia.

Luckily for me, I had a great group of friends who force-fed me
and helped me get through it. I was so out of it during that
period (probably from lack of calories) that I don't remember that
much.

Now I know that anorexia and cutting myself came about as two
things I could control (being a control freak) and that would also
get me attention.
```

The next section provides startling information about some of the most dangerous threats on the web, the sexual deviants who prey on unsuspecting netizens.

Sexual Deviants on the Web

As noted previously, the web is a haven for sexual predators of all manners, and the natural anonymity of the Internet has facilitated thousands of sexual attacks in the United States.

TheFreeDictionary.com defines a pedophile as "an adult who is sexually attracted to children." Everyone should remember being told to stay away from strangers. Many schools today spend time teaching schoolchildren about "stranger-danger", and that they should avoid all contact with unfamiliar adults. Sadly, this advice has not been extended to the Internet.

Research is clear that the web has become an important vehicle in the enabling of child molesters:

"Technology itself does not create pedophiles.

However, the Internet reinforces negative behavior and negative arousal patterns and gives these sex offenders a place to express themselves."

Excepted from *Monitor on Psychology*
Volume 31, No. 4, April 2000

On the Internet, the distinction between stranger and "new friend" can blur. For example, a new friend in a chat room might tell a child they are 14, but in reality, this new friend is middle-aged and recently released from prison.

Internet access can be a wonderful tool for all manner of education and fun. Tutoring, learning about other cultures, gaining hands-on experience in technology, etc. are just a few of the many advantages the web offers children.

The instinctual trusting nature of children combined with the anonymity of the Internet makes cyberspace the perfect target-rich environment for technology-enabled predators. Chapter 10 is entirely devoted to protecting children on the web.

Web Addicts

There is some debate about whether excessive Internet use deserves its own addiction label; Internet Addiction. It has been suggested that the Internet itself is not addicting, but rather it is personal behavior, which directs online usage or abuse. The thought being that the person addicted to online gambling, for instance, is in fact, addicted to gambling not the Internet and merely uses the web as their vehicle of choice.

What about those who spend hour after hour online; in chat rooms, playing games, or just simply web surfing? Over-use of the Internet now has a label,

Pathological Internet Usage (PIU). Honestly answering the following two questions will allow a person to see if they are at risk:

- Is some amount of Internet use causing stress among family and/or friends?

- Is use of the Internet causing poor grades or affecting work performance?

If the answer to either of these questions is yes, reducing time spent online is advisable. If any combination of family, friends, school, or work is being significantly affected, then it is time to seek professional help for ways to reduce that dependence.

Kimberly Young, PhD, and Executive Director of the Center for OnLine Addiction, has a more comprehensive test for those who believe they may have a problem. This test can be accessed at, www.netaddiction.com/resources/internet_addiction_test.htm.

An Internet addiction test administered online may appear paradoxical, like holding a gamblers anonymous meeting in a casino or an Alcoholics Anonymous meeting in a tavern. Yet, in reality, it is more like passing out information regarding Gamblers Anonymous to those in a casino, or passing out information regarding Alcoholics Anonymous to those in a saloon.

Those who think they may be addicted to the web will more than likely take the test online rather than anywhere else. Hopefully, if confirmation of addiction is confirmed, they will seek additional treatment and support for their PIU.

Web Gambling Addicts

Gambling made available on the Internet seven days a week, twenty-four hours a day is a serious danger to an addict. Gambling is not universally permissible in the United States, so there are not many legalized casinos available to those who enjoy gambling. Other than the weekly card game among friends or a wager placed on a sporting event, the temptation to gamble is less prevalent.

Now, however, the easy availability of the Internet provides opportunities to place bets on sporting events around the world, or to play a couple hands of poker any time of the day or night. The temptation has become too difficult for many to resist.

With this new accessibility, many who did not allow gambling to negatively influence their lives before the Internet now have to face this compulsive addiction. The following are a few characteristics of a compulsive gambler:

- Impulsiveness.

- Poor problem-solving capabilities.

- Anti-social behavior.

- A history or family history of substance abuse and/or depression.

- People from a lower socioeconomic status tend to spend a higher proportional amount of their disposable income on gambling activities

- Gender. Males are more likely to develop a gambling addiction than females.

- Age. Youths are more susceptible to high-stakes, high risk activities such as gambling, substance abuse, etc.

Knowing whether a person is addicted to gambling or addicted to online gambling is not as important as knowledge of the potential financial and emotional damage that could be inflicted on that person and their family.

If a person is faced with this compulsive disorder, seeking help from a professional is just one avenue to assist in getting the destructive behavior under control. Another available option is the support group, Gamblers Anonymous (www.gamblersanonymous.org).

Web Pornography Addicts

Anyone who has been online for any length of time has likely seen e-mail messages advertising pornographic websites. It has been said that if the total energy spent on Internet pornography could be converted into usable fuel, the energy crisis would be solved.

Online pornography is an area that benefits greatly from the perceived anonymity offered by the Internet. Many people, who would not feel comfortable walking into an adult bookstore or purchasing pornography from their local convenience store, barely hesitate before opening up a web browser and viewing the same sort of material online.

In much of the world, pornography depicting exclusively adults is legal. However, there are countries in which simply logging onto a pornographic website could subject them to criminal prosecution. Whether legal or not, study after study has demonstrated the negative impact of pornography. Among the psychological ramifications are the development of anti-social attitudes and an increased aggressiveness towards women.

Clearly, where pornography is legal, people need to make up their own minds about their exposure to the materials. However, when the viewing of pornography becomes a compulsion and begins to impact work and personal relationships, it can be as destructive as any other addiction.

Don't let addiction rule your life.

It is commonly argued that pornography is a "victimless" crime. The models that pose for the pictures are consenting adults who are paid rather well for their trouble. The magazines that publish the material are businesses that pay taxes, hire employees and contribute to the economy as do all other businesses. Opponents of the industry are thus hard pressed to locate the "victim."

The problem with this assessment is that viewing pornography has become a destructive addiction for many people. Pornography can become a part of a person's life that demands engagement again and again, whether that person wants to or not. This is of course, the very nature of an addiction.

Studies indicate that indulging in pornography is a progressive behavior, much like drugs or alcohol. The types of images that one views escalate over time and become more explicit and sometimes deviant. Material that once inspired a certain level of satisfaction no longer does the trick. Eventually, what may have once seemed shocking becomes mundane.

No count morals that are out to lunch

They're sliding away cause everything is okay

It was taboo back then but today you say "What the hey"

Lyrics to the song "Socially Acceptable" by DC Talk.

Once a person is desensitized to hard-core pornography, they may begin to seek alternatives, and try to recapture the sensation it once provided. Some people have been known to act out according to the material to which they have been exposed. Some kinds of pornography depict images of violence against women and focus on the domination of helpless victims. Although this is not universally the case, there are many instances where pornography has been identified as a contributing factor in sex crimes.

Along with the victims of these crimes, the addicts themselves also suffer. Personal relationships can be pushed to the edge by the stresses caused by an ongoing addiction. A spouse may be left with feelings of disgust and betrayal when a pornography habit is discovered. In addition to all this, it is understood that the financial resources of the addict are stretched. A pornography addict will, like all other addicts, spend money with abandon, seeking to satisfy what drives them.

CyberSexualAddiction.com offers many helpful articles, facts and a self-assessment test, all designed to give support to online sexual addicts as well as their spouses, family members and friends whose lives become affected by pornographic addiction.

Pornography has both its advocates and opponents, and its potential effects will undoubtedly be argued for years. Nevertheless, it is imperative to understand the addictive qualities of pornography and the personality traits that can lead not only to addiction, but also to progressing sexual deviant behavior.

The next section provides important information to those looking for love so that they might be better able to identify the predator lurking among the sincere lonely hearts.

Looking for Love on the web

Is that wonderful new girl that one meets online as attractive in person as her picture? Is she as nice as she seems online? Is she close to the age she says she is? Is she really a woman?

"I'm a twenty-year-old non-smoker..."

These are all important questions when people start looking online to find a relationship. There are a myriad of services available designed to help anyone find their soul mate. Some of these are simply personal advertisements; an online version of the classified section in some newspapers. Others provide comprehensive personality assessments to help find someone with compatible personalities.

Is there a better name for online dating?

Online meeting might be more accurate. If one is sincerely looking for a relationship, after an interesting initial online contact is made, there will likely be a date *in real life* (IRL). Dates IRL are not online by definition.

The Internet is rampant with stories about relationships that started online. Some of these stories are about good relationships while others take a negative turn. Even when the Internet is not involved, most individuals know people with good relationships and people with bad ones.

The difference is that if one meets a person face-to-face, generally, they cannot or will not lie as much about themselves as they can online. Online, they can send an old picture from their high school or college days or even the image of a supermodel. Online or in real life, they can lie about their job, income, and current relationships. Online, it is difficult to determine whether any of what they say or send is true. The real truth about whether they have been lying about their height, weight, economic status or anything else will be unknown until a meeting occurs in real life (IRL).

The online Romeo may have a dark side in real life.

As with anything found on the Internet, care should be taken not to give too much credibility to a source that one does not personally know and trust. Be especially careful of stories that are not from the person in question. Many of the Internet's urban legends are told as something that really happened to a "friend of a friend" (FOAF).

There are many sites designed to inform people about the dangers of meeting people online. Some sites are offered by people that have been burned by online meetings and others by people that have witnessed the unfortunate aftermath of an online meeting, short courtship, and sudden marriage.

Internet dating or online introductions do have their success stories. The following are important examples of the positive impact that the Internet can have.

A Way to Meet: A Real World Case

Tim had decided to look outside of his usual hangouts to find a new romantic interest. He had a few matches that looked good via e-mail and through telephone calls, but they ended up not "clicking" in person for various reasons.

Finally, he started a dialog with a girl and after they spent some time getting to know each other through e-mail conversations and phone calls, they agreed to meet in a public place.

That date and the many that followed have resulted in what is currently a two-year relationship. It is not a perfect relationship, but none are, regardless of whether they originated online or off. By all accounts, this relationship is going well and may very well last many years or decades.

Tim considers this a true success story of online dating. He attributes this success to some factors that could be beneficial to others considering online dating:

Give it time. Spend time getting to know the other person's personality, likes, and dislikes before arranging an in-person meeting.

Do not look for a twin. Variety is the spice of life and a relationship with a lack of spice can be a bad recipe. If he likes jazz music and she likes classic rock, there is room in the CD caddy for both.

Do not look for an opposite. Identify features where one does not want the opposite. These things are what matter the most. If religion is important, look for someone with a compatible religion or at least a tolerance of such beliefs.

Public meeting. Make sure that the meeting place will allow either person to make a quick exit if something does not feel right. One may decide that if the other obviously lied about their height or appearance, they do not know what else they may have lied about and may want to pass on this date.

Finally, Tim says that if a relationship does not work out, try again. Do not avoid Internet dating. When learning to ride a bicycle, most people fall down at least a few times. If people quit trying to ride because they fell down once, there would be a lot of bike companies going out of business.

Ensuring Safety from Cyber-nuts

Many safety guidelines are important when first meeting someone in real life that one has only known via e-mail, chat, or telephone. Many of the guidelines are good ideas all of the time, while some may not be important if one feels like they already know the other person.

Lisa Hupman is the operator of a website that informs people about the possible dangers when a relationship is initiated online. To be fair, some of these dangers exist regardless of how or where two people meet, but www.wildxangel.com is a site that contains a lot of information from people who wish they had been more cautious.

Some tips for a first face-to-face meeting are shown in Figure 3.1.

First Meeting Safety

- Always Meet in a Public Place! Don't even agree that the parking lot is a good idea, you have NO protection from anything in a parking lot and no, your car is NOT safe! You can be easily overpowered, you don't know if other cars in the parking lot are safe and nobody from within can see you.

- Always Tell a Friend or Relative where you will be and write that information down!

- Never allow yourself to be picked up for the first meeting. If you don't own transportation, get a ride from a friend, take a cab, or bus. Do not become a statistic! It is NEVER SAFE to leave your home with a total stranger or to give a total stranger your address. If you plan on drinking, get a ride from a friend though I would strongly advise against becoming inebriated in the presence of someone who is, basically, a stranger to you.

- Never leave your purse unattended, even if the person you are meeting tells you they will watch it for you. Contained within your purse or whatever you carry is not only the obvious personal information, but your car and house keys. You may not notice they're gone.

- NEVER EVER leave your drink on the bar! If you have to go to the bathroom, or leave for whatever reason, take your drink with you. If that is not possible, dump it out! Order a fresh one when you return. Rophynol is not the only drug you need to be concerned about, homemade knockout drops are very vogue now! Be safe, be smart, be aware.. Remember, knowledge is power, forewarned is forearmed.

Figure 3.1 - *Safety Tips.*

Copyright Chamade, reproduced with permission

Conclusion

This chapter presented a brief overview of the many types of "weirdos" lurking on the web. Equipped with this set of guidelines and making use of some old fashioned common sense, netizens can avoid these undesirables and maintain their own web presence unencumbered by the likes of the following:

- Social Incompetents and Neurotics

- Pseudo Stalkers

- Narcissists

- Dopers

- Sexual Predators

In additional to web weirdos, this chapter also briefly covered various web addictions, online relationships and over-use of the Internet, identified as Pathological Internet Usage or PIU.

The next chapter will present in-depth information on hard-core web stalkers and what can be done to identify a threat and protect against predators.

Web Stalkers

MILWAUKEE -- In April, a Marquette senior came home from class to find a friend in her apartment clutching a knife.

The senior, thinking that he was her friend, had turned to him when she started receiving threatening e-mails.

Police now believe that the *"friend"* who pretended to help find her stalker, was actually the woman's cyber-stalker and, ultimately, her rapist.

Introduction

United States Federal law uses the term "facility for Interstate Commerce" to encompass the web for Stalking actions:

> "Uses the mail or any facility of interstate or foreign commerce to engage in a course of conduct that places that person in reasonable fear of the death of, or serious bodily injury to any person."

Stalkers do not always become violent. While in many cases the progression of events will tend toward an escalation in aggressive behavior that can lead to violence, there are things that can be done to prevent this from happening. Responding in a strongly negative manner to unwanted and inappropriate overtures may, at times, be all that is necessary to put an end to the problem. It can also be effective to inform the would-be stalker that law enforcement has been notified and action is being taken to track them down.

Not all offenders will be so easily dissuaded, however. There are those who become so fixated on the person they are stalking that even the threat of discovery and punishment will not discourage them. These are dangerous people, and every available resource must be employed to ensure safety.

Knowledge is a powerful tool and being aware of the many possible threats that stalkers propose will empower people to remain safe in the cyber-world as well as IRL (In Real Life). The following is a list of important information this chapter will cover:

- Ways to recognize a stalker.

- Action to take when stalked.

- Types of stalkers.

- Other types of unpleasant people.

- Safety requires vigilance, online and off.

What Is Web Stalking?

Deviants have been around for a very long time, but it was not until the 1990's that a particular set of socially deviant behaviors were identified and grouped together under the general heading of "stalker".

The dictionary defines stalking as "to move threateningly or menacingly" and "to follow or observe (a person) persistently, especially out of obsession or derangement," (*The American Heritage® Dictionary of the English Language*, Fourth Edition Copyright © 2000 by Houghton Mifflin Company.)

This definition applies universally, whether one is on a dark street at night, or in front of a computer at work. While the focus of this book is the online environment, the threat is no less real and is often the first step in a more menacing scenario.

Stalkers often begin to research the object of their attention online, gathering information or sending harassing e-mails, and then they proceed to engage their subjects In Real Life (IRL).

Technology Enables Web Stalking

The incredible information gathering ability afforded by the Internet has become a powerful new weapon in the arsenal of the stalker. Phone numbers, addresses, financial and employment information and even hobbies and interests may be available online, depending on how poetic one may have waxed while filling out a user profile for an e-mail group or blog. In addition, the stalker may contact an agency to search for information, and for a fee, the agency can obtain facts regarding property ownership, history of criminal activity, civil proceedings and the like.

John Wayne Gacy would have loved the Internet.

It is also possible that a stalker may seek information directly by contacting an intended victim through e-mail or in a chat room. In most cases, a stalker requires only a thin veneer of secrecy created most often by merely saying

---

they are someone they are not. With a false identity established, they may interact freely with whomever they wish.

A healthy dose of caution and little skepticism can go a long way in protecting the online public.

The Credible Threat Doctrine

Some web stalkers have been stalking and terrorizing people for years, and they are familiar with the ins-and-outs of the criminal system. If a person is unfortunate enough to become a victim of a web stalker, their first line of defense is the police.

Many victims are surprised when the police choose not to take action, even on a seemingly obvious threat. The police use the threshold of *credible threat* when evaluating web stalkers. When evaluating any complaint, the police are not going to mobilize a team for protection, unless it appears that the person is in clear and present danger.

"The Cops won't touch me.
They don't think that I'm a credible threat."

Sometimes, presenting evidence that the tormentor has a mental problem can backfire. Many police officers will dismiss the threat as the ramblings of a harmless crazy person, leaving it to the victim to convince them that there is a credible threat. In some cases, police will not act until it is too late.

Netizens should bear in mind that web stalkers may escalate their attacks. Many people encounter weirdos every day, and even the seriously disturbed flashers may be seen as a nuisance but otherwise harmless. However, real-world studies have shown that many deviants eventually progress from flashing to rape.

When does the flasher become a credible threat?

Likewise, many stalkers start out as merely annoying with excessive e-mail, gifts, and phone calls; but may eventually progress to threats and violence. The big question is, "Do they pose a credible threat?"

Real World Case: Web Harassment

Several years ago, a woman and her husband were awakened by the telephone in the middle of the night. The wife had appeared on national TV that month in connection with an experimental program to train seeing-eye horses for the blind. The calls were coming from miniature horse owners who were offended by a web page they found on her website. Call after call ensued and some of the callers were obscene, threatening and lewd.

Terrified, the next day the wife started collecting evidence and discovered that the calls originated from one of their toll-free business hotline number. The couple tracked all of the callers and found the source of the harassment to be the moderator of a Canadian message board. At about midnight, this moderator published the number and a challenge to her forum members:

I see they have a toll-free number 800-xxx-xxxx.

Let's all call her, let her know our feelings and run her phone bill sky-high.

Armed with complete evidence including names and addresses, the wife went to the authorities, expecting immediate aid only to find that:

The Sheriff – The local sheriff took a report but said that there was nothing they could do, not until one of the stalkers entered the county in which the couple resides.

The State Police – The trooper said that a single call does not constitute harassment, and as long as any person does not call multiple times, there was nothing that could be done under the law.

The FBI – The FBI agent said that while annoying and threatening, they could not investigate because the threat had originated from a foreign country.

In this case, the stalking escalated and the wife had to file U.S. Federal complaints against more than a dozen people to get the court's attention. Apparently intimidated by the wife's evidence, complete with IP addresses, URL's and other technical jargon, many in law enforcement had no idea about how they should pursue the matter.

Arresting the Web Stalker

Web stalkers are bold, and they believe that they can get away with things online they cannot in real life. Online, they can take on a new persona and hide their true identity. However, the online names used by web stalkers can provide clues about their agendas. Some pick a nickname like they would for a personalized license plate. Their screen name says something about who they are or what they like; truckguy, TXsoccermom or queenquilter. In the following true story, the web cretin chose the macho name Vito to communicate his agenda of mafia-like terrorism.

Of course, there is no real anonymity on the web. Despite Vito's perceived anonymity on the web, law enforcement and Cyber detectives in California were able to track suspected web stalker Mark Johnson, AKA Vito:

"Johnson has admitted creating the persona of Vito because it "'sounded like a Mafia name'" and would be hard to trace," court papers allege.

> "The arrest -- which has attracted nationwide attention -- caps an eight-month "cyber-space" investigation by the Economic and Computer Crimes unit of the Fresno Police Dept." the Fresno Bee reported.

This arrest is an example of how law enforcement can use their technical specialists to support an investigation. However, this story does not end with the arrest. An arrest is only the beginning. With evolving Internet laws, many prosecutors are afraid to go into this predominantly uncharted new territory.

After Arresting the Web Stalker

It is not over, even after the police investigate and arrest the web stalker. Here is another story from the *Fresno Bee* where the District Attorney could not find enough justification to charge a web stalker.

> "Fresno police last Thursday arrested Mark Johnson, 39, on charges of grand theft, 44 counts of fraudulent use of a credit card, 52 counts of making fraudulent credit applications, distributing obscene material to a minor, attempted oral copulation with a minor and attempted sodomy with a minor."

Sounds clear-cut, right? That is not necessarily so. In this case, the DA said that there was not enough evidence at that time to sustain the charges.

> "I sent the case back [to police investigators] for more work," said Deputy District Attorney, Greg Bixler, who reviewed the credit card fraud charges against Johnson.

> "The charges involving sex with a minor also needed additional work before they could be sustained in court", said Elizabeth Mitchell, chief deputy district attorney.

Despite the evidence, the alleged web stalker's attorney made a huge fuss over the arrest of his client.

> "The police must have a vendetta against my client."

The article says that the arresting officers in the case are furious with the turn of events.

It becomes apparent that reporting, capturing and prosecuting a web stalker can be a huge uphill battle.

The information in the next section will delve into the types of web stalkers in an effort to help understand their personalities, motives and weaknesses.

Types of Web Stalkers

Almost all web stalkers have a personality disorder and many have more serious mental health issues. These issues range from neuroses to a full-blown delusional personality. Dr. Patricia Farrell, a licensed psychologist and educator specializing in medical psychology, notes that most web psychos do not believe that they have a problem.

There are many kinds of stalkers, and they can be categorized according to their maladies. Netizens should note that all varieties of stalkers have a high degree of instability, and their behavior is not likely to fit neatly into any one profile. To put it briefly, because they are unpredictable, they can shift from category to category while stalking their victim.

The Insane Among the Sane

Those individuals with documented cases of severe mental illnesses make the scariest web stalkers. These individuals are characterized by delusions such as hearing voices or talking animals, bizarre belief structures, and the manifestation of inappropriate actions like the stereotypical maniacal laugh of the mad scientist. True delusional insanity is most common in teenagers and older people who have suffered from a brain disorder such as a blockage or Alzheimer's dementia.

Even a child can spot insanity

According to Silvia A. Tomai of Wellesley College, there are four main types of schizophrenia. This psychiatric classification is not a cut-and-dried diagnosis because many insane people may manifest symptoms from each category. Plus, the lack of face-to-face interaction makes it very difficult to know if a stalker is insane. The following is Dr. Tomai's summary of the types of insanity:

Undifferentiated Schizophrenia - This type of schizophrenia is defined as a gradual reduction in the sufferer's interests and relations with the outside world. In addition, these people experience a reduction in the vitality of their personality and emotional responses.

Hebephrenic Schizophrenia - This type of schizophrenia is characterized by the person's grossly inappropriate, shallow or ridiculous emotional responses to the outside world and their incoherent thought and speech. In addition, this type of schizophrenia displays hallucinations and delusions.

Catatonic Schizophrenia - This type of schizophrenia is characterized by unusual motor behavior. People suffering from this type of schizophrenia sometimes remain in a state of complete immobility for long periods of time. Other common symptoms include an inability to talk and a lack of all voluntary actions. These periods of inactivity are commonly interrupted by episodes of excessive excitement and motor activity. These actions are often impulsive and very unpredictable. Therefore, patients in this state of schizophrenia require special care and supervision in order to prevent self-harm or harm to others.

Paranoid Schizophrenia - This type of schizophrenia usually does not develop until later in the person's life. It is characterized by prominent delusions or hallucinations of personal harassment in conjunction with illogical and unrealistic thinking. These delusions may be numerous, but are normally centered around a common theme or idea.

While classifying the deviant who is stalking a person may be interesting, more importantly it can help the victim understand the type of person they are dealing with and prepare appropriate defenses. It is important to remember that a person who is judged insane may not be legally responsible for their actions.

Obsessive Personalities and Web Stalking

According to the available statistics, 60% of all stalking cases are of the simple obsessive type. These typically involve a fixation on a person with which the stalker has previously been involved; very often an ex-wife or husband, girlfriend or boyfriend and so on. Many of these cases are actually an extension of a previous pattern of behavior involving domestic violence or psychological abuse, but now the stalker has learned of a new way to reach out and touch their victim.

*"I told her I was a doctor.
She couldn't resist the temptation to meet me."*

Low self-esteem is often a motivating factor for the stalker. Through a twisted series of mental exercises, they decide that the way to enhance their own sagging self-image is to dominate and demean others. Along with the feeling of power and control they get from this type of bullying, the stalker gains an improved sense of self. When a victim of this type of repression tries to free themselves from the situation, the bully often feels that the very foundation of their self esteem is threatened. They may feel their whole life is tied up in the failed relationship, and that if it is lost, they have nothing left for which to live. A desperate psychotic like this, can become a dangerous stalker very quickly. Their behavior will become increasingly erratic as they feel their control and own sense of worth slipping away. If, in the end, they cannot intimidate or threaten their former victim into returning to them, it is likely they will become violent and try to destroy the victim.

In the rogue's gallery of stalking categories, "simple obsession" has distinguished itself as the one most likely to result in murder. The familiar phrase "If I can't have you nobody can" applies to this situation in spades. All too often, once a stalker decides to become violent, it does not end until the victim is killed. Faced with a life alone, stalker suicides often follow close on the heels of these murders.

Love Obsession Stalking

The love-obsessed stalker is not normally as well associated with the object of their desire as is the simple obsessed individual. In most cases, they have only the most cursory acquaintance with their victim or are complete strangers to them. This type of stalker admires from afar, but desires to be much closer. Similar to the simple obsession stalker, the love-obsessed stalker will have low self-esteem. They see a potential relationship with a person possessing strong personal qualities and of a higher social standing than themselves as a way to advance their own prospects. They wish to "hitch their wagon to a star" as the saying goes. When the affection is expressed and not reciprocated, a stalker can be born.

Love-obsessed stalkers cannot accept rejection and go on with their lives. They become so driven to have a relationship with the object of their desire, that in the absence of the real thing, they may invent a fantasy relationship and delude themselves into believing it is real.

They stalk their victim in an attempt to make them participate in the illusion and act out the role assigned for them in the stalker's imaginary world. Of course, this sort of psychotic behavior only results in an even stronger negative response from the victim. The love-obsessed stalker becomes so desperate to have any relationship at all with the victim that they will assume an adversarial role and become an enemy, rather than have nothing to do with the object of their obsession.

Authorities have surmised that this may explain why somebody like John Hinkley could believe that shooting President Ronald Reagan would win the affection of his love obsession, Jodi Foster. It may also shed some rather bizarre light on the motives of the man who shot John Lennon, all the while claiming to be his biggest fan.

Erotomaniacs and Web Stalking

The clinical name for a particular type of love-obsession web stalker is erotomaniac. This stalker believes that their victim is in love with them.

"She loves me, I know it.
That Restraining Order is just
her way of playing hard to get."

More precisely, an erotomaniac is a person who relentlessly pursues the false notion that the object of their affection reciprocates their romantic feelings and fantasies. Erotomaniacs are often delusional, and nearly all suffer from serious mental disorders such as paranoid schizophrenia. Paranoid schizophrenics are not always the obvious "Napoleon" stereotypes.

Paranoid personalities can happen at any age and for many reasons, including genetic predispositions, major life stress, post traumatic stress disorder, or organic brain problems such as Alzheimer's senility.

Unlike the simple and love-obsession stalker types who are seeking to establish or re-establish personal relationships with their victim, erotomaniacs fool themselves into believing that the relationship already exists between themselves and their targets.

Fortunately, this type of stalker is somewhat rare and they account for less than 10% of all stalking cases. Erotomania stalking cases frequently receive public attention because the target is usually a celebrity, and the media knows that stories about celebrities help drive sales.

Here is a new story documenting how law enforcement cooperated with a web provider to locate a web stalker accused of murder.

Daily Mirror 08/02/00

"JILL POLICE NET WEB STALKER"

A SUSPECT who traced Jill Dando's address through the Internet has been tracked down by murder squad detectives.

The stalker has been quizzed on why he wanted to know where the TV presenter lived.

He gained the information in November 1998 - five months before Jill, 37, was shot outside her home in Fulham, west London.

He visited the tracing specialist website 192.com, whose owners happen to be Fulham-based, and paid by credit card.

The search was reported by 192.com the day after the murder.

Until yesterday, it was believed that details of the caller were destroyed after 14 days.

But Scotland Yard worked with computer firms to track the Internet call back to its source.

The Yard confirmed yesterday that the searcher has been interviewed, but refused to say where he was found.

A spokesman added: "He has not been arrested."

Similar to love-obsession stalkers, erotomaniacs attempt to increase their self-esteem and status by associating themselves with people who hold a higher social status than they do. While the behavior of many erotomaniacs never escalates to violence, or even to threats of violence, the irrationality that accompanies their mental illness represents unpredictable behavior that might become a threat to victims.

Vengeance and Terrorism Stalking

Stalkers that fall into the category of vengeance and terrorism are of a different ilk altogether than those that have been discussed thus far. Vengeance stalkers are not trying to create or restore a relationship. They have been injured, or think they have, and rather than seek reconciliation or at least restitution, they are out to settle the score. When vengeance is the goal, punishment is the means for its accomplishment. They seek to hurt their victim, and extract pain as payment for whatever wrong has been done by them.

One scenario that is commonly seen among vengeance stalking cases is that of a disgruntled employee who has recently been fired. They believe they have suffered an injustice, and that a group or individual can be blamed for their trouble, usually a boss. They are unable to reconcile their own feelings about the wrong they feel has been done to them, and become driven by their own consuming desire to make the offending party pay.

On December 26, 2000, Michael M. "Mucko" McDermott murdered seven of his coworkers with a firearm after learning that his employer had been instructed by the IRS to garnish his wages to pay back taxes. It is believed that Michael McDermott suffered from several psychotic disorders including paranoid schizophrenia and a history of depression, which is believed to have contributed to his deadly behavior.

At times, the motivation for a vengeance or terror stalker may be less personal. Some people have been known to adopt stalking strategies in order to promote a political or ideological agenda. This type of activity is more in line with what are considered 'traditional' terrorist tactics.

Stalkers who employ these methods are usually trying to influence the actions of others. For the political terror stalker, they may see the threat of violence as a kind of a trump card that allows them to influence the decisions of highly placed power brokers far more effectively than through legal channels. Other stalkers may have an ideological objective to pursue and target anyone they think may be able to direct affairs in a manner that aligns with their particular bias.

Predatory Web Stalking

Predatory stalkers are those who incorporate a stalking tactic into their preparations for an attack. They are not stalking so much for the sake of stalking, but to lay the groundwork in order to accomplish their true objective. They may also be motivated in part by the feeling of control they get when their stalking begins to have an effect and the victim starts to behave differently.

As with other stalker personalities, this type of stalker will likely suffer from low self esteem and perhaps poor social skills. Unlike the love-obsessed stalker, the predatory stalker is not interested in meaningful one-on-one time with the target, stalks for a shorter period of time and is more likely to commit sexual assault. However, during the early stages of events, they tend to keep some physical distance between themselves and the victim.

Surveillance is a major component of the predatory stalker's plan. This can be a weakness. It can also be exploited if the victim becomes aware that they are being watched. Any suspicion that this is the case should heighten the alert level with which daily activities are performed.

Anyone feeling as if they might be watched should practice some common sense defense tactics. They should take note of cars in traffic and ask themselves if any of them look more familiar than they should? While in public places, they should look around; observe, know what is normal and what is out of place. Their actions and activities should not be predictable. They should take a different way to work now and then. It is also good to vary lunch hours and leave the office early on occasion, if possible. It sounds strange in today's schedule-oriented society, but one should make sure a watch cannot be set by the things they do. If anyone has reasons to believe they are being observed, they should call the police and at the very least make an official record of the problem through a police report.

Regardless of which category a stalker falls, the unique information-gathering capabilities of the Internet have made the task easier. While not every stalking case results in physical violence, the unpredictable nature of the beast makes it imperative that every precaution be exercised.

The next section will present information on the law as it applies to criminal activity and the Internet. It will become clear that law enforcement in this area is an evolving entity, much like the Internet itself.

Legal Issues on Web Stalking

Among the significant findings of the 1998 National Institute of Justice (NIJ) study, *"Stalking in America"*, was that:

> "Less than half of all stalking victims are directly threatened by their stalkers, although the victims, by definition, experience a high level of fear."

This has motivated some states to strike the "credible threat" requirement from the language used to define stalking under some state stalking statutes. (Tjaden & Thoennes, (1998), *"Stalking in America"*, NIJ.)

More flexible legal terminology is now being used that allows for the inclusion of a broader range of activities to fall within the legal definition of stalking. The new concept revolves around the idea of determining whether a reasonable person has justification to feel in jeopardy because of the actions of another.

Recognizing a Stalker

> In the summer of 2004, Catherine Zeta-Jones and Michael Douglas were the repeated objects of national news-worthy reporting. Because of their celebrity status, their personal stalking case was of interest to the entire world, which is why performing an Internet search on the subject will return over 100,000 hits.

While many of the stalking cases that make it into the headlines center on high profile targets like celebrities and movie stars, this is only the tip of the iceberg. Most stalking cases do not garner public attention and people's perception about the seriousness of the problem is skewed.

Netizens should consider the following clues to be potential indicators of a problem. They should be taken seriously:

- Persistent e-mail of an aggressive or disturbing nature.

- Someone impersonating the individual or others, and then acting irresponsibly.

- Mail bombs (Denial of Service/DOS).

- Spamming (someone signs the individual up for unwanted e-mails at pornography or other potentially offensive sites).

- Comments like "I know where you live" or "I know what kind of car you drive" are strong indicators.

As soon as a person becomes aware that a problem is developing, they must notify local law enforcement. While there may not be enough evidence to locate and arrest the perpetrator, officials advise that it is extremely important to begin the documentation process as early as possible.

When dealing with many web stalkers, it is impossible to avoid confrontation. It is a no-win interaction because the web stalker will use any excuse that they can find to start attacking their victim. It can be as simple as buying something online or responding to a message in a chat room. Once people engage with the stalker in any way, they lose.

It takes little or nothing to provoke the web stalker. In this real-world message from a Usenet newsgroup, the following individual was targeted by a web stalker because of their choice of letter fonts. In the case below, the victim's contact information was located via a Google search and they were bombarded with threatening and obscene e-mails. Sadly, the victim was unable to stop the web stalker because they lived in a country with lax enforcement of stalking laws:

```
btw... a**hole, why don't you type in a normal font?
```

The following discussion captured from a Google Usenet Newsgroup shows two people hurling serious threats and accusations at each other.

```
You are a stalker. Maybe not by the legal definition. I'm not a
lawyer so I can't say.

However let's look at just the word stalker and how it applies to
you.

- You have said you will post the addresses of some people.
- You have posted where some people work.
- You have continually harassed some people.
- You have impersonated some [people] and
  posted on the boards as if you were them.
```

As one might expect, the accused person, web stalker or not, feels compelled to retaliate in kind. In this case, if the accused real life identity was revealed, the web stalker would have a cause-of-action for libel and defamation of character, provided that the allegations were false.

Web stalking is a serious felony, and the excerpt from an online conversation quoted below illustrates the danger of making direct allegations to a stalker. The accused stalker replies:

```
Now you are alleging that I am a "stalker". Please post your proof!!

Since I have never been arrested or charged what would lead you to
post that very defamatory allegation???

Rest assured that legal action will soon be instituted on behalf of
myself and others who have endured suffering as a result of this
witch hunt.
```

Based on other reports about this event, it is likely that neither of these two people are criminals or web stalkers. In this case, the real web stalker stole the identity of the person accused above and the accuser was not technically savvy enough to understand Internet impersonation. Impersonation is a common stalker method that can be used both to disguise their identity and to enjoy watching others be accused of their crimes.

In this case, the accuser made a serious error with their accusations and opened themselves up to a costly civil court action. A web stalking victim is already under tremendous stress, and it is easy for them to make false assumptions about the identity of their tormentor. In the wild-west atmosphere of Google Groups, it is easy to overreact to a message. Never make accusations that cannot be proven, and the temptation to retaliate against any presumed attacker should be resisted. There is always the chance that even the most logical conclusions can be in error.

Another lesson from this real-world case is never to trust third-parties. Just because someone says that they are an expert does not make them one. Savvy netizens always seek independent confirmation of someone's identity. Just because an e-mail says it is from someone does not mean that person actually sent the message. Many systems have been setup insecurely or have been compromised by viruses or hackers and can be used to spoof e-mail to make it appear that someone else sent it.

The ability to identify a stalker is a valuable skill. But just who are these shadowy figures that slime about the murky depths of the cyber pool wreaking havoc where they can? Alarmingly, the next section will illustrate that they could be just about anybody.

Demographics of Web Stalkers

The demographics of stalkers show that there is a potential for anyone to become a stalker. Web MD's, Dr. Patricia A. Farrell says,

"Stalkers and their victims come from every area of life, every socio-economic, educational group".

Therefore, no one is immune from potentially being stalked or becoming a stalker when driven by external factors.

By Day   *By Night*
"Many Web Stalkers lead a double-life."

Data from Patricia Tjaden and Nancy Thoenne's report, *"Stalking in America*: Findings From the National Violence Against Women Survey",* states that stalkers fall within very specific demographic groups:

- 80% are white.

- 87% are male.

- 50% are between the ages of 18 and 35.

- Most are of above-average intelligence.

- Most earn above-average income.

The type of victim also crosses all demographics, but the same report provides this interesting information about the typical web stalking victim:

- 78% are women.

- 83% are white.

- 74% are between the ages of 18 and 39.

- 59% are married.

It is surprising to note, according to the statistics, that nearly one quarter of the stalking victims are male, and demonstrates that no one kind of stalker has a monopoly on the practice. Some conjecture that the percentage of male stalking victims may be even higher since there is a tendency among men to under report the crime.

The Scope of Web Stalking

It is estimated that around 1 million women and 400,000 men in the United States are being stalked in one form or another at any given time. This estimate is based on a 1998 National Institute of Justice study that surveyed more than 16,000 adults. These are staggering statistics and bring into stark relief the enormity of the problem.

With the explosive growth of the Internet, the declaration of an accurate number of people online is very difficult to make, but estimates range between 80 million and 600 million people. This represents the community world-wide, including both cyber stalkers and their victims.

The Motivations of Web Stalkers

So what makes a stalker? From earlier information, it would appear that they often suffer from a mental illness of one kind or another, and typically have low self-worth.

Like everyone else, they have been confronted with life's disappointments; but somehow they have not managed to keep a proper perspective on these let-downs. As a result, they have seemingly been sent careening head-first into a world of delusion.

There are those with a predatory bent, seeking to destroy the object of their fixation. This chapter has introduced us to the concept of those persons obsessed with wanting a love relationship with another, often out of their league; but somehow unable to grasp that fact or deal with the obvious and inevitable rejection.

The range of personality types and motivating factors that go into the interactions between people can make it difficult to determine whether a person is a stalker or merely socially inept. If it is merely a problem with a socially inept person, and one has conveyed to them a lack of interest, maybe a visit from the police will reinforce the borders of normal social behavior.

Indeed, often times the stalker will be unaware that they are doing anything wrong, and may be thoroughly confused about their own motivations. So, what constitutes a stalker?

The following section will illustrate the natural progression of web stalker from initial contact to the escalation into violence. This will relay an idea about the mind-set of the web stalker, and will show how they justify their actions.

The Web Stalking Progression

The web stalker always follows a similar pattern of behavior toward their victim. It is relatively predictable, and can sometimes escalate into direct violence:

- They become agitated or enamored with their victim.

- They publish threats, insults or invitations on the Internet.

- They obtain personal information regarding their victim.

- They begin unsolicited e-mails or telephone contact.

- The rejections received enrage them and they begin overt attacks.

The following are a few examples of the web stalker's progression.

E-mail Harassment and Web Stalking

Engaging a web stalker in discussion on a message board or in a chat room is sometimes all that is needed to mark an individual as a potential object for harassment. Should such a situation develop, document all the details possible, and begin an official history of the problem by filing a police report.

Another web stalking technique is the veiled threat. The following is an actual example of a veiled threat from a real-world web stalker. In the case below, the web stalker resides in the Middle East country of Jordan; therefore, it was impossible to prevent the threats and harassment:

```
By the way, say high to Mrs. Fitz; I hope she received the gift; how
is douching for the bitch coming along?
```

The problem with taking any formal action in response to this type of threat is the "Credible Threat" doctrine established by law enforcement. Only when the web stalker's correspondence is judged to present a credible and immediate threat to an individual's safety will law enforcement investigate the web stalker. Many unfortunate victims have lost their lives because of this requirement; however, the sheer volume of Internet threats makes it prohibitive for the FBI to investigate them all. The following is another real-world example of a veiled threat, cloaked in sarcasm:

```
Oh, I see that you only live a few hours drive from me.

Since we are becoming great friends I thought me and some of my
Green Beret friends might stop over and meet you in-person.

We are really looking forward to getting to know you at a more
personal level.
```

When reporting these sorts of incidents, make sure to specify that the threats were received via Internet technology. This may help route your case to the Computer Crime Unit. These officers are in tune with what is taking place on the net and are equipped to take action. They are also aware of the special procedures that apply in cyber-cases such as the subpoena of IP addresses and archived server logs.

What an Individual Can Do

Once the web stalker escalates into direct threats to a netizen's family and indicates that they know personal addresses, always notify the police immediately. It is unfortunate, but most law enforcement will convey the fact that little or nothing can be done until a credible threat exists.

Blocking unwanted email from a stalker is always an option. Configuring a web browser and setting up rules for email handling can be very effective at accomplishing this. If the disturbing overtures were only from a prankster with too much time on their hands and a bad sense of humor, this may be all that is needed. This type of joker is looking for fun, and having their e-mails bounced and other forms of prodding ignored, is not it.

On the other hand, if one has been specifically targeted by a stalker, the stalker is not likely to be discouraged so easily. They have a more sinister objective and must be confronted at some point. Preventing all contact through the Internet may seem like a solution in the short term, but could also mean missing the opportunity to identify valuable clues about the person's identity or intentions.

In the end, it may be that a specialized law enforcement department designed to handle these sorts of cases will be best suited to help users decide if the offender is a dangerous threat or an annoying wannabe, and what can be done to stop the harassment.

The legal language varies by location concerning when law enforcement is authorized to act in web stalker cases. It is always advisable to err on the side of caution. As stated earlier, if an Internet user is receiving unsolicited, unwanted attention that is causing a problem for them or their family, the police should be contacted. The consensus of the law enforcement officials and a licensed psychologist interviewed for this book was unanimous on this point.

Preventing Web Stalking

When a stalker makes first contact with their target, it is often after some initial research. While it may be at this point that the victim begins to think about the security of their online information, in all likelihood, the horse is already out of the barn, and their information is in the hands of the bad guy.

The guidelines that follow are designed to help law-abiding netizens reduce the volume and increase the security of their personal online information.

Do Not Threaten the Web Stalker

In some cases, the victim might fabricate a story to scare the web stalker into submission. This "throwing down the gauntlet" approach may give one some personal satisfaction, but it rarely works. The following is an actual example of a victim's "Don't mess with me" message from a Usenet newsgroup:

```
About five years ago, somebody cut me off on the freeway and I
flipped him the bird.

He followed me home, yelled out his car window "I know where you
live." I maced him, dragged him out of the car by his hair, cuffed
him (on the way home from work, had my tools with me).

Called the cops. He spent five days in jail for menacing. Bitching
all the time to the judge, "I didn't do anything!"

This is a very nice way of saying that if any of you wackos show up
anywhere near my property or me, you're going to jail.

You really don't know the law, do you? And do you think that anyone
will take you seriously after seeing a compilation of your continual
harassment of me?

I'm reporting you to the police as an Internet stalker who is
possibly a danger to me and my friends.

Consequences, nutcase. Consequences.
```

In this case, the web stalker became even more enraged and made a direct threat to his victim:

```
If you are such a tough motherf***er, why hide behind the police
now? Or are you so ****ing fat that you really are a "Big" man?

You always talk big Scott xxx, come up with good stories but have no
proof that you have the balls to do anything.

> Called the cops. He spent five days in jail > for menacing.
Bitching all the time to the
> judge, "I didn't do anything!"

Boy do you sound scared. I can't wait to see how brave you are when
I show-up in person.
```

While this may seem self-evident, one should always resist the temptation to tell the web stalker to "Bring it on." Instead, one might consider exposing their anonymity, a tactic that works remarkable well for web psychos who would never have the courage to engage in a real-world confrontation.

Always Stay Anonymous on the Web

Whenever performing an online function or conducting business that requires a username, be sure to choose a name that reveals as little as possible. Tom Smith for example, would not want to identify himself as T_Smith, since this could be easily guessed by anyone trying access his accounts.

Internet security advisors also suggest that a username be gender neutral. This practice, known as "gender-blurring", is a sensible precaution for everyone, but is especially prudent for women since they are statistically more likely to be the target of Internet harassment.

In general terms, the more non-descript a person's username is, the less likely it is that their username will be a factor in their being chosen as the target of Internet harassment.

Having said that, by all means, never choose usernames like "young-and-hot" or "loose-girl". These labels will draw stalkers out of the woodwork like a bucket of chum draws sharks. A person who chooses a name like this is plainly seeking attention, but there is no way to predict the outcome. Safety is not a game, and playing on the Internet can have unintended consequences.

Do Not Reveal Personal Demographics

It should go without saying that some things are better left unsaid. Many of the online activities in which groups of people interact over the Internet will have a registration and/or a profile process to complete. The idea is that one is joining a community of sorts, and that other members of like mind and interest will want to know more about each individual user.

Perhaps there was a time when volunteering personal information was a friendly gesture. Today, it can be dangerous. When participating in instant messaging groups, blogs or any other online communities, provide the absolute minimum information allowed. Remember that security cannot be taken for granted, and in some instances, it may be possible for even unregistered lurkers to access individual profiles.

If demographic information is required as a prerequisite for membership in the group, at the very least investigate who will have access to it and how it is protected from those who do not.

Do Not Accidentally Reveal Personal Identity

Privacy minded users must make it a point to understand the security policies in place at their local Internet provider. They should also have a company representative from each online business they deal with to explain how the company keeps sensitive data secure. Banks and credit card companies will most likely have a high degree of security associated with their online businesses. However, an online dating service or a free business sponsored email account may not. Each user should spend some time thinking about who has their information, and then find out what each of them are doing to protect it.

As mentioned previously, weblogs, Usenet groups, e-mail discussion groups and Internet guest books maintain information on members. They can also capture some types of information about any person that stops by. All netizens should be cautious. Understand that any information surrendered is now controlled by someone else. When considering what to submit to one of these sites, one should consider if it would be wise to post the identical information in the classified section of the local newspaper.

The newspaper is local; the Internet is world-wide. The newspaper runs ads for a brief period of time; the Internet may archive personal information for years. The Internet is an information-gathering machine of unparalleled abilities, and can be used to combine a bit here with a byte there, and assemble a profile more detailed than most people might feel comfortable with; the newspaper cannot. So if one does not want any particular piece of information to be public knowledge, one should simply not post it.

Report the Web Stalker

The web stalker relies on the safety and anonymity of the web to make them bold, so a formal complaint can often make them stop.

Complain about the Stalker to Their ISP

The following is a complaint published by someone claiming that they were harassed with unwanted e-mails.

```
Dear postmaster at bigpond.com:

Howard xxx continues to violate my previous requests of not sending
me uninvited private e-mails.

This constitutes HARASSMENT by Howard xxx.  I am hereby notifying my
Internet service provider of this HARASSMENT, which also constitutes
invasion of my privacy.

Please take action on this matter immediately as this continued
HARASSMENT is particularly disturbing.

Please note that I am not asking Howard J. xxx any questions, and do
not thus want any replies from him, as well as demand he immediately
stop his further violation of my prior requests.

Again, Howard xxx is HARASSING me with his uninvited private e-mails
to me. Please bring his violative behavior into check immediately.
```

Even if all precautions are taken, it is still possible to become the target of a web bully or a stalker. If this occurs, collect and record as much evidence as possible. Save and print hard copies of all suspected documents. Make sure to include all header information when printing. The data collected may be the most valuable tool law enforcement officials have in the event of an inquiry.

The Stalking Resource Center is a department of The National Center for Victims of Crime (NCVC). They can provide valuable advice on how to proceed as one gathers electronic evidence for use in a potential prosecution. The NCVC also works with a nationwide network of local advocacy groups that can help victims receiving protection and support.

Complain about the Stalker to Their Employer

Netizens can use the same tricks as the web stalker and use Google to find their personal information. In the United States, the stalker's employer may be liable for the actions of their employees if the threats were made during working hours or if the stalker was using the company's equipment. Many courts have ruled that vicarious liability may be imposed on employers for the defamatory actions constituted by an employee's use of the Internet and e-mail facilities, especially when the stalking is done during business hours or when it is done using the company's electronic equipment (PC, network, etc.).

Almost every employer has an e-mail policy. The policy usually includes a clear statement that derogatory, obscene, defamatory and/or harassing communications are prohibited and will lead to disciplinary action up to and including termination.

The following is a sample letter that was successfully used to stop a web stalker and receive a settlement from the web stalkers employer for facilitating his actions:

```
Dear HR Department,

I am an attorney representing Ms. Jane Doe in this complaint against
your corporation.  This is a formal letter of complaint regarding
damages resulting from the actions of your employee, Mr. Di Irtbag,
one of your employees.

I have proof that Mr. Irtbag is publishing these remarks during his
standard office hours while working for your corporation.  We also
have evidence that he is using your computer equipment to facilitate
his unlawful attacks against Ms. Doe.

The following are samples of Mr. Irtbag's threatening comments,
published on an Internet Usenet newsgroup.

    "This dame sounds hot, and I really like her "go away"
messages.  We all know that she wants it, and wants it bad"

    "I looked-up her hometown and found Jane's home address and
phone number.  I'll be getting some nookie soon, for sure."

Mr. Irtbag then escalated into direct e-mail and telephone threats
and the line-item detail from her phone records clearly indicate
that the calls are coming from your corporation, using your
corporate assets.

Upon opinion and belief, your corporation is wholly responsible for
these threatening publications and obscene contacts by Mr. Irtbag.
Please have your attorney contact me at their earliest convenience
so that we may access the extent of Ms. Doe's emotional distress and
arrive at appropriate compensation from your corporation.

Sincerely,

Ima Litigator

DEWIE, SICUM and HOWE
A Professional Limited Liability Corporation
```

Conclusion

The Internet has been compared to America's Wild West of a century ago; a place where the law could not always be found and the bad guys sometimes get a leg-up on the good guys. And just as settlers in the old Wild West had to accept responsibility for their own protection, so citizens of today's Internet communities must take the initiative in securing their identities, their resources and their lives against the stalkers that threaten them all.

In this chapter, details have been presented about web stalkers, their various personalities and motivations and some things that can be done to protect against them.

Specifically, the following areas have been touched upon:

- Definition of a web stalker

- The credible threat doctrine

- Types of web stalker personalities

- Legal issues effecting stalker investigations

- Progression of web stalker behavior

- Ways to protect against web stalkers

The next step is to look at other criminals who inhabit the web. In the next chapter, Cybercrime will be introduced as well as information on how law-breakers use the Internet to facilitate their evil deeds.

All About Cybercrime

"Man, when perfected, is the best of animals, but, when separated from law and justice, he is the worst of all." Aristotle

Introduction

The Internet has provided an unparalleled vehicle for criminals to inflict harm on the unsuspecting. With lightning-fast speed, personal information can be accessed, with web forums being regularly used as platforms for coordinating criminal activity.

This chapter provides an overview of the major areas of Cybercrime. The information presented will start with the most onerous criminal activities, and then move on to lesser crimes such as invasion of privacy and defamation. It will also include important issues surrounding theft and vandalism. Web-related crimes will be examined and information on how even an innocent website can violate the law will be presented.

Options on how to collect evidence, determine the right jurisdiction, and report crime to the appropriate authorities will be included. The main topics in this chapter include:

- An overview of Cyberlaw

- Internet Scams

- Cyber Stalking

- Internet Harassment

- Libel and Defamation

- Invasion of Privacy

- Web Identity Crimes

- Tortuous Interference

- Web Conspiracies

- Victims Rights in Cybercrimes

- Collecting Evidence

- Reporting Cybercrime to Law Enforcement

- Penalties for Cybercrooks

Unfortunately, most law enforcement agencies have limited resources and must prioritize their caseload by the amount of the loss to the victim; in most cases $100,000 or more. In addition, many law enforcement officials face some of the following hurdles:

No Sympathy – Victims of greed-based scams often get little sympathy from the police.

No Technical Education – Due to limited funding, many law enforcement officers do not receive the training necessary to investigate cybercrime.

No Concept of the Law – Anyone who attended law school before 1995 is unlikely to understand Cyberlaw. Many of these judges and prosecutors try to apply brick-and-mortar principles to cybercrimes, often with unsatisfactory results.

While Federal and State laws contend with cybercrime, it may be very difficult to get assistance for a minor violation.

"No, this agency can't investigate until you've actually been murdered."

In the wake of the 9/11 attacks, the FBI and other Federal agencies spend much of their resources fighting cyber terrorism; therefore, reporting a minor web crime can be an exercise in futility.

Unless there has been a financial loss of more than $100,000 or a direct and credible threat against an individual, federal agencies are unlikely to investigate the complaint.

Sadly, cyber criminals know this and many operate with impunity, knowing that traditional law enforcement is often forced to turn a blind eye to their criminal activities. Smart Cyber-crooks know that they can make millions of dollars by perpetrating hundreds of small crimes. As long as no one makes a connection between the crimes, the cyber-thief is safe from investigation.

Unfortunately, there are plenty of trusting people who will readily fall for a scam. As P.T. Barnum once said, *"There's one born every minute",* and the Internet has no shortage of greedy and gullible people looking for a deal.

The following section provides an overview of Cyber Law within the United States and how these laws rarely protect against attacks.

Internet Scams

Chapter 7 of this book, *Internet Scams,* has been devoted entirely to the issue of web scammers; however, this section will give a quick tour of the phenomenon in order to tie together how scams fit into the evolving world of Internet law.

Nigeria has distinguished itself as one of the world's chief hotbeds of fraudulent Internet activity through its proliferation of highly effective cyber-scams. One Nigerian swindle that appears on the scene with startling regularity is the *Advanced Fee* scam, which is also called the *419 Fraud.* It is so named in honor of the section of the Nigerian criminal code that it violates. Nigerian President, Olusegun Obasanjo has vowed to improve Nigeria's record of law enforcement in the cyber realm. Recently, he announced the creation of a specialized 15-member committee focused exclusively on Internet fraud. This committee will work alongside existing law enforcement agencies, assisting them in their effort to stem the tide of cyber crime in their country.

Despite these efforts, Nigerian based cyber-crime continues to flourish. The architects of these ongoing schemes have even incorporated the government's publicity about its beefed up efforts into yet another variation of the same old trick. This new adaptation of the *Advance Fee* scam comes in the form of an e-mail claiming to be from a Nigerian government official. A sample of the content of one of these emails is presented below.

This e-mail claims that recent law enforcement efforts are meeting with success and that some of the stolen money has been recovered. It goes on to explain that in a good faith effort, the Nigerian government is making an attempt to return the recovered funds to the rightful owners.

Comment: good day sir/ma,

my name is usman abdulahi i am the chairman of the financial aid in nigeria.

my aiim of writting this lettrer is to inform you that thje rate which nigerians has been sending scam mail is much and has also been collecting money from people in other countries. we are sending this lettrer to every body who has nigerians must have stolen their money to please send us a mail and the information on how they collected yoiur money and the money will be sent to you.

the number of 1000 m,en has been caught running scams and has been arrested .we also went further on and saw the sum of $32million in their account and now this money has to be shared to every body who has lost their .i want you to send me a mail; if your was stollen so that we refund the money to you and also send us full information on how they collected it .i am expecting to hear from you to refund you your money if you have lost any.

thanks
usman abdulahi

Figure 5.1 - *A sample Nigerian scam*

If successful, this unfortunate scheme will have the potentially devastating effect of hitting the same target twice. Should the victim of a previous *Advance Fee* scam receive such an e-mail, their sense of relief and exuberance may short-circuit their clear thinking, allowing them to fall into the same trap yet again.

For the record, at the time of writing this book, the Nigerian government has not reported the recovery of any of the stolen money and has no plan to seek restitution of any kind.

Remember, scams work because they appear legitimate. One cannot always rely on instinct or gut feelings to alert them when something is not right. There may not be any clues or errors to raise warning flags within the fraudulent e-mail or the web page promoting the scam.

"....Nigeria is still ranked as one of the most corrupt countries on earth. U.S. citizens lose approximately $2 billion ($2,000 million) a year to Nigerian fraud -- be it credit card fraud, insurance fraud, or 419 scam letters, or counterfeiting, which totals about two and one-half times the value of our total U.S. exports to Nigeria."

Nov. 1999, Robert L. Mallet, Deputy Secretary of Commerce

Verify through a third party anything that sounds too good to be true, because in all likelihood, it probably is.

To obtain additional information about specific governmental laws as they apply to international cybercrimes, consult the official government website for the country of interest. To obtain a brief overview of how these laws apply in more than 20 countries around the world, log onto www.mcconnellinternational.com/services/Updatedlaws.htm.

Real-World Case: Nigerian Scam

When Dianne opened her e-mail and read the earnest plea from a religious man in Nigeria, she responded immediately. A trusting and caring type, she was also already planning how she would spend the millions of dollars she would get in return for helping this man in desperate need of assistance.

She sent the poor Nigerian fellow all of her cash and even took out cash advances against her credit cards. It was only after spending thousand of dollars in fees and charges did she begin to suspect that this was not a legitimate proposal. After she told the police her story that she realized her poor judgment and ultimately greed had backfired on her.

The attitude of the law enforcement agency was not sympathetic. They considered Dianne as culpable as the criminal because of her desire to make a fortune without earning it. For the second time in less than a decade, Dianne quietly filed bankruptcy and left the system to make up for her poor judgment.

The following section provides a closer look at information on more traditional cybercrimes, starting with the web hacker attack.

Hackers on the Web

Computer intruders were around long before the introduction of the web. Back in the ancient days of data processing (the 1970's), computers at the prestigious Massachusetts Institute of Technology (MIT) were infected by an annoying software program called the Cookie Monster.

The first recorded computer network hacking software, Cookie Monster was designed to randomly choose a user's terminal session and interrupt it with the text display:

Gimme Cookie!

If the user ignored the demand, the message would continually interrupt them at more frequent intervals. Students at MIT soon learned that responding with the word *"cookie"* would stop the harassment. The Cookie Monster would politely reply *"Thank You"* and disappear back into a hidden alcove in the network.

Once the World Wide Web was opened, computer hackers have become far more sophisticated and their attacks have become far more dangerous.

Denial of Service (DOS) Attack – The DOS attack is an extremely simple attack. By capturing a request to the web server and placing it in a loop, the same URL request can be sent over-and-over in rapid succession, clogging the web listeners.

Virus Attacks – Using one of the hundreds of vulnerabilities in Windows web servers, hackers can introduce Windows viruses to wreak havoc on any MS-Windows-based web server. Today, UNIX and Linux-based web servers are relatively immune to these attacks, but there have been fears that as Linux become more popular, hackers will create Linux-based viruses.

Root Kit Attacks – In a root kit attack, the operating system is compromised. For example, a root kit attack can install a daemon process that constantly accesses confidential information and e-mails it to others such as a company's competitor.

While hackers have fun interrupting the operation of websites, the real threat comes from their obsession for stealing personal and financial information. The following section outlines how hackers steal information.

Outside-In Hacker Attacks

Kevin Mitnick, a noted computer felon, likes to show how security breeches are commonly the result of employee errors. In his book, *The Art of Deception*,

Mitnick writes about the techniques he used to finesse trusting employees into disclosing confidential information and privileged passwords.

In one case, Mitnick was able to secure a privileged password using the name Lemonjello, and then bragged about the naïve employee who handed-over a system password to someone called "Lemon Jell-O." The IT staff was never able to ascertain the root cause of the breech because their mechanism for the dissemination and auditing of secure information was inadequate.

Of course, outside threats from hackers remain a major concern, especially threats from overseas countries in Eastern Europe and Asia. Some companies report access attempts by automated hacker bots every few minutes as these rogue programs constantly sweep the Internet looking for ports with access vulnerabilities.

Windows PCs are especially vulnerable to attack. Many Windows XP computers are considered a *honeypot*, the slang term used to describe a Windows XP computer connected to the web with the default security settings. In a study reported by Australian PC authority, a Windows XP computer with the default settings can be taken over by a hacker in less then four minutes:

"In some instances, someone had taken complete control of the machine in as little as 30 seconds," said Marcus Colombano, a partner with AvanteGarde, and, along with former hacker Kevin Mitnick, a co-investigator in the experiment.

"The average was just four minutes. Think about that. Plug in a new PC, and many are still sold with Windows XP SP1, to a DSL line, go get a cup of coffee, and come back to find your machine has been taken over.

Windows XP SP1 with the for-free ZoneAlarm firewall, however, as well as Windows XP SP2, fared much better. Although both configurations were probed by attackers, neither was compromised during the two weeks"

These automated bots contain very sophisticated logic and are designed by criminals to identify and exploit weaknesses in online computer systems. Some of the common exploits include:

Tipping the User ID – This is where a telnet or FTP access attempt tells a user that they have entered a valid ID, but provided an improper password.

No Password Disabling – Hacker routines love systems that do not disable a user ID after repeated password attempts. On these systems, they run bots to try hundreds of thousands of passwords until they gain entry.

Man-in-the Middle Attacks – Hackers can gain access to computer systems by guessing the IP address of a connected user and sending a TCP/IP packet with that user's IP information.

Trojan Horse Access – Once a hacker gets a user's IP address, they can map-out phony sign-on screens to their boss and get a privileged password. These attacks are usually easy to use tools such as ASP and Active-X that allows HTML pages to be redirected to the user's IP address.

Buffer Overflow Attacks – In these attacks, the web cache buffer is deliberately overloaded to gain unauthorized entry to the system.

Injection Threats – Many database systems have vulnerabilities in which access to confidential data can be gained via a SQL injection, a technique where a "1=1" string is added to a sign-on string. For example, this query might return the real password for a user named Jane:

```
select
   userid, password
from
   dba_users
where
   userid = 'jane'
and
   password = 'xxx'
OR 1=1;"
```

Hacker attempts against web-enabled systems are constant, and many companies report thousands of attempts every day. A comprehensive auditing system will record all illegal access attempts and include the time, referrer IP address and all other relevant information. The following is a real-world case.

Real-World Case: The Extortion Attack

In this case, a hacker exploited a web server vulnerability, started siphoning confidential information from a corporate database, and shipped it via e-mail to a foreign country that did not honor U.S. copyright law. A foreign cohort then extorted the company, proving that they had the data and threatening to disclose proprietary secrets to a competitor unless they were paid a significant sum of money.

Faced with the loss of their competitive advantage, the company contacted the FBI and was told that there was no reciprocity with the nation and that Interpol would not be able to investigate or arrest the extortionists. The webmaster had not detected the data leakage, and he had no idea how the thieves had accessed the database.

Surprisingly, this is not an uncommon occurrence, and many multi-national companies keep accounts for bribery and extortion expenses because they are a legitimate requirement for doing business in some overseas nations. In this case, the company quietly paid the extortionist in return for the promise to destroy the data and details about how the data was stolen.

While there are always opportunities for attack from the outside world, one is unable to discount attacks from within the company firewall. In practice, "inside jobs" are more common than external attacks, and they can often have devastating consequences. The following is a real-world example.

Real-World Case: The Rootkit Attack

In 2004, a call came in from a client who was complaining of performance problems on their web database, which was running on a standalone Linux server. The company was in the business of providing credit information to third-party companies to assess an individual's probability of financial default.

Upon accessing the server, it was apparent that something was terribly wrong. Even when idle, the database was performing I/O operations and the processors were active, even though Linux did not show any active processes.

After a Linux expert was consulted, the real issue was discovered. A time-bomb was activated by a hacker, and the attack was both clever and devastating. The attacker placed a Linux daemon process called "Hoover" on the Linux server and this process was constantly polling the Oracle database, vacuuming up new data, and e-mailing it to an overseas mailbox!

The attack was very sophisticated and unobtrusive. The malicious employee had replaced the standard Linux commands with a root kit, an attack method readily available on the Internet. In a root kit attack, the Linux commands are replaced with an alias to disguise the presence of the data stealing mechanism.

This attack had disclosed the entire database of confidential information to an unknown party! In this case, the company lost its entire database to a competitor and went out-of-business within a month.

Web Privacy Legislation

The Computer Fraud and Abuse Act is very specific about penalties for anyone who enters a web server without consent. Section 1030, Fraud and Related Activity in Connection with Computers, makes it a serious crime to break into a website.

How serious is it, really? It is shocking to discover just how impaired law enforcement officials are, especially in light of the fact that most hack attacks cannot be prosecuted because of:

- **Age of Offender** – A large amount of US hackers are under the age of 18.

- **Foreign Origin** – Long-arm statutes are largely ineffective in developing countries.

Because of these issues, local, state and FBI enforcement officials will only investigate hack attacks that result in financial losses that exceed $100,000. Even then, they are often unsuccessful because of the right of juveniles and the lack of cooperation in foreign lands.

Additionally, the ease at which someone can enter the web anonymously is incredible. For example, at a midtown Manhattan hotel in 2004, it was possible to access 8 wireless routers, none of which required any user ID or password. This was accomplished in less than 5 minutes! Had the individual that accessed these routers had malicious intent, it would have been possible to hack a website or start a virus and no one would have known the identity of the perpetrator.

The Problem of the Wireless Web

The proliferation of wireless technology has opened an entirely new way for hackers to perform anonymous attacks. Simply driving through a neighborhood with a laptop running and within a few minutes someone's home wireless network will be found to be open and ready for use.

A large section of Chapter 9 is devoted to this issue. For now, suffice to say that until people start getting sued for allowing open wireless connections, it is very easy to launch an anonymous web attack.

The following is a real-world case that happened in 2004.

Real World Case: Website Hacking

Just to show that no one is exempt, this incident involved someone who is considered a technology expert. While the experience left him feeling violated and abused, he acknowledges that he learned a great deal about the underworld of web criminals. This individual decided to use a service for his website. He assumed that the web hosting service would plug all security holes and protect his websites against foreign invaders.

The user was shocked one morning to get an early call saying, "I think you've been hacked. Just take a look at your home page and you will see!"

 Well, this technology expert went to his home page and saw an image, roughly like this, where a profanity was added to the header on more than 3,000 web pages:

He joked out loud to himself that he liked it, but deep down inside he felt really scared. He immediately had the header replaced and then sat back to plan his next step. Having one's personal space violated, whether it's a home burglary or a website invasion leaves one feeling violated and angry.

He decided that he was going to make this a learning experience and understand exactly what happened, how they did it, and how the FBI would respond to the crime. To start, he accessed the File Transfer Protocol (FTP) log file on his web server. He discovered:

- The attacker entered by web domain at 5:38 a.m. using a valid password.

- The attacker FTP'd a copy of the altered header.

- The attacker downloaded the secure directory with an eCommerce shopping cart.

The following is a representation of what his FTP log looked like:

```
[17950] Login Wed Jul 28 05:47:32 2004
[17950] To 666.56.173.106( dba-admin.com )
[17950] From modemcable004.85-202-24.mc.video.ca( 77.202.85.4 ).
[17950] PWD[17950] FEAT
[17950] REST 100
[17950] REST 0
[17950] PASV
[17950] LIST
[17950] CWD /dba-admin-secure
[17950] PASV
[17950] LIST
[17950] PWD
[17950] CWD /dba-admin-secure/disk_files
[17950] PASV
[17950] LIST
[17950] CWD /dba-admin-secure/cart
[17950] PASV
[17950] LIST
[17950] TYPE I
[17950] PASV
[17950] RETR shop.tar
[17950] TYPE A
[17950] CWD /dba-admin-secure/cart/admin
[17950] PASV
[17950] LIST
[17950] CWD /dba-admin-secure/cart/admin/CVS
[17950] PASV
[17950] LIST
[17950] TYPE I
[17950] PASV
[17950] RETR Root
[17950] TYPE A
[17950] CWD /dba-admin-secure/cart/admin/admin
[17950] PASV
[17950] LIST
[17950] CWD /dba-admin-secure/cart/admin/admin/includes
[17950] PASV
[17950] LIST
[17950] CWD /dba-admin-webmail
[17950] PASV
[17950] LIST
[17950] CWD /dba-admin-webmail/_webmail_sessions
[17950] PASV
[17950] LIST
[17950] CWD /www
[17950] PASV
[17950] LIST
[17950] REST 0
```

```
[17950] REST 0
[17950] REST 0
[17950] PASV
[17950] LIST
[17950] CWD /www/images
[17950] PASV
[17950] LIST
[17950] TYPE I
[17950] SIZE index_text1.gif
[17950] MDTM index_text1.gif
[17950] PASV
[17950] RETR index_text1.gif
[17950] PASV
[17950] RETR Jones_logo2.jpg
[17950] PASV
[17950] LIST
[17950] TYPE A
[17950] PWD
[17950] TYPE I
[17950] PWD
[17950] REST 0
[17950] REST 0
[17950] PWD
[17950] REST 0
[17950] TYPE I
[17950] TYPE I
[17950] SIZE _header.jpg
[17950] CWD /www/images/_header.jpg
[17950] CWD /www/images
[17950] PASV
[17950] STOR _header.jpg
[17950] TYPE A
[17950] PASV
[17950] LIST
[17950] TYPE I
[17950] SIZE index_text1.gif
[17950] MDTM index_text1.gif
[17950] PASV
[17950] RETR index_text1.gif
[17950] REST 0
[17950] TYPE I
[17950] REST 0
[17950] TYPE I
[17950] REST 0
[17950] PWD
[17950] PASV
[17950] LIST
[17950] REST 0
[17950] PWD
[17950] PASV
[17950] LIST
[17950] RNFR /www/images/header.jpg
[17950] RNTO /www/images/___header.jpg
[17950] TYPE A
[17950] PASV
[17950] LIST
[17950] TYPE I
```

```
[17950] SIZE index_text1.gif
[17950] MDTM index_text1.gif
[17950] PASV
[17950] RETR index_text1.gif
[17950] SIZE header.jpg
[17950] CWD /www/images/header.jpg
[17950] CWD /www/images
[17950] PASV
[17950] STOR header.jpg
[17950] TYPE A
[17950] PASV
[17950] LIST
[17950] TYPE I
[17950] SIZE index_text1.gif
[17950] MDTM index_text1.gif
[17950] PASV
[17950] RETR index_text1.gif
```

The next step was to get the IP address of the attacker. The FTP log showed the Internet Protocol (IP) address as 666.56.173.106 and a whois search on InterNIC (www.internic.net/whois.html), showed that the attacker was hosted by a service in Montreal Canada.

However, when he researched the Canadian Internet Service Provider (ISP), he was dismayed to find out, using a Google search, that they were an open relay, which is a technical term for an ISP with bad security. These ISPs are a favorite of hackers who wish to remain anonymous.

Dismayed but still hopeful, he notified the FBI and spoke with an FBI agent in the FBI Internet Fraud center in Charlotte, North Carolina. She was very helpful, but immediately played the terrorist guilt card:

> "We are very sympathetic to your situation, but since 9/11 the FBI must concentrate our efforts on Internet terrorism."

Since his shopping cart was empty and he had not suffered any financial damages, he was not expecting the FBI to put a task force on it, but he seized the opportunity to learn about how the FBI handles these issues.

> "These attacks are very common and almost unavoidable."

> "If a hacker wants to get in bad enough they will find some weakness to exploit. Even www.fbi.gov was hacked once."

This statement hit him hard. All these years, this technology expert was living under the illusion that his Linux-based websites did not have any vulnerabilities, and he was immediately concerned about the safety of his website. The agent continued:

"In your case, the hacker placed the profanity on your header as a signal to other criminals.

Their M.O. is to hack a site, steal the shopping cart credit card numbers and then alter the header to prove that they have the stolen goods.

Next, they post an offer on a chat board, offering the header as proof and then selling the credit card numbers.

In your case, the thief is probably stealing from the buyers, offering-up fake card numbers."

Apparently there is no honor among thieves. The FBI agent continued:

"We have tracked these cases before, and they almost always originate in a foreign country.

To confound the matter, even when we trace the hacker it usually is a minor, and they are very difficult to prosecute.

It's very frustrating and we can only help victims who have suffered large losses."

She informed him that he could continue to pursue the matter with an attorney, and the next step would be to obtain a subpoena from a U.S. Federal District court to get the account name, mailing address and the telephone number used by the attacker.

He could then serve it on the Montreal ISP. A reciprocity agreement requires Canadian citizens to comply with U.S. court orders. Of course, the ISP could always claim that they lost the record of entries.

He figured if the ISP knows the account holder and the phone number that they used, he should be able to trace it directly to the house where the attack originated! Not so fast, the FBI agent cautioned.

> "It's very likely that the hacker used an open wireless connection and the home associated with the phone number will be an innocent third-party."

Most people would have quit at this point, but he called a Federal attorney and had a subpoena prepared anyway. There was always a chance, however slim, that he would be able to find his attacker. His lawyer also told him that they would be able to collect damages wherever the trail ended:

- **The Montreal ISP** – If the ISP failed to keep proper logs of system access they would be wholly responsible for the actions of the hacker.

- **The Phone Number Owner** – If the owner of the telephone number that was used to access the ISP had an open relay wireless network, they would be responsible for the attack because they did not lock-down their Internet gateway.

- **The ISP User** – The owner of the User ID and password could be held responsible for the actions used by their account.

This individual was not a litigious person, but he really wanted to see what happened. To date, the Montreal ISP has failed to comply with the U. S. court order, and he is pursuing an "Order to Compel" from the U.S. Federal District Court. He hopes to know who hacked into his web, but he suspects that it might take the better part of this decade.

One must wonder if the web hackers know how difficult it is for their victims to find them?

Next, information will be presented on other serious cyber-crimes and will illustrate how criminals use the web to harass, intimidate and threaten.

Cyber Law and Harassment

In plain English, Cyberstalking is the act of using the web to harass, intimidate or threaten an innocent party. What the law states about the use of the Internet for this sort of activity is the subject of this next section.

> United States Code Title 18, Chapter 110A, Section 2261 - Interstate domestic violence
>
> (a) Offenses. -

(1) Travel or conduct of offender. -

A person who travels in interstate or foreign commerce or enters or leaves Indian country with the intent to kill, injure, harass, or intimidate a spouse or intimate partner, and who, in the course of or as a result of such travel, commits or attempts to commit a crime of violence against that spouse or intimate partner, shall be punished as provided in subsection (b).

(2) Causing travel of victim. -

A person who causes a spouse or intimate partner to travel in interstate or foreign commerce or to enter or leave Indian country by force, coercion, duress, or fraud, and who, in the course of, as a result of, or to facilitate such conduct or travel, commits or attempts to commit a crime of violence against that spouse or intimate partner, shall be punished as provided in subsection (b).

The above statute is applicable in cases in which the Internet has been used as a tool to facilitate a crime of domestic violence. As previously discussed, the Internet has been categorized as an instrument of interstate commerce. USC 2261, shown above, applies in cases of domestic violence. USC 223, listed below, applies to stalking situations within federal jurisdictions.

United States Code Title 47, Chapter 5, Section 223 – Obscene or harassing telephone calls.

(a) Prohibited acts generally

Whoever –

(B) by means of a telecommunications device knowingly -

(i) makes, creates, or solicits, and

(ii) initiates the transmission of,

any comment, request, suggestion, proposal, image, or other communication which is obscene or indecent, knowing that the recipient of the communication is under 18 years of age, regardless of whether the maker of such communication placed the call or initiated the communication;

(C) makes a telephone call or utilizes a telecommunications device, whether or not conversation or communication ensues, without disclosing his identity and with intent to annoy, abuse, threaten, or harass any person at the called number or who receives the communications;

As an example, consider the following statute addressing the legal issue surrounding harassment and stalking. Arizona Revised Statutes 13-2921 is excerpted here:

"A person commits harassment if, with intent to harass or with knowledge that the person is harassing another person, the person:

Anonymously or otherwise communicates or causes a communication with another person by verbal, electronic, mechanical, telegraphic, telephonic or written means in a manner that harasses.

Continues to follow another person in or about a public place for no legitimate purpose after being asked to desist."

Violations of this section of the Arizona statute will usually be categorized as a misdemeanor. Stalking cases are generally comprised of activities defined under the law as harassment. The Arizona revised statute 13-2923 defines stalking in the following terms:

"Would cause a reasonable person to fear for the person's safety or the safety of that person's immediate family member and that person in fact fears for their safety or the safety of that person's immediate family member.

Would cause a reasonable person to fear death of that person or that person's immediate family member and that person in fact fears death of that person or that person's immediate family member."

A person experiencing problems along these lines would benefit greatly from a brief study of the law as it applies to these situations. Doing so will make it less difficult to determine when harassment has become stalking as defined under the law.

Many states make these and other laws a matter of public knowledge on their official state websites. Locating the website for any state can be easily accomplished by using an Internet search engine such as www.google.com. A person interested in California state law for example, might use Google to search for "State CA Gov". Another useful resource is The

Library of Congress State and Local Governments list located at www.loc.gov/global/state.

The Arizona laws quoted above shows that legal language can be a bit obscure for those not familiar with its interpretation. If a part of the law that applies to an individual's circumstance seems difficult to understand, they should consult a lawyer to evaluate their position as the best course of action.

Threats over the Web

No one wants to be the recipient of threatening or hostile messages. Sadly, many people know what it is like to be the target of this sort of intimidation. For some, the natural response is to delete these kinds of messages and try to forget they ever existed. If the person who sent the message is a jokester with bad taste, this might be all that is necessary.

If, on the other hand, an individual has become the target of a more determined, perhaps distorted personality, ignoring the messages completely could be an invitation for more trouble.

The obvious question then is, how does a person know what they are dealing with, and therefore what to do about it? In most cases, the victim will have no way of figuring that out. They will simply not have enough information to make that kind of determination.

"What do I do now?"

In addition to the lack of information, fear can affect judgment. If someone is rattled because of the messages they are receiving, it can be difficult to

---

know exactly how to proceed. It can, in fact, be difficult to do anything at all, even normal daily activities, depending on the level of the threat.

Are intimidating e-mails a matter for law enforcement? For a person receiving these sorts on messages, feelings waver. On one hand, going to the police might be an over reaction. On the other, not doing something may be foolish and place the recipient in serious danger.

The checklist below is designed to help take some of the guesswork out of the question. Working through the list provides answers that can help with the decision of how to proceed. Remember that this is only a checklist and a general guide at best. If, after going through the list, the results are not agreeable, then take action according to what seems best. In the final analysis, the experts consulted for this book agreed; err on the side of caution. No one should ever let themselves be talked out of going to the authorities if they feel it is the right thing to do.

Threat Analysis Checklist

	YES	NO
1 Did the message contain specific threats? (Watch out, I know where you live)	____	____
2 Did the message contain veiled threats? (It's a good thing I'm nice. Others might get mad.)	____	____
3 Did the message contain personal information? (How do you like that new convertible?)	____	____
4 Have you asked the sender to stop contacting you? (Only once, but clearly)	____	____
5 Has there been any escalation in recent communication? (From asking for a date to talking about personal issues)	____	____
6 Did the message make you uncomfortable or concerned?	____	____

Note: The purpose of this checklist is to assist in determining whether a given problem is something you should take to law enforcement. If you feel there is an immediate threat to your safety or the safety of someone else, call your emergency service.

Figure 5.2 - *A "yes" answer to any of these questions indicates a serious problem.*

Once law enforcement becomes actively involved, all messages received will be evaluated by one or more computer crimes technicians. These tech-enabled officials know how to extract what evidence there is to be had from these messages, much like another kind of detective might lift fingerprints from a glass. This information may help lead law enforcement officers back along the pipeline through which the message passed, and hopefully, to the original sender.

Victims should not send copies of suspect messages to friends or any other mailbox for that matter. It is possible the messages are tainted, possibly with a virus or that the sender of the original is able to cipher if and where the message has been forwarded. Additionally, copied messages are of less value evidentially, as seems intuitive; copies of copies only mire the picture.

If a pattern develops, it may become possible to recognize messages from the perpetrator without opening them. If the person sending the messages is at all technically sophisticated, they may attach scripts that will be executed when the message is opened. These scripts can be written to reduce the usability of the message as evidence in the event of an investigation. If the recipient knows the message is from the person harassing them, they should just leave it alone and pass it on directly to law enforcement.

A "Troll" is always fishing for victims.

Another type of pesky troublemaker lurking about on the Internet today is known as a troll. A troll sends obnoxious messages to a large group of people, knowing that at least some of the recipients will respond in kind; which as it turns out, is exactly what they are hoping for.

A troll is looking for a fight, and anyone will do. Deleting a message from a troll is exactly the right thing to do. The problem is, just as before, it is hard for anyone to know that they are dealing with a troll or something more dangerous. It takes time for patterns to develop and clues to fill in the picture.

As an alternative to immediately deleting suspected troll messages, save them in a special folder. Never respond to them in any way, because this will only feed the fire. If the situation develops into a legitimate threat, the early messages will be there ready for law enforcement to use as evidence. If the messages dwindle in number and eventually dry up completely, it is likely that the perpetrator hailed from a lower rung of the pest ladder and is now hurling insults at someone else.

Threats are undeniably a little unsettling for most people, but often they are just that and nothing more. In the next section, details will be presented on a group of Internet criminals who engage in more damaging practices.

Internet Harassment

Those who publish private information about an individual in areas of the Internet that are known hang-outs for criminals can be responsible for any damages against that individual. For example, if someone finds a user's home address and posts it on a forum populated by known sex offenders, the user then has an instant case against that poster for harassment.

Harassment is defined as the repeated, unwanted contact from a person or group of people. Many netizens falsely believe that if they form a conspiracy against any individual and they get all 100 people to call that person one time, then they are not committing harassment.

Intentional Infliction of Emotional Distress

The tort of Intentional Infliction of Emotional Distress (IIED) has been used successfully in many web cases, but it is often misunderstood. Sure, an obnoxious e-mail may make the recipient angry, or a threatening message board post may cause them to lose sleep at night, but the level of emotional distress must be very serious for one to win a lawsuit.

In most cases, the emotional distress must be so severe as to require psychological or psychiatric treatment.

Unsolicited E-mail Crimes

Last year the *Controlling the Assault of Non-Solicited Pornography and Marketing Act of 2003* law was passed. This law, also known as the *CAN-SPAM Act of 2003,* takes direct aim at those that flood e-mail inboxes with unsolicited marketing messages, including the graphic portrayal of pornography. It also makes it an offense to send un-requested sexually oriented material where the originator of the message cannot be traced, or the subject line is intentionally deceptive.

There are instances when the legality of an e-mail may not be readily apparent. Pornography, for example, is legal in some venues. It is not necessarily illegal in all circumstances when one person e-mails pornography to another. The rules, regulations and laws that apply to both the sender and recipient, the computers both are using and the nature of the material itself must all be taken into account.

Threats and harassment are unpleasant experiences, but libel on the Internet can cause more damage than either. In the next section, this burgeoning area of Internet law will be presented in greater detail.

Libel and Defamation on the Web

Defamation is defined as making a false statement about someone, which hurts or damages that person's reputation. When a false statement is made verbally, it is called slander. If a false statement is made in writing, it is called libel.

Libel laws were first instituted in England to provide honorable men with an alternative to dueling. The practice had been outlawed, but it still continued to flourish in certain circles. There are several criteria for Libel:

- The statements are false;

- The statements "were made maliciously and intentionally with full knowledge of their falsity or in complete and reckless disregard of their truth or falsity, for the purpose of injuring and destroying a personal and professional reputation";

- The person "acted with actual malice".

To be defamatory, the statement must be clearly stated as a fact, appear believable, and the statement must rise to the level that an ordinary person would think less of the victim as a person. Traditionally, the courts have used the standard of a horrible illness (AIDS, Venereal Disease) as an example of statements that defame.

The Courts have the right to restrict speech if the speech constitutes "Fighting Words." Fighting Words means speech usually intended to be a personal insult and directed to a specific person, which by their very utterance inflict injury and tend to incite an immediate breach of the peace. Fighting Words are not protected under the First Amendment because their slight social value is outweighed by the government's compelling interest in social order.

Remember, some states allow filing civil charges against someone who commits defamation, even if the statement is true. Under the false light invasion of privacy laws, a court judgment can be won against anyone who publicly discloses embarrassing facts with malicious intent.

Peter D. Kennedy, an Attorney with a law firm in Texas whose practice includes the areas of Internet and libel, points out that in cases of cyber-libel, several challenges and factors are different from traditional libel cases.

- **Identity** – One must be able to penetrate the cloak of anonymity to know the true identity of the person.

- **Jurisdiction** – One must establish personal jurisdiction for the offender.

- **Other Responsible Parties** – One must be able to identify other parties who may conspire to defame them.

Now that some definitions have been presented, the next step is to take a closer look at the legalities concerning libel in cyberspace.

Libel and the Internet

Recent laws have been enacted to limit the liability of Internet providers (i.e. Yahoo forums, etc.), and many people mistakenly conclude that the web is now wide-open for anyone to publish defamatory information about anyone else.

People are still responsible for their words, and the anonymity of the Internet can easily be broken by a court order. More information on how to identify people who post in a libelous manner is contained in Chapter 1, *The Illusion of Anonymity*.

The emerging web has now made it possible for anyone to become a publisher. Sitting in a prison cell, convicted felons can post terrible things about specific people, causing great damage to the reputation of others.

Even if a netizen has never read a book, they can now go to a newsgroup on the Internet and publish content that is almost instantly accessible to millions of people across the globe.

With respect to the Internet, defamation claims are generally filed for comments made in message boards or other posted material. This would make them libel, so these cases are frequently termed cyber-libel. Often people will disagree with a statement made about them either in the printed media or on the Internet. Their reaction is to talk about a lawsuit for defamation of character. Even if the statement is false, it does not automatically mean that it is defamation. In order for a written statement to be libelous, it must not only be false; it must also be harmful.

One common trick of libelous conspiracies is to use circular references and republishing to avoid direct responsibility for their acts. These acts have no protection under US laws and the courts are recognizing that republishing libel, even through linking to a libelous article, is a legitimate cause for action.

Malice and Libel

There are several criteria used to determine liability for false publications about anyone on the Internet:

- **Malicious Intent** – The offender intends for publication of the statement to result in harm to the victim's personal interests.

- **Reckless Disregard for Truth** – The offender knows that the statement is false or acts in reckless disregard to its truth or falsity.

There is an additional standard for public figures (politicians, celebrities) whereby actual malice must be proven for a Libel charge to be valid. In recent U.S. cases, a new concept called Limited Purpose Public Figure (LPPF) has been created.

If an individual is deemed to be a LPPF then they have the additional burden of proving actual malice on the part of the offender. The U.S. Supreme Court developed a two-part inquiry for determining whether a defamation plaintiff is a LPPF:

- Was there a particular "public controversy" that gave rise to the alleged defamation?

- Was the nature and extent of the plaintiff's participation in that particular controversy sufficient to justify "public figure" status?

Under some state laws, an individual may become a LPPF by his purposeful activity amounting to a thrusting of his personality into the vortex of an important public controversy.

This section has included some of the intricacies of how liability law works. Another step is to investigate its application to websites.

Website Liability for Cyber-Libel

The matter of corporate or personal liability in cyber-libel cases often rests on the issue of content control. Even in cases in which the crime of libel is proven, the questions regarding who is responsible and how far the culpability extends still remains.

An illustration may help explain this concept. Consider the case of a newspaper charged with libel. Assume that the crime has been committed and damages are to be paid. Who is liable? The newspaper itself, the editors on staff, the writer of the story, the research assistant, the distribution manager, the newsstand operator, the paper delivery boy?

All of these people played a role in the distribution of the newspaper containing the libelous content. In this case, the answer seems obvious, but the example demonstrates the point clearly. The liable party or parties are those who were in a position to know the truth and prevent the libel from occurring.

If one applies this example to the Internet; if a libelous statement is posted to a moderated forum, who is liable? The answer is the same as before, but the layers of responsibility may be in question. Certainly the moderator, if in a position to know the statement was libelous, should have removed it immediately. Precisely who else may share in the guilt in this and similar situations will be a question for inquiring legal minds in the years ahead.

Undoubtedly, mistakes will be made by publishers and others, and lawsuits will result when inaccurate information makes it to the intended market. When this occurs, the law in many places allows for the source of the information to be protected from liability by issuing corrections to or retractions of the problematic statements. This helps protect against frivolous legal actions that might result from genuine mistakes in the form of factual errors or even typos.

The Judgment-Proof Libeler

In many cases, the source of the libel is a semi-indigent person where it is not worth the effort and expense involved with seeking damages. It may be that the accused does not have the financial resources to cover legal expenses, let alone compensate their victim for losses. They know this, of course, and use their legal status as "judgment proof" to harass anyone they like. It is similar to what Bob Dylan said in his popular 1960's song, "When You Ain't Got Nothing You Got Nothing to Lose".

Libelers with limited financial resources may inspire those seeking damages to look elsewhere for compensation; hoping to find deeper pockets to raid. In the world of print media and newspapers, senior editors have been targeted. When libel appears on the Internet, some have taken aim at the ISPs; reasoning that ISPs facilitate participation in the Internet by providing access to the forums in question, and ultimately enable the libel itself.

U.S. law put an end to that kind of reasoning with the passing of the Communications Decency Act (CDA), which states in part that no ISP

"shall be treated as the publisher or speaker of any information provided by another information content provider".

In other words, ISPs may make the communication of libel possible through the facilities they provide, but they are not themselves responsible for that libel.

This concept seems to hold up to intuitive reasoning. The sheer volume and variety of information passed along through the myriad interconnected systems that comprise the Internet; not to mention the legal considerations that apply to the monitoring of communications and other privacy issues, render this sort of regulation by ISPs completely untenable.

This has led some to shift their focus to the moderator of a forum in which the libel occurred. The moderator's function may at first seem well-suited to stopping libelous information soon after it hits the net. Consider the following, however, to see if that is really the case:

> First, remember that for a statement to be considered libelous under the law, a number of conditions have to be met. It must be shown that malicious intent motivated the accused and that they knowingly made false statements or engaged in reckless disregard for the truth. The mere falsehood of a statement is not enough. Whether these conditions apply in a given instance can take months for even courtroom proceedings to determine. Without some sort of special insight, a moderator is in no position to make these kinds of judgments on the fly.
>
> Secondly, moderators are no more likely to have the financial resources to cover damages than the libeler themselves. If one can't get blood from a turnip, going after another turnip doesn't make a lot of sense.

The laws that apply to Internet communications are still in the developmental stages in some cases. It remains for the legislators, judges and juries in the courtrooms of the world to construct a legal framework on which to build upon in the years ahead.

Challenging the Defamers

Whenever someone's reputation has been damaged by individuals on the Internet, attorneys say that the first step is to allow the offender to retract and mitigate the damage.

The following is a sample libel demand letter:

```
March 6, 2005

Ms. Eurethera Badvibe

_____

_____
```

```
    Re:      Defamation

Dear Ms. Badvibe:

    We are legal counsel to Mr. Joe Dogood.  In that connection, we
are in possession of a copy of the article written by you and
published in xxx.

    We have reviewed the article and discussed its contents with our
client.  We believe the article contains damaging, false statements
about Mr. Dogood, and it misquotes Mr. Dogood in a manner that
places him in a false light.  As such, the article may form the
basis of a defamation claim against you.

    We also understand from Mr. Dogood that you have threatened to
"put Dogood out of business."  Please be advised that we and Mr.
Dogood take these threats seriously and will use whatever legal
means necessary to protect Mr. Dogood's reputation, including filing
suit to recover any damages caused by defamatory statements made by
you or others.

    If you would like to discuss these issues, please feel free to
call me, and in the future, please direct any correspondence for Mr.
Dogood to me.  In the meantime, we will continue to monitor any
articles or other publications by you (including statements on
public bulletin boards and other public displays on the Internet).

Sincerely,

DEWEY, SICUM and HOWE
A Professional Limited Liability Company
```

Jurisdiction and Internet Law

Questions regarding the applicability of international law to the use of the Internet in various jurisdictions continue to plague attempts to arrive at a universally accepted benchmark. The world is a diverse place. Various forms of government set differing standards of behavior. They establish systems of reward and punishment to promote the accepted practice of politics, religion, business and morality in all arenas of life.

How then are these divergent interests and the laws they inspire to be fairly and evenly applied to the global medium of the Internet? Each citizen in every nation cannot be subject to the laws of every other nation.

The Internet makes it possible for a foreigner, not subject to the laws of a distant country, to interact with the citizens of that country whenever they choose. They may conduct business, maintain advantageous political alliances or promote an agenda that suites their interests. In short, they may exercise influence at some level without being subject to the laws that govern the systems of that nation. It goes without saying that this situation will, and does, create problems.

Even neighboring countries with very similar value systems can have differences in their legal codes that can cause problems. For example, the United States and Canada agree, for the most part, on the major ideologies underpinning their laws, but definitions and technical points can vary. Canada and the United States have slightly different definitions of what constitutes defamatory remarks.

Suppose a statement is made on an Internet forum by someone in the United States that negatively impacts the interests of a party in Canada. Suppose further that the statement meets the requirements of defamation as defined by Canadian law, but because of differences in the legal language of the two countries, the statement does not qualify as defamatory according to U.S. laws. Should legal proceedings ensue, plaintiffs may wish to consider these subtleties.

Whenever one is the victim of a Cybercrime, they may have a choice of jurisdictions. For example, if they are defamed (libeled), one normally has a choice of filing the action in the defendant's jurisdiction or the victim's home jurisdiction. Of course, the choice is largely determined by the laws within each jurisdiction and the propensity of the courts to find in the victim's favor. his act of choosing jurisdictions is commonly called "forum shopping", and it is one of the first steps when one has been harmed on the Web. In fact, jurisdictional issues warrant a more detailed look.

An important factor in cyber-law cases is the intersection of geography and contact. The UCLA Cyberspace Law & Policy Institute has a wonderful description of Jurisdiction:

In order to establish personal jurisdiction over a non-resident defendant, he or she must either have

(1) "substantial, continuous and systematic" presence in the forum state, which would give the court general jurisdiction over the defendant, or

(2) certain "minimum contacts" with the forum state such that maintenance of the suit does not offend "traditional notions of fair play and substantial justice."

International Shoe Co. v. Washington, 326 U.S. 310 (1945).

Source: Lexis

To determine whether a person or business is continuously and systematically present in a forum state, a court will not look solely at the number of hits or customers that a website will receive from a particular state, but will evaluate the "totality of circumstances" to evaluate the relationship among the defendant, the forum and the litigation.

When a URL request is sent from one website to another, a referrer URL is attached. These referrer statistics allow a website to see the number of hits coming-in from other web domains.

Significant Contact and Personal Jurisdiction

In one famous Supreme Court case (Calder vs. Jones), the Court found just the act of publishing defamatory remarks is enough to establish jurisdiction. In this case, a defamatory article was published by the *National Enquirer* about actress Shirley Jones. The reporters for the story knew that Jones lived and worked in California and that she would bear the brunt of the injury in California; therefore, they should have "anticipate being hauled into court there to answer for the truth of their statements."

For example, consider a libel action. After confirming the identity of the person who made the statement in question, the next challenge is to find that person. If they live in the same country as their victim, the courts of that country will most likely determine that they have jurisdiction.

With the Internet, the world has become smaller. Someone in another country can easily make statements about any other person that are false and harmful. If they successfully assert that their local laws apply to their conduct, then to continue to pursue a case, one would need to do so in their country. The cost of a foreign lawsuit will make many decide not to pursue the case further.

Fairness and Substantial Justice with Jurisdiction

In addition to meeting the burden of "minimum contacts", the victim's court must find that their jurisdiction is a fair forum for the action. This issue is aggravated by the vastly differing laws across the globe.

For example, Australian and United Kingdom courts are seen as favorable for libel suits due to the difference in laws and free speech rights. Accordingly, in December of 2002, when the Australian high court ruled that the Australian-based mining entrepreneur, Joe Gutnick, could sue the American multimedia company, Dow Jones, in the Australian state of Victoria over an article published on its WSJ.com website, this was seen by many in the American media and free speech supporters as a defeat. The WSJ.com website is posted in New Jersey, and Dow Jones attempted to get this suit transferred to New Jersey on this basis.

Determining jurisdiction is not an easy task in the global community, especially when applicable laws are conflicting. But applying the law or even determining what the law is can be difficult, regardless of jurisdiction, as will be shown in the next section.

Real-World Case: Web Deception

In 2004, during a Google search on a familiar subject, one savvy Internet user noted an unfamiliar website in the Google results. When he clicked on the link, he was taken to a web page that shocked him.

The site was offering an article that he had read before, on another website, but it looked as if the article had moved.

On Fetching, Storing, and Indexing

Available for Members. ● See Related Articles

▸ Article Abstract:

(Tom Kyte) Our technologist fetches sequentially, stores inline, and indexes globally.

We've got a problem concerning an ORA-01002 error in a PL/SQL block. We learned that this error sometimes happens under special circumstances when updating selected data, such as when using a SELECT for an UPDATE. But this is not the case here. The strange thing is that we're getting this error only when reading data from a cursor, without any updates on the cursor data.

▸ Read this article...

Key (Please note):
(R) - registration may be required for access at the target site
($) - target site may require paid membership for access to this or other content

Curious, he clicked the "Read this Article" link and was directed to a payment page and asked to pay at least $9.50 to see the article:

⊙	Monthly **$9.50/Month**
⊙	Quarterly **$19.50/Qtr.** (32% discount)
⊙	Annual **$69.50/yr.** (39% discount - only $5.79 / month)

As it turns out, there was no article on this website. If he had paid the $9.50 fee, he would have been redirected to the real article on the Oracle Technical Network (OTN).

This gentleman was personally taken-aback to find that this site was re-selling hyperlinks, and he wondered if it was illegal.

- The content looks like an original article with no disclosure about the legitimate owner of the content.

- It is never mentioned that the article is nothing more than a hyperlink. There is no value-added content whatsoever, no commentary, nothing but the fee.

While doing some research, he consulted an attorney, Internet Law expert Nicholas Ackerman, who told him:

- It's not against the law for a website to collect and sell collections of related hyperlinks. Websites such as "News Clipping Services" sell hyperlinks to the works of others.

- It may not be legal, however, to represent these hyperlinks as if they were the proprietary property of the website. This practice might fall within the realm of U.S. consumer fraud laws. There are strict state and federal statutes against unfair or fraudulent business practices, as well as truth in advertising laws that are designed to protect Internet users against deception.

Selling the work of others and presenting it as original content violates an honest user's sense of justice. In the next section, guidance will be presented on how to seek justice for a whole host of offenses.

Real-World Case: Cyber-libel and Tortuous Interference

In the Pets Warehouse Message Board libel case, there is an excellent example of a web-based allegation. The facts of the case are recited here:

On May 15, 2001, according to court documents, XXX, a computer scientist at Virginia Commonwealth University in Richmond, posted a message that made a blunt recommendation:

"Thinking of buying plants from Pet Warehouse? Don't."

He went on to detail his gripes about the company's customer service, based on what he said was a delayed shipment of plants he'd ordered.

In classic Net slambook fashion, other members of the list responded to XXX's messages by sharing their own experiences with Pets Warehouse. One post on May 22, 2001, as recorded in court documents, quotes YYY, sloganeering: "Remember petSWEARhouse, buy their plants and you'll be swearing!"

The owner of Pets Warehouse felt that he was violated and served the mailing list owners and participants with a $15,000,000 lawsuit for libel and defamation. From the court papers:

Defendants have conspired to, and have joined together into an illegal agreement to, intentionally injure the business and goodwill of Petswarehouse.com by a variety of tortious and other unlawful acts.

> Each member of the illegal conspiracy has economic incentives for their actions, all of which are at the expense of Robert Novak and Pets Warehouse mark
>
> Specific charges are Computer fraud; Trademark; Tortious Interference; Civil Conspiracy; Product disparagement; Linking; Defamation; False Light; Invasion Of Privacy; Intentional Infliction Of Emotional Distress; Harassment; Libel; and Trade Libel.

In this landmark cyber-libel case, the victim was able to settle out of court with many of the defendants.

With that introduction to cyber-libel, the next step is to examine a related offense, the act of False Light Invasion of Privacy.

Invasion of Privacy

With the increasing ability of people to damage others on the web, many states have created a "false light" law for the protection of Internet users.

There are four types of invasion of privacy laws that can be used to prosecute an offender:

- **Appropriation of an individual's name or likeness** – While this encompasses the idea of blatant identity theft, false light appropriation is more subtle. For example, the following are some common appropriation cases:

    - Someone could use an individual's name and e-mail address and post bigoted remarks as if they were coming from that individual.

    - Someone could take an individual's photograph from their web page and use it in a story about plastic surgery disasters.

- **Intrusion on solitude** – This area of false light involves unauthorized disclosure of an individual's private affairs. An example would be publishing private bank records or a personal home address.

- **Disclosure of embarrassing facts** – In this false light challenge, a person could be liable for disclosing true facts about an individual if the disclosure was made with malicious intent.

- **False publicity** – Judges have used the false light laws to award damages against those who publish false or misleading information about an individual. For example, having one's face featured in an article about leprosy damage could be actionable, even if it did not identify that individual by name.

The most common defense in a false light action is to claim First Amendment freedom of speech, but the courts are quite clear about offering no protection for false speech:

"false speech, even political speech, does not merit constitutional protection if the speaker knows of the falsehood or recklessly disregards the truth."

"The use of a known lie as a tool is at once at odds with the premises of democratic government and with the orderly manner in which economic, social, or political change is to be effected.

Hence the knowingly false statement and the false statement made with reckless disregard of the truth, do not enjoy constitutional protection."

This information shows how it is possible to implicate oneself in a crime by invading another's privacy as defined by the law. Another interesting phenomenon on the Internet is how some people are making themselves out to be somebody else altogether.

Identity Crimes

People make statements all the time. Whether chatting over the fencepost or the Internet, today's society is filled with communication junkies, and there is no end to the rivers of information that flow through and around everyone every day.

But what if, within the context of all this interaction, it becomes apparent that some of the information diffused into the mass of overlapping forums is not true? What if, in addition to not being true, it is damaging and intentionally so?

If a person or organization is to be held accountable for the things they say or the information they communicate, it is vital that their identity be known. A blurb freely floating about, no matter how often it is repeated, cannot be dealt with. The source of the blurb must be discovered, and identifying them can sometimes be a slippery job.

Traditional media has been around a long time, and the laws that apply to the attribution of credits and the citing of sources have had hundreds of years to evolve. This is not so with the Internet. It is possible to post information in a variety of forums with comparative anonymity and cover one's tracks rather thoroughly upon retreat. The information, however, is still there, doing its work, benefiting or harming the interests of others; and no one can be held accountable. This can lead to abuse on a grand scale.

The problem then becomes a simple matter of identifying the sources of various forms of information commonly occurring on the Internet. While the concept is straightforward, accomplishing the feat is another beast altogether. A complete discussion of identity crimes is covered in another chapter.

It should be becoming clear now that anonymous sources of information present a problem for everyone. What about those who make it their business to remove, from others, a level of anonymity the law protects; their privacy? This subject will be explored in the next section.

Tortuous Interference

Tortuous interference is the unlawful interference into one's contractual or business affairs. For example, someone who uses the web to defame an individual's business and contacts their customers (or prospective customers) may be violating this law. A special case of tortuous interference called "Tortuous Interference with Prospective Advantage" is available in some states to punish those who seek to damage one's ability to find and retain new customers.

The elements of the tort of interference with contract are:

- A valid contract between the plaintiff and a third person that confers upon plaintiff a contractual right against a third person.

- The defendant knows of the contract.

- The defendant intentionally induces the third person not to perform the contract.

- The defendant acts without justification.

- The defendant's conduct causes actual pecuniary harm to the plaintiff.

Web Conspiracies

The web has made it incredibly easy for those with similar malice to join forces against an individual. For example, participants in a web forum may conspire to defame someone by using the forum as a platform for attacks against them or conspiring to harass them.

The web provides immediate communications worldwide, and one can often see how these criminal websites are used for illegal purposes.

Even on the net, a conspiracy only takes two people.

Whenever a web forum is used as a communications device to violate the rights of innocent people, they can be prosecuted under the U.S. Communications Decency Act:

"It is the policy of the United States – to ensure vigorous enforcement of Federal criminal laws to deter and punish trafficking in obscenity, stalking, and harassment by means of computer."

Criminal Conspiracies on the Web

Crooks and scammers are using the web with increasing boldness and using the fast worldwide communications of the Internet to facilitate crimes, great and small. The following are actual samples of postings from message board criminal conspiracies, this one for Felony Grand theft:

> "That's a ridiculous price. Now, I'm absolutely NOT telling you to do this!!! (wink), but you should go, quietly, at night, and just take it.
>
> It is then up to her to prove it is her property. She has no proof of ownership and, possession is still 9/10 of the law.
>
> BUT I AM ABSOLUTELY NOT SAYING THIS IS WHAT YOU SHOULD DO BECAUSE IT IS ILLEGAL!!!"

Here is another actual forum conspiracy to commit fraud:

> "I would have him bring some crack along and pretend to get smoke with him, and then buy the car cheap while the guy is stoned. . . .
>
> Marvette is on the phone right now with the "man" that I suggested we use to pose as a buyer.
>
> I think he agreed."

To prove a civil conspiracy, one must show that two or more persons have combined to accomplish a purpose that is unlawful, immoral or oppressive.

Conspiracies Against One's Civil Rights

Conspiracies against the Civil Rights of the disabled and minorities are becoming increasingly common, and the web is used as a vehicle for all sorts of Civil Rights violations, from petty violations to first-degree murder. The U.S. Civil Rights Act, specifically the penalty for Conspiracy against rights, makes this a serious Federal offense:

> "If two or more persons conspire to injure, oppress, threaten, or intimidate any person in any State, Territory, Commonwealth, Possession, or District in the free exercise or

enjoyment of any right or privilege secured to him by the Constitution or laws of the United States, or because of his having so exercised the same; . . .

They shall be fined under this title or imprisoned not more than ten years, or both;"

Conspiracies are also used to violate the rights of disabled people, especially in light of new expansion of the Americans with Disabilities Act (ADA) laws. Specifically for disabled people, the ADA law has a section titled "Rights to access to public accommodations and prohibition against retaliation and coercion":

(b) **Interference, coercion, or intimidation** - It shall be unlawful to coerce, intimidate, threaten, or interfere with any individual in the exercise or enjoyment of, or on account of his or her having exercised or enjoyed, or on account of his or her having aided or encouraged any other individual in the exercise or enjoyment of, any right granted or protected by this chapter.

Illustrations of conduct prohibited by this section include, but are not limited to:

- Coercing an individual to deny or limit the benefits, services, or advantages to which he or she is entitled under the Act or this part;

- Threatening, intimidating, or interfering with an individual with a disability who is seeking to obtain or use the goods, services, facilities, privileges, advantages, or accommodations of a public accommodation;

- Intimidating or threatening any person because that person is assisting or encouraging an individual or group entitled to claim the rights granted or protected by the Act or this part to exercise those rights; or

- Retaliating against any person because that person has participated in any investigation or action to enforce the act or this part.

These Civil Rights crimes carry serious penalties and many are facilitated by the Internet.

- North Carolina man pleads guilty to racial harassment of African-American family - The defendant participated in the hanging of a rope noose on the victim's front door. The victim had just moved into a previously all-white neighborhood of Richlands, North Carolina. The defendent admitted that he and his co-conspirators intended to frighten and intimidate the family into moving away from Richlands.

- Conspiring to violate the civil rights of several individuals by carrying out a campaign of intimidation - Alexander James Curtis, 25, of Lemon Grove, Calif., admitted that from 1997 to 1999 he conspired to injure, oppress, threaten and intimidate persons because of their race, color or national origin. Curtis pleaded guilty to three felony counts of a conspiracy to violate civil rights. The maximum statutory punishment is 10 years in custody and a maximum fine of $250,000 for each felony count

The following a quick look at how the web is used to facilitate crimes against disabled people's civil rights.

Conspiracies against the Blind

It is well known in the blind community that it is almost impossible to get a taxi with a Guide dog in some major cities. Many cab companies do not like having animals in their vehicles and they use Internet forums to find legal ways to bypass the ADA and deny rights of access to blind guide animal users.

The following is a sample of such a conspiracy. By publishing this information in a prominent forum, blind people everywhere can be discriminated against.

"Just say that you are allergic to dogs.

The ADA has an exception when the animal endangers the health of others and all you have to do is claim that you are allergic to dogs".

Conspiracies Against the Mentally Ill

On May 9, 2003, the Department of Transportation (DOT) published new guidelines concerning service animals, ruling that Emotional Support Animals (ESAs) fall within the scope of the ADA and must be allowed in all places of public accommodation.

To qualify, the disabled person must have a psychological neurosis as delineated by the American Psychological Association diagnostic guidelines, and the animals must provide a legitimate service. For example, a person who was traumatized by a mugging could get diagnosed with Agoraphobia and gain the right to keep an Emotional Support Animal in an area where no pets are allowed.

Many business owners, especially hotels and restaurants, are against this law and some are using Internet forums to circumvent the new laws.

Conspiracies are a clear violation of the law, but questions about the legality of website content are more complex.

Illegal Websites and Cybercrime

Since laws vary widely between countries, websites that are legal within one country can be highly illegal in others. Here are some common examples:

- **Gambling** – While this activity is acceptable in many countries, it is prohibited in many states in the U.S.A.

- **Child Pornography** – Many nations have no specific laws against child pornography, while it is a serious offense in the USA. This is an especially dangerous area because just clicking a URL to a kiddie porn site can be a crime.

- **Access Rights** – Many countries have differing laws on website content and it is impossible to enforce these laws on a global level.

The following section provides some examples of how website laws vary by jurisdiction.

"Foreign Decrees are often ignored by Netizens"

Website Laws

Varying vastly between jurisdictions, many national and local laws have been enacted to restrict website content. The following are just a few examples:

- **France** – The French require that all websites be accessible in French.

- **Canada** – All Canadian websites must be bi-lingual; available in both French and English.

- **USA** – The Americans with Disabilities Act may soon be expanded in scope to require that all USA websites meet minimum accessibility standards for the visually and hearing impaired.

The following section details the USA website accessibility guidelines for the blind.

Website Accessibility in the U.S.A.

Groups of disability rights advocates are fighting to expand the scope of the Americans with Disabilities Act (ADA) to cover the rights of the visually and hearing impaired to have equal access to websites.

Just as the owner of a business can be sued if they do not provide wheelchair ramps, the owners of computer systems on the web might be exposed to legal action if their system is not accessible to the blind or deaf.

The International Center for Disability Resources on the Internet (ICDRI), has published a great article on this topic titled, *Is Your Site ADA-Compliant ... or a Lawsuit-in-Waiting?* This site sums-up the issue quite elegantly:

> "That beautiful new law firm site that your high-priced designer just created may be impossible for a person using screen reading technology to navigate; particularly if they are blind/low vision or have a specific learning disability.
>
> Those "frames" or neat drop-down Java menus on your site may be impossible to use via voice command software.
>
> Your fancy "streaming audio" online CLE courses or video conferencing events may be impossible for a deaf person to hear."
>
> *Source: The Internet Center for Disabilities Resources on the Internet*

Around the country, businesses are publishing standards for accessibility of their Internet websites. Even cities are passing standards for development, and the City of San Jose in the heart of Silicon Valley published the *City of San Jose Web Page Disability Access Design Standard* in 1996. From this standard, there are seven minimum requirements that are meant to ensure accessibility for the disabled:

- Provide an Access Instruction Page for Visitors which includes email hyperlink for visitors to communicate problems with web page accessibility.

- Provide support for text browsers.

- Attach "Alt" tags to graphic images so that screen readers can identify the graphic.

- Hyperlink photographs with descriptive text "D".

- Caption all audio and video clips by using "CC" hyperlinks.

- Provide alternative mechanisms for on-line forms such as email or voice/TTY phone numbers.

- Avoid access barriers such as the posting of documents in PDF, table, newspaper or frame format or requiring visitors to download software. If posting in PDF, the HTML text or ASCII file must also be posted.

U.S. Disability Laws and Cyber Torts

The federal circuit courts are now split over whether the ADA can be "stretched" to cover electronic systems and the Internet. The ADA clearly covers all public places such as restaurants, hotels, and parks, but the case law is evolving.

The National Federation for the Blind (NFB), a leading advocacy group, has instituted lawsuits against purveyors of public electronic communications, with mixed results:

- **Diebold** - The manufacturer of Automatic Teller Machines (ATMs) was sued by the NFB because their ATM machines were not usable by the blind. In a settlement, Diebold agreed to donate $1,000,000.00 to the NFB and agreed to equip ATM's with voice-guidance capabilities.

- **America Online** – AOL was sued by the NFB and nine blind people because they were unable to use AOL without the assistance of a sighted person.

- **Access Now vs. Southwest Airlines** - In a landmark decision, U.S. District Judge Patricia Seitz said the Americans with Disabilities Act (ADA) should apply only to physical spaces, such as restaurants and movie theaters, and not to the Internet.

Pornography and obscenity crimes on the web are presented in the following sections which will explore the issue and illustrate how one can protect oneself.

Obscenity on the Web

Obscenity is in the eye of the beholder. In 1964, Supreme Court Justice Potter Stewart tried to explain obscenity with his famous quote:

"I shall not today attempt further to define the kinds of material I understand to be embraced . . . but I know it when I see it."

Nudity, per se, is no longer considered obscene and the Venus De Milo remains unclothed in the Louvre in Paris. Society has come a long way since Victorian ancestors placed shirts on table legs because all legs, even wooden ones, should be covered.

However, obscenity is not just about nudity. When the controversial artwork *Piss Christ* was unveiled in New York, protests erupted at the vulgar and obscene paring of excrement with sacred religious icons.

Regardless of the definition, it is clear that obscenity is big business. Industry experts say that obscenity and pornography are extremely profitable on the web, one of the few web industries to be financially successful.

Officially, obscenity was defined by the U.S. Supreme Court in the *Miller vs. California* case. The court rules that in order to be judged obscene the content as a whole must be considered, and three conditions must be met:

- The content must appeal to a prurient interest in sex.

- The content must contain patently offensive depictions or descriptions of specific sexual conduct as judged by the contemporary standards in the affected community.

- The content must have no serious literary, artistic, political or scientific value.

Material that meets these conditions is illegal, whether obtained at an adult bookstore or on the Internet.

Child Pornography

Regardless of what a person thinks about pornography, the fact remains that specific laws make particular types of pornography illegal. It is a criminal offense in many places in the world, including Great Britain, Australia and the United States to have any dealings of any kind with child pornography. It is illegal to produce, sell, buy or view child pornography. While legislators have extended a measure of protection to other types of pornography as a form of free speech, the law remains unequivocal in its view of child pornography; it is illegal.

Some have protested that the definition of child pornography is too restrictive. For the purposes of the law, anyone under the age of 18 is considered a child. Advocates for the pornography industry have argued for lowering the age of adulthood, ostensibly to keep in step with the standards in other parts of the world. One wonders if these newly defined adults would be entrusted with other responsibilities associated with their new status. Experts on sex crimes against children disagree and paint a dark picture of this sordid underworld.

Some use the Internet to spew forth trash.

The fact remains that laws vary from country to country, and what is legal in one location is against the law in another. The questions of jurisdictions, whose laws apply where, and what laws take precedence when, are still being argued and resolved day by day. There is, as yet, no end in sight to the problems associated with the world-wide regulation of the World Wide Web.

Sexual Addiction and the Internet

For many people pornography is a problem. Like alcohol, gambling or drugs, it can take control of a person's life and drag them kicking and screaming or voluntarily into the gutter. The addictive and progressive (or should that be regressive) nature of pornography is well documented.

There are a number of things netizens can do to limit their exposure to potentially harmful material. One very effective measure that can be taken is the use of Internet filtering devices.

For those who already suffer from an addiction, other useful resources that have helped people who wrestle with pornography addiction are support groups and programs. Sexaholics Anonymous (www.sa.org) is one such organization that leads struggling people through a 12-step recovery process based on the widely successful 12-step program developed by Alcoholics Anonymous. Numerous resources are available at their website, including a self-assessment test designed to help those who suspect they have a problem determine if they actually do.

Cyber Attacks and Terrorism

Some experts believe that the use of the term cyber-terrorism is inappropriate. They argue that terrorism is a class of crime so grievous that computer related offenses do not deserve the title; therefore, they argue the term cyber-terrorism is a misnomer. While cyber-attacks are typically associated with computer viruses and other malicious scripts, they can often have real world consequences.

Cyber attacks can have gargantuan consequences.

"New York City and much of the Northeast were paralyzed by a sudden blackout yesterday that stopped 50 million people in their tracks. From New Jersey all the way to Toronto, trains stopped, computers crashed, planes were grounded, air conditioners cut off and thousands of homes and businesses were plunged into darkness by the largest power outage in the nation's history".

Excerpted from, www.nydailynews.com story about the August 14th 2003 power failure.

A major failure of the power grid like the one experienced in the northeastern United States and parts of Canada in 2003, provides a stark reminder of how completely dependent society is on the public utility systems. Transportation systems grind to a halt, businesses of every kind shut down, security systems fail and as a result, public officials have their hands full.

Initial suspicions that this black-out may have been terrorist related turned out to be unsubstantiated. The fear remains, however, that a major terrorist assault with severe real world consequences could be launched against the computer systems that control the infrastructures on which everyone depends.

Preventing Cyber attacks

There are many sectors of the computing society and all bear a responsibility to themselves and others to be on the alert for security risks. While it is unquestionably in the interest of individual computer users to protect their personal systems against these sorts of attacks, there is a larger benefit to doing so. Viruses spread through the Internet by making use of inadequately protected equipment. A network of well-protected machines, results in a well-protected network.

Government agencies need to be especially vigilant in guarding against cyber attacks. They are likely to be probed by more virulent bugs, and a successful breach of security is likely to have more dire consequences.

Corporations and businesses own and operate some of the largest computer network systems known. These users must maintain a high degree of awareness and be ready for the worst. A company that does not mind its own security is not only putting itself at risk, but offers itself unintentionally as a platform from which others may be attacked.

In February 2003, the Department of Homeland Security released *The National Strategy to Secure Cyberspace* report, which presented recommendations for protecting the United States against cyber attacks. The report can be accessed on line at www.dhs.gov/interweb/assetlibrary/National_Cyberspace_Strategy.pdf.

Knowing about illegal material or activity on the Internet is one thing, getting the relevant information to the proper authorities in a timely manner is quite another.

Reporting Web Crimes to Law Enforcement

There may be a tendency on the part of some people to feel a sense of shame when they realize they have become a victim of cyber crime. Rather than give in to this temptation, try to learn from the experience. Discover the areas of vulnerability that made the crime possible and make the adjustments necessary to keep the incident from being repeated. The first step in the process is often the reporting of the crime.

While the victim will certainly benefit from reporting a crime, it may be an encouragement to remember that others will benefit as well. Hundreds of people who might otherwise have suffered a similar attack may never become a target. Timely and accurate reporting of crimes gives law enforcement the information they need to stop the perpetrators more quickly, and that means less victims.

As soon a person realizes they have been successfully targeted and are now a victim of cyber crime, they need to contact local law enforcement and ask for the Computer Crimes Unit. As may be the case, if no such crime unit exists, one should at least attempt to locate a detective who is cyber-savvy and has experience along these lines. If nothing else, the local authorities may be able to refer the victim to another agency more suited to handle computer crimes.

Michael Rayball, commander of the Maricopa County Sheriff's Office Computer Crimes Division states that for some local police departments, the resources to support a dedicated computer crimes unit are just not available.

The next section provides a quick look at the right of victims of cybercrimes.

Victims' Rights and Cybercrimes

Cyber crimes can be dangerous, leaving victims with a sense of helplessness. Law enforcement needs to be involved if the perpetrator is to be caught and punished, but to which agent of the law ought a victim to go? The answer is: it depends.

Local law enforcement may handle many or all aspects of the crime, particularly if both the victim and the criminal are within the same local jurisdiction. If the perpetrator has committed related crimes in other locales, the law enforcement agencies associated with those areas will also become involved.

If all offenses related to a string of violations appear to be contained within a state, most likely state authorities will oversee the investigation. This is not always the case, as crimes involving violations of federal laws can involve the FBI, regardless of other jurisdictional considerations.

When crimes span interstate boundaries, the FBI and possibly other federal agencies, depending on the nature of the crimes, will be involved in the investigation.

In some cases, law enforcement agencies themselves may be unsure how to proceed, especially if they are not accustomed to handling these sorts of offenses. A victim may be referred to a special crimes unit, or less satisfactorily, they may simply take a report and then not act on it at all.

A better option may be to contact the Internet Crime Complaint Center (www.ic3.gov). Specially trained staff members will record the details of the crime and refer the case to the correct law enforcement agency.

Local, Regional or International Crimes

Questions of jurisdiction in criminal proceedings involving Internet crimes are complicated by a number of factors. The Internet is a global forum, spanning international jurisdictions, each with their own laws and codes.

To complicate matters further, cyber criminals are able to spoof e-mail addresses, making it appear that messages they send are originating from a different address than they actually are. An e-mail that appears to have been sent from outside the country may in fact have been sent from across town.

Deciphering the genuine properties of a message can be a challenge, but it is only the first step in a long chain of events that may or may not lead to identifying the bad guy. For cases like this, IC3 may well be the best starting point.

Separate jurisdictions may attach penalties of differing severity to the same crime. In cases involving financial loss for example, the level of damage that must be incurred before the crime is considered a felony can be different from state to state. Researching which jurisdiction carries the tougher penalty for a particular crime can result in a more robust sentence. Any victims of such crimes should contact their state's Attorney General to advise the course of action.

In cases with international considerations, the questions associated with inconsistent penalties can be very difficult to answer. It is possible for an act to be categorized as a serious crime in one country, and not even illegal in another.

IC3 and Cybercrime

These wildly divergent laws and penal systems may seem like insurmountable challenges under the current arrangement. Thanks in part to the efforts of IC3 and others, there is a growing level of coordination between foreign and domestic officials aimed at prosecuting cyber crimes. Laws already on the books are often applicable to these cases, but a lack of evidence-gathering expertise on the ground can mean a weak case even if the law is clear. IC3 can help foreign law enforcement build stronger cases by sharing their extensive knowledge of how to go about the business.

IC3 also partners with the U.S. State Department to increase internal awareness about the issues surrounding the problems of domestic and international cyber crimes. This heightened sensitivity can help the department navigate the treacherous legal landscapes that often confront anyone attempting to investigate or prosecute an international cyber crime.

In addition to the jurisdictional quandaries, there are other aspects of cyber crime that tend to muddy the legal waters. As a Supervisory Special Agent with the FBI and a Unit Chief for the IC3, Dan Larkin points out that one significant difference is the traditional damage priority assessment process.

When conducting traditional criminal investigations, prioritizing criminal activity on the basis of the damages makes sense. A crime involving the loss of a fortune will outrank a petty theft when it is time to allocate law enforcement resources.

With cybercrime, says SSA Larkin, it's not that cut and dried. Crooks of the cyber type may strike at thousands, perhaps hundreds of thousands of targets in a single shot. Playing a numbers game of percentages, they potentially swindle huge amounts of money in short amounts of time, without cheating any single person badly enough to cause a major stir.

Unless an astute cyber investigator puts it all together and realizes that many small scams are being run by a single operator, the resources needed to bust the bad guys may never be brought to bear. On occasion, enough pieces of the puzzle fall into place and form a picture of what is going on. It may be well after the fact however, with vital evidence having long since been destroyed. The trail goes cold, as they say, very quickly. Thus time is of the essence when investigating cyber crime.

This need to expedite cyber investigations is at the heart of IC3's philosophy of acting quickly; building cases in real time as the crimes are occurring. IC3 is often able to glom diverse and seemingly unconnected reports together to form a cohesive picture. If the trail that begins to develop leads overseas, IC3 may still be able to work alongside foreign government's officials and continue to pursue the case further. Feasibly, the days of automatic immunity from U.S. laws for overseas perpetrators are drawing to a close.

The United States is not alone, however, in taking a dim and serious view of cyber crime. India is just one foreign government that has taken steps to counter the problem. In 2000, India passed the Information Technology Act, which removes some of the ambiguity of the law by establishing legal definitions for many cyber offenses, including hacking, tampering and the distribution of obscene material. Under this act, India has established an array of punishments for convicted offenders ranging from fines to imprisonment for up to 10 years.

The criminals are out there wreaking all the havoc they can muster. The victims know it is happening, but how do they take advantage of the legal resources that are available? This topic will be covered in the next section.

Enforcement of Internet Crime Statutes

As a former chief of security for Microsoft Corporation and longtime soldier in the war against cyber crime, Howard Schmidt says that most areas of the country have sufficient laws in place to protect against common forms of cyber crime. The problem lies in the enforcement of those laws.

Victims of cyber crimes need to be of as much aid as possible to the law enforcement agencies that will be handling their case. Make sure every scrap of evidence in whatever form it may exist is available to investigators. Cyber crimes are difficult to investigate and prosecute, even when all the pieces are in place. Victims should be careful not to compound the difficulty by providing shoddy information. Provide a journal outlining events and timelines.

Be vigilant with your evidence.

As the problems associated with cyber crime continue to grow, the FBI has intensified its efforts, and has formed a partnership with IC3 to help facilitate data gathering.

Penalties for Cyber Criminals

The Identity Theft Penalty Enhancement Act of 2004 was signed into law in July of that year by President Bush. At the time of the signing, President Bush commented on the new law, remarking that,

"It reflects our government's resolve to answer serious offenses with serious penalties."

The act toughens the sentences that will be imposed on those convicted of identity theft. It also defines a new crime known as "aggravated identity theft", which occurs when a person steals an identity specifically for the commission of a crime. Conviction of this new crime results in a mandatory minimum two-year prison sentence on top of the judgments that may result for the crimes committed while acting under that false identity.

The penalties imposed for cyber crimes are dependant on a number of factors including the specifics of the offense and the jurisdiction in which it occurred. In Arizona for example, a person need not profit in any way through the use of another person's identity. The simple presentation of oneself as someone else is all that is necessary to be charged under identity theft laws.

Juvenile and first time offenders may find clemency before the court, receiving probation or a suspended sentence for cyber crimes. Such offenders should not, however, take this as a license to continue their ways. The laws are getting tougher, and an increasingly dim view is being cast on unruly netizens.

Cybercrooks and Security Assessment Tools

Some computer programs categorized under the heading of risk assessment tools are designed to probe other computer systems and networks for weaknesses and vulnerabilities. These programs were originally intended to help technology professionals identify security risks in their own systems. Corporations have also been known to hire computer security companies who use this type of software to attempt break-ins, as a means of testing their own defenses.

Criminals have gained access to these sorts of programs in the past and used them to perform illegal hacking operations. This use of these programs violates their intended purpose as a security-enhancing tool. Some have argued for the eradication of this type of software, citing problems associated with its misuse. But most experts agree that while the problem exists, it does not pose a grave enough threat to outweigh the benefits.

Conclusion

There are many individual and corporate netizens helping to make the Internet a safer place to navigate. Specialized law enforcement units and companies that develop security and anti-virus software, as well as consultants and security experts all make the Internet a less threatening environment. Additionally, there are hundreds of responsible corporations like banks, retailers and others who contribute by maintaining a high level of security awareness in their Internet dealings.

And then there is the individual netizen. When a user maintains a clean, protected system with application and operating system patches installed; anti-virus software and Internet security programs up-to-date and running, they make their computer a hard target to hit. On the Internet, ensuring the personal security of each individual user is the best way to promote the security of all users.

In spite of all these precautionary efforts, cyber crime happens. When it does, Internet users must report it in a timely manner and cooperating fully with law enforcement in their efforts to investigate and prosecute the perpetrators.

Many of the larger issues impacting the world of cyber-crime today have been presented in this chapter. Some of the key topics covered were:

- Criminal terms and definitions.

- Civil matters of defamation and libel.

- Reporting cyber crime to law enforcement.

- Cyber crimes involving identity theft.

- Cyber crimes involving conspiracies.

- Jurisdictional concerns and international Internet law.

The next chapter the growing problem of cyber theft will be addressed and it will illustrate how crooks use the web to steal from honest consumers.

Cyber Theft

What is mine is mine and what is yours is mine!

Introduction

This chapter will cover copyrighted property, creative and software licensing, plagiarism, and trademarks as well as the various tricks that web thieves employ to steal websites, otherwise known as web page hijacking. This first section begins with an overview of web page theft.

Web Page Hijacking

Unfortunately, for the Internet user, web page hijacking is a fairly simple and common criminal activity. How does it happen?

"Let's you and me make a deal."

Opportunists simply wait for an Internet name, also called a domain name, to expire and then they pay the fee and take it over. If the previous owner wants their web presence restored, the new owner may accommodate them "for a processing fee". This could be considered blackmail. Taking over an expired domain name is, of course, perfectly legal. The new owner of the domain may simply have wanted to establish a web presence with that particular name. If that is the case, they will then replace the previous content with information on their new company, association, group or hobby.

Taking over a website becomes a legal issue when the new owner uses the content already in place on that web page, which could result in infringement of copyright, trademarked names or even text.

In addition, if the domain name is unique and unlikely to be used fairly by another party, this may be case for a legal challenge. For example, the name Coca-Cola is unlikely to be used for anything other than the soft-drink vendor and thus it would be difficult to avoid returning www.coca-cola.com to the company that owns the name Coca-Cola.

To a politician, appearance is important. Most candidates are leveraging the Internet to some degree to communicate on issues that are important to their constituents. Some are not aware that when their domain registrations expire, anyone can pay the required registration fee and take over the domain.

Some people may not care, especially if the election year was part of the domain name (for example www.johndoe2003.org). The risk is that many times, there will be other links to the site and if it is taken over and used for different purposes, it may reflect upon the former owner.

This happened to one Colorado politician whose site was taken over and converted into a site containing pornography. One of the organizations that supported her candidacy was a Christian organization and they had a link to her campaign web page. That could be embarrassing to some and potentially a major hindrance to future campaign success.

Where, in many cases, the opportunist may be within the extent of the law, another class of pagejacker exists who is clearly not. These hackers search for a web page which is on a web server with a security hole. They use the security vulnerability to take over control of the machine. With control of the machine, they are free to do whatever they want to the web pages contained within.

These pagejackers may create a link from a legitimate web page to one that is specifically created to scam people. Unsuspecting users may type www.mybank.com in the address bar of their browser and unknowingly be re-routed to www.hackersbank.com where their username, password, account number and anything else they type in is recorded. In this type of instance, this information will most likely be used for the financial gain of the criminal.

Copyrights and Cyberspace

According to the United States Copyright Office's extensive online site, www.copyright.gov/:

"Copyright is a form of protection grounded in the U.S. Constitution and granted by law for original works of authorship fixed in a tangible medium of expression. Copyright covers both published and unpublished works."

While content is copyright protected from the moment of creation, most feel more secure with registering their work and thus giving themselves a public record and certificate of copyright, which will benefit them in case of an infringement lawsuit.

Copyright protection has both civil and criminal repercussions. Civil damages can be awarded in excess of any actual amount earned or profited by the copyright violator. It is important to realize that U.S. law specifies that felonious criminal violations of copyrighted material involves more than 10 copies and is valued over $2500.00.

Before the growth and popularity of the Internet, copyright law frequently dealt with paper copies of books and magazine articles or cassette copies of music from records or radio. The Digital Millennium Copyright Act provides both civil and criminal penalties for violations. For the first offense, violating this law can be penalized up to $500,000 and 5 years in prison. In addition, the U.S. has reciprocal agreements with many other nations and honors the copyright of other countries' material.

Music and the Web

In the era of vinyl records and cassette tapes, people routinely made copies of records onto cassette tapes for a variety of reasons. Some wanted to protect the more sensitive vinyl from being damaged. Others wanted to be able to listen to their music in the car. Some people wanted to avoid buying their own music and chose to disregard copyright law by making copies of artists' records.

Music Downloads

A recent trend has been to offer free music downloads in conjunction with another purchase. These free downloads require a specific program. The programs are free, but they require the user to create an account.

Free music had some artists singing foul.

This disregard for the law, while not endorsed by the record companies and other copyright owners, was generally considered to have a minor monetary impact on record sales. This was for a couple of reasons.

- One reason was the limited quality of the copied music. Stereo equipment capable of reproducing music at a high quality was very expensive and not very common. This meant that the quality of most copies was inferior to what could be obtained by purchasing legal music.

- Another reason for the relatively minor impact was the scale of these copies. Most illegal copies produced amounted to a person's circle of friends. The justification many people expressed when asked about the legality of making copies of music for a friend was usually something like this;

"So what if I make a few copies? I'm not charging any money. The record companies have bigger fish to fry than me."

Advances in technology, however, changed the record companies' attitudes towards downloading free music. Higher quality and readily available equipment for playing and copying music combined with master digital CDs now results in pristine copies. Computers and technology can make a digital copy of music into a format any computer can read. This facilitated the spread of illegal music. Online services were created that allowed people to share their digital music collection with anyone in the world who wanted it. Whereas, illegal copies used to be limited to a small circle of friends, these online services made it possible for one legal album or CD to be shared illegally with every person in the world who has Internet access.

These changes forced copyright owners to sit up and take notice. The Recording Industry Association of America (RIAA) is the trade group that represents the U.S. recording industry. Its mission is to foster a business and legal climate conducive to their members' creative and financial vitality.

> "In order for legitimate services to continue their growth, we cannot ignore those who take and distribute music illegally. There must be consequences to breaking the law, or illegal downloading will cripple the music community's ability to support itself now or invest in the future."
>
> RIAA President Cary Sherman

In recent years, the RIAA has brought legal action against thousands of individuals and companies that have participated in illegal music exchanges. They are taking aggressive action to slow the spread of illegal music sharing.

To combat the illegal distribution of music, digital protection is being developed, which will protect copyright holders. Some methods will limit the number of copies that can be made. This has drawn some criticism from consumer rights advocates who fear that customers will not be able to make copies of music for personal use.

Another approach is to imbed an identification code into the digital music itself. This will allow law enforcement the ability to identify the source of the copy. Of course, the problem with any solution is convincing all the parties involved to agree to a standard. For example, there are problems with some solutions that will not let music be saved to certain mp3 digital music players from some software programs.

The days of freely downloading any song without fear of reprisal are over, and the days of making copies of CDs may soon be over or, at the very least, closely restricted.

Software Licensing and the Internet

Most of today's software programs are covered by software licenses. These licenses protect software development companies from unauthorized usage of its software. This protection from unauthorized usage is important because most often the financial investment in a program is huge. If these licenses are not enforced, people will not purchase the programs and the software companies will not be able to stay in business.

To help enforce these licenses, many software companies use copy protection devices to slow or stop illegal copies from working. This slows down the process of installing legal as well as illegal software. It is also problematic when a computer is replaced, as the owner will sometimes need to contact the vendor to obtain a new license key for installing existing legal software on the new computer. Installing on a second computer is usually not legal unless it is a replacement for the first. Each software company has their own rules, so users should be sure to read the software license and call the vendor if they have any questions.

One organization that works against software theft is the Software & Information Industry Association (SIIA). SIIA is the principal trade association for the software and digital content industry. They work to promote, protect, and inform the software and digital content industry.

The SIIA web page on piracy includes information on how to report corporate or Internet piracy. This includes the possibility of being eligible for a reward of up to $50,000 USD. For more information on reporting violations, visit their web page at www.spa.org/piracy.

The costs of software programs run the gamut from moderate to extremely expensive. If high cost is a deterrent, users can consider alternative programs as some vendors have different versions of the same products to meet the needs of a wide variety of customers.

For example, a family holiday letter requires a word processor with different features than a weekly newsletter with multiple authors, editors, and reviewers. Writing a corporate memorandum requires different features than writing a book. Users should consider how the program in question will be used, and then shop for different products that will meet their exact needs.

Computer games are particularly susceptible to theft because the top games are often hyped-up through expansive advertising campaigns. Fans on Internet game-discussion lists supplement this advertising. Players in these forums often promote the game as they tout their skills and discuss strategy.

As the demand for the latest games grows, the game manufacturer and retailers have little reason to discount the selling price. Often, the result is piracy. Once this happens, some over zealous fans will rush to download a copy of the game from the pirate's website, causing the sales for the legal version of the game plummet.

Freeware

Another way to legally fight the high cost of programs is to use freeware. Freeware is, as the name implies, a type of program that is free. Free is a word that is usually associated with financial cost. While free software is free to acquire, the free part of the name refers also to freedom from restrictions.

The question most people have is, "How do programmers get paid if the software is free?" There are many ways that free software creates paying jobs, but they are beyond the scope of this book so only one example will be given.

When software is free, the source code of the program is accessible to anyone who wants to see it. If someone encounters a bug or problem with the program, anyone with the required programming skills is able to overcome the problem. This means a company wishing to provide paid support for users of an application that is freeware needs no authorization or cooperation from the developer of the program. They can hire programmers to fix bugs as they appear.

The open-source movement represents a major implementation of free software. The Free Software Foundation and their General Public License, GPL, established an early presence in what became known as the "open source movement".

One of the features of free software is what the leading figure in the open source movement, Eric S. Raymond refers to as the benefit of having many people looking into a problem. He says, "Every problem will be transparent to somebody." Who hasn't faced a difficult problem only to have a friend or associate suggest a viable solution that they had not thought of?

This is of value to some companies because trouble with a program can take months or years to fix. Frequently, the only solution is to buy or license a newer version of the program. Free software often has a solution within days and sometimes even hours after the problem is discovered.

E-Books

Electronic books, or e-books, are becoming more common. Sometimes e-books are simply an electronic copy of a printed book, and the only benefit is that they can be carried on a CD ROM. Other times, they are fully searchable, which provides a huge benefit over hard copy books where the index is simply a compilation of words the publisher thought were important enough to list.

While there are benefits to e-books, there are also downsides. Making photocopies of even small, one-hundred page books, would be time-consuming enough that it would not be done very often. However, Google is doing just that in an attempt to create a vast online, totally searchable, library.

An e-book, like digital music, could be quickly shared across the world. If the e-book is copyrighted, that sharing is illegal. The ease at which it can be done makes this a potentially risky venture for copyrighted material.

Like the music business, the publishing world is working on technical solutions that would protect the copyright. The key is to find a solution that will protect the copyright, and still give the purchaser the ability to use the product in a way that allows them to derive the benefit they expect.

Plagiarism and the Web Revolution

Web plagiarism has become an epidemic in academia largely as a result of the high precision and recall of the Google search engine and the huge volumes of intellectual property on the web.

According to Northern Kentucky University (library.nku.edu), many students think that it is acceptable to "paraphrase" the works of others and they have one of the best definitions of paraphrasing:

Students anxious about committing plagiarism often ask:

"How much do I have to change a sentence to be sure I'm not plagiarizing?" A simple answer to this is: If one has to ask, one is probably plagiarizing. This is important.

> Avoiding plagiarism is not an exercise in inventive paraphrasing. There is no magic number of words that can be added or changed to make a passage "original".
>
> Original work demands original thought and organization of thoughts.

Plagiarism, by its very definition, cannot be an accident, and it is an intentional act of theft. No amount of excuses or pleas of ignorance can exonerate a plagiarist from their fundamental dishonesty.

The Semantics of Plagiarism

The act of plagiarism involves the stealing of "original work and thought." Plagiarism can be subtle, and many students believe that they can change one or two words in a sentence and avoid detection. So, how does one detect the work of the sly plagiarist who replaces words with synonyms and alters the sentence structure?

- **Synonyms** – A reference to "house" could be changed to dwelling, abode, apartment, etc.

- **Word Stems** – A reference to "house" could be changed to housing, home, etc.

- **Semantic Structure** – Adverbs and adjectives can be replaced and altered to conceal the crime.

Fortunately, despite these attempts to hide their wrongdoing, the plagiarist can still be detected thanks to sophisticated web tools and the world of applied Artificial Intelligence. Sophisticated software programs, such as those found at Turnitin.com, employ pattern-matching algorithms that glean the meaning of each phrase and compare it to existing works on the Internet.

Software such as the *Princeton Wordnet* provides hierarchies of synonyms that can replicate the plagiarist's attempts to conceal their theft. This author worked extensively with semantic networks and they can often lead to surprising results.

Other web search engine companies are developing search tools that have the surprising side-effect of being able to detect plagiarism. Their goal is to allow web users to highlight a paragraph of text and press a button called "Show me more like this." Internally, these tools analyze the paragraph, apply structure, word stem and synonym rules, and scour the web for a suitable match.

The Epidemic of Web Content Theft

According to a televised investigation report on the hit TV show *Primetime Thursday*, their investigation revealed a growing problem of cheating and plagiarism, facilitated by the massive volumes of content on the web. From junior high schools to the Ivy League, *Primetime* found that students find the temptation to copy-and-paste from the web to be an irresistible temptation. According to the *Primetime Thursday* report, many students believe that everyone plagiarizes, and they use this as an excuse for their theft:

> "It's unfair on your part, if you're studying, you know, so many hours for an exam and everybody else in the class gets an 'A' cheating," says Sharon, a college student. "So you want to get in the game and cheat, too."

The web is a double-edged sword. Just as it has facilitated the theft of content, it has also enabled tools for publishers and professors to quickly detect stolen content.

Detecting Plagiarism

Fortunately, it is just as easy for someone to detect plagiarism as it is to copy it off other people's web pages. There are many websites which aid in detecting plagiarism.

- **Amazon** – The Amazon "search inside the book" feature has resulted in dozens of lawsuits for plagiarism as unscrupulous authors were caught within days of the introduction of the feature.

- **Google** – The Google search engine is used by almost all College professors today and the new Google Print facility is now indexing thousands of books into the Google engine.

- **Turnitin.com** – This wonderful website is available to academics everywhere and provides instant web content matching for papers and College essays. (www.turnitin.com)

Now that the web has given users tools with which to detect the plagiarist, the threat of getting caught has acted as a deterrent. However, the punishments for the plagiarist can run the gamut from a slap-on-the hand to criminal prosecution.

A Question of Honor

The punishments for plagiarists are the most severe at schools that employ and enforce the Honor Code such as the U.S. military academies.

"We will not Lie, Cheat, Steal, nor Tolerate Among us those Who Do."

The Honor Code requires any student to turn-in any other student who they suspect of lying, cheating or stealing. The code creates a self-policing system to ensure personal honor and integrity.

Col. John Garmany, a noted author with Rampant TechPress and a Graduate of West Point, notes that the Honor Code made plagiarism virtually non-existent:

"We were well versed in plagiarism and we would never think of using someone else's work without giving them credit.

"An honor code violation meant dishonor and dismissal from West Point and we took it very seriously. For example, we were allowed to ask another cadet for help, but we were required to mention the helper by name, even if we did not use any of their ideas directly."

Sadly, enforcement of web content theft is sporadic at best, even among the top schools.

Punishment for Plagiarists: Real World Case

In one Adjunct professor's experience, plagiarism is largely tolerated at major U.S. colleges and universities, and he found it to be extremely frustrating.

There was one particular case where a U.S. Military officer submitted a computer program that matched the work of another, line for line. Upon investigation, the professor discovered that he had lifted someone else's work from a trash bin and copied it, adding only his name, as the author.

This professor was especially offended because this officer was a graduate of a U.S. Military academy, and was completely familiar with the Honor Code and the ethics of an officer. Upon confrontation, he was completely unremorseful and gave the lame excuse, "everyone does it."

In this case, the professor attempted to flunk the student and file a complaint against him with the university. The professor was fully aware that the Armed Forces would not be favorable to the officer, that he would lose his security clearance and could be summarily dismissed from the armed forces, perhaps losing his retirement and most of all, his personal honor.

Unfortunately, the Dean of the college was far more tolerant than the professor was, and he refused to allow the professor to pursue his complaint. To this professor, it seems that the web thief was enabled by the lack of threat of consequences.

Plagiarism, intentional or not, is considered stealing and can expose one to serious liability. In 2004, a noted author and publisher was reviewing a job interview book and discovered an entire page that he had written which had been stolen and published by one of the world's largest publishers. Fortunately for the publisher, he was also one of their authors and was familiar with their contract that holds the author solely responsible for ensuring that their content is their own work.

Victims of plagiarism are entitled to the following remedies:

- To have the offending book recalled from distribution – This can cost the publisher over $100k, and the author is required to pay for it.

- To receive an official published apology – The plagiarist must publicly admit their theft and acknowledge the rightful creator of the material.

- Civil damages – In one case, the victim sued the author and received over a quarter of a million dollars. The author lost his house and savings and was ruined by his act.

Laws Against Plagiarism

According to the United State Constitution,

"The Congress shall have power to promote the progress of science and useful arts by securing for limited times to authors and inventors the exclusive rights to their respective writings and discoveries".

The U.S. Supreme court has also addressed the plagiarism issue, and also uses the Lanham Act to justify punitive damages for plagiarism.

In 1948, Doubleday copyrighted and published General Dwight D. Eisenhower's book, *Crusade in Europe*, which was about the D-Day invasion. Fox Television later created a TV series based on the book.

For the fiftieth anniversary of World War II, a third party company named Dastar edited the *Crusade in Europe* television series, added some new material, and released a video set called *World War II Campaign in Europe* without attribution to Fox.

In the famous *Dastar vs. Twentieth Century Fox* case (539 US 23), the court found Dastar guilty of plagiarism for copying Twentieth Century Fox material without giving them proper credit:

---

their complaint [...] claims that Dastar's sale of Campaigns "without proper credit" to the Crusade television series constitutes "reverse passing off" in violation of § 43(a) of the Lanham Act, 15 U.S.C. § 1125(a)

In this case, the U.S. Supreme court doubled the amount of the damages. When plagiarism is intentional and with malice, courts are allowed to impose punitive damages, doubling and even tripling the amount of the actual damage to punish the plagiarist:

"The ultimate test [...] is whether the public is likely to be deceived or confused".

The court awarded Dastar's profits to respondents and doubled them pursuant to § 35 of the Lanham Act, 15 U.S.C. § 1117(a), to deter future infringing conduct by petitioner.

Another common type of Internet theft is cybersquatting. The next section details how cybersquatters are punished by the U.S. courts.

Cybersquatting

Cybersquatting is the illegal appropriation of protected website names, URLs, content, trademarks or copyrighted material. The U.S. *Anticybersquatting Consumer Protection Act* (ACPA), which was passed into law in November 1999, contains a provision that allows judges to order large damage awards against cybersquatters. This ACPA defined cybersquatting as:

"registering or using with a bad faith intent to profit a domain name that is confusingly similar to a registered or unregistered mark or dilutive of a famous mark."

Since this landmark 1999 law was passed, the ACPA has been used many times to punish web thieves. The ACPA requires "bad faith" intent, and this malice is a prerequisite for punishment of a web crook.

In the famous case of *Coca-Cola Co. v. Purdy* (382 F.3d 774), the investigation revealed that Mr. Purdy has published counterfeit web pages including drinkcoke.org, mycoca-cola.com, mymcdonalds.com, mypepsi.org, and mywashingtonpost.com, a website designed to appear like the Washington Post:

During a telephone conversation with counsel for the Post entities on July 8, Purdy acknowledged that he had published a counterfeit front page at mywashingtonpost.com and claimed that his actions were protected by the First Amendment.

Purdy appears to be one of the zealot types of cyber-personalities as detailed in Chapter 2, *Understanding Web Personalities*. His fake Washington Post website proudly proclaimed, "Abortion is Murder." Even more distasteful, it contained disgusting and offensive photographs of aborted fetuses next to the Coca Cola logo with this caption:

Things Don't Always Go Better With Coke.
Abortion is Murder —
'The Real Thing.'

In typical cyber-crook fashion, Purdy draped himself with the First Amendment and said that the right to free speech allowed him to copy the Washington Post's website and appropriate the Coca Cola logo and slogan.

Unfortunately for Purdy, the district court found that Purdy's logos were both distinctive and famous and that the domain names Purdy had registered and used were identical or confusingly similar to those the legitimate trademarks.

The court also found that Purdy had "bad faith intent" and desired to use the Coke logo to promote his personal agenda:

---

a strong likelihood that plaintiffs would prove that Purdy and others acting in concert with him had registered the domain names with a bad faith intent to profit by tarnishing and diluting plaintiffs' trademarks and by relying on their good names and goodwill to achieve the personal gain of promoting their messages, generating publicity, and raising money for supported causes.

Source: Lexis

In summary, the courts are very clear that the First Amendment not protect the use of another's trademark in a domain name to attract an unwitting and unwilling audience to the message of the domain name holder.

Deceptive Domain Names: Real World Case -

This case involves the creation of deceptive domain names, geared to divert web traffic from legitimate websites.

In what may be the largest award yet under the ACPA, a federal judge in Pennsylvania found John Zuccarini guilty of cybersquatting and ordered him to pay $500,000 to Electronics Boutique for registering five domain names that were similar to the retailer's trademarks of ebworld.com and electronicsboutique.com. Zuccarini had registered the domain names electronicboutique.com, eletronicsboutique.com, electronicbotique.com, ebwold.com and ebworl.com. The court subsequently ruled that these deceptive URL's constituted cybersquatting.

The purpose of these deceptive domains comes into full effect when web users accidentally miss-type a domain name.

> "Mr. Zuccarini's bad-faith intent to profit from the domain misspellings is abundantly clear," the court wrote. "Also, Mr. Zuccarini has no bona fide business purpose for registering the domain misspellings, as he does not and has not offered any goods or services that relate to [Electronics Boutique] or electronic products."

Cybersquatters will change the title, keyword and description tags on web pages to include trademarked phrases in order to take web traffic from a legitimate website.

No matter the type of content on the web, be it domain names, web pages, content, software, music or trademarks, one thing remains clear; the explosion of the popularity of the Internet has brought about an entirely new form of theft and as a result, a wide array of burgeoning laws and punishments for cybercrimes.

Conclusion

In this chapter, various ways thieves can steal valued web property and the laws that protect the online user have been introduced. The following topics covered:

- Web page hijacking

- Copyright and cyberspace

- Music on the web

- Software licensing

- E-books

- Plagiarism

- Cybersquatting

The next chapter introduces one of the most damaging areas of cybercrime, the "Internet Scam."

Internet Scams

I am Princess Abdulahi of Nigeria.
Why did you not answer my e-mails?

Deception at Work

The very power that makes the web a wonderful tool also makes it a perfect breeding ground for criminals. The ability to have world-wide, instant communication has made it possible for scammers across the globe to prey on unsuspecting consumers.

At this time, Internet law has not evolved to the point where foreign scams can be prosecuted and it is reported that a measurable segment of the Gross Domestic Product of some third-world nations is related to organized crime scams on the Internet.

This chapter will examine the technology that enables web scams, the typical methods used by scammers and the currently inadequate Internet laws governing worldwide commerce. Tips and tricks will be provided that can be used to help avoid becoming a victim of a web scam.

The Horrors of Internet Fraud

The global nature of the web has created a situation where it can be nearly impossible to bring an Internet scammer to justice. The epidemic of scams is facilitated by the limited resources of third-world countries who are unable (or unwilling) to investigate these sorts of crimes originating within their borders.

In the USA, there is the Internet Crime Complaint Center (IC3), which was originally named the Internet Fraud Complaint Center. IC3 was established as a central reporting agency for Internet-related complaints. This provided a reporting mechanism for those who had been the victim of web scams. Largely limited to collecting and reporting the statistics of web scammers, IC3 has reported a marked increase in web scams over the past several years. Nearly 100,000 scams were reported in 2004. See the graph in Figure 7.1.

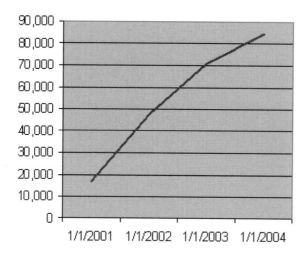

Figure 7.1 *There has been a dramatic increase in Internet scams reported since 2001*

Unfortunately, the IC3 often cannot help scam victims. Since this information is widely known, many users do not bother to report their losses. Consequently, the real number of web scams is potentially much higher.

While the medium has changed, the concept of the scam has been around for centuries. Professional con artists have preyed on people displaying the following characteristics:

- **Greed** – The number one factor upon which web scammers play is a person's desire to make a fast buck.

- **Guilt** – Many scammers play upon personal guilt. Charity scams are notorious for tugging at heartstrings.

- **Entitlement** – Many people feel cheated by society and want to get nice things that they feel that they deserve. In fact, the phrase "Get what you deserve" is directly targeted at this type of person.

- **Poverty** – A large percentage of web scam victims come from lower socioeconomic levels.

- **Ignorance** – Many victims of web scams may not have the benefit of an adequate educational background and are easily fooled by a slick sales pitch.

- **Incompetence** – All else being equal, web scammers often prey on those with diminished mental capacity.

 Phineas T. Barnum remarked "There's a sucker born every minute." Scammers are constantly trying out new methods and techniques for deception, and the potential gullibility and greed of Internet users is a great asset in this pursuit. When a new scam proves itself to be successful, it will spread across the globe like wildfire. The IC3 tracks new web scams and attempts to classify them. Whenever a new scam is detected, it is named and an alert is issued.

The next section explores the world of the web scammer to see how they operate.

Inside the World of the Web Scammer

The temptation to scam from people in wealthy nations is too strong to resist. Even highly religious people in third world countries will justify their thievery by rationalizing that their wealthy victims have too much money. Ironically, many scammers adopt the same mindset as their victims, believing that they deserve the money.

Just like a fisherman, web scammers troll the web with spam and deceptive offers hoping to lure naïve and greedy netizens.

By many estimates, Internet scams are a multi-billion dollar business which attracts criminals from all over the world. According to the Federal Trade Commission's (FTC) records of complaints, the following are the top 10 internet frauds committed in 2004 along with some advice from the FTC for how to avoid becoming a victim:

- **Internet auction fraud** - Consumers say they've received an item that is less valuable than promised or don't receive the item at all.

- **Internet service provider scams** – Consumers report being trapped into long-term contracts of ISPs with big penalties for cancellation.

- **Web site design/promotions -- Web cramming** – Consumers report that getting a custom-designed Web site for a 30-trial period could be more than what was bargained for.

- **Internet information and adult services -- credit card cramming** – Consumers report being required to use a credit card to prove they are over the age of 18 years.

- **Multilevel marketing/pyramid scams** - Some multilevel marketing programs are actually illegal pyramid schemes. When products or services are sold only to distributors, there is no way for anyone else to make money. Netizens should avoid any online recruiting for anything that appears to be a multilevel marketing scheme.

- **Business opportunities and work-at-home scams** - Promises of earning "big money" while sitting at home are almost always too good to be true. Anyone interested in trying one of these business opportunities should talk to other people who have dealt with the company or consult an attorney.

- **Investment schemes and get-rich-quick scams** – These schemes involve making an initial investment in a day trading operation that claims to offer huge returns. The FTC advises: Always check with federal securities and commodities regulators to determine the level of risk associated with any investment.

- **Travel/vacation fraud** - The lure of a cheap trip, with various extras, at a bargain-basement price often does not reveal hidden charges and additional requirements. The FTC advises: Reputable companies will provide references upon request, as well as a written cancellation policy.

- **Telephone/pay-per-call solicitation fraud** - Free access to adult material and pornography by downloading a viewer or dialer program is cause for concern. After downloading such a program, consumers reported their modem being disconnected, then reconnected to the Internet through an international long-distance number. The FTC advises: Every online customer should review phone bills carefully and not download any program to access a free service without reading all disclosures.

- **Health care frauds** – This scheme involves the sale of items not sold through traditional suppliers. These products are advertised as proven to cure serious and even fatal health problems, but in actuality, people simply lose money to these sites. The FTC advises: Always consult a health care professional.

Source: www.ftc.gov

The next section looks into eCommerce in general to examine how it offers opportunities for web scammers.

All about eCommerce

The ubiquitous nature of the Internet has permeated every aspect of society in the 21st Century. The Internet has evolved into a respectable medium for commerce, and companies all over the world are going online.

The phrase "Brick and Mortar" is now used to refer to the old-fashioned ways of retailing and virtually every major retail chain has a web presence today.

- **Retailing** - Huge multi-billion dollar retail conglomerates including eBay, Amazon, and kmart.com rake-in billions of dollars each year from online sales.

- **Entertainment** – The web has been a huge and successful source of revenue for online music, gambling and the sex industry.

- **eBanking** – Large banks including eSchwab, Ameritrade, and Chase Online are providing online financial services across the USA.

- **Service Industries** - Medical advisory web sites such as WebMD are booming, as are insurance, travel, and online legal services.

eCommerce is slowly changing the face of employment in America. Traditional face-to-face occupations such as bank tellers, travel agents and stock brokers are rapidly disappearing, and are being replaced by secure web pages.

The eCommerce revolution is also creating new industries such as *Cybercash*, a service for collecting funds from online shopping carts, and expanding existing industries such as web hosting and email services. The postal industry, including package delivery services, has benefited significantly from eCommerce as millions of new customers start shopping online each year.

The next section provides a review of some of the common perceived risks with eCommerce and then examines the positive role that online shopping has played in 21st Century society.

The Risks of eCommerce

Still, there are many people who fear the anonymity of the Internet and the risks of giving out their private contact and credit card information on a faceless web form. From computer scientists to laymen, there seems to be a generic fear of the web and the daily news reports of web scams fuel the uncertainty and doubt among the consumers.

Real-world case – The "actual size" deception

Even the savviest consumer can get taken on the web, especially when dealing with an unknown seller. The explosion of web portals that claim to be "the worlds largest flea market" have also become the "world's largest source of consumer deception."

The following is a story that demonstrates how easy it is to be deceived online. A man who was an avid clock collector also considered himself to be aware of the subtle scams employed by most private sellers on the web. One day when he was browsing a popular web auction site he saw an opportunity to get a pair of very nice clocks at a great price. Here is the information that was placed in the ad:

Wonderful Pair of Antique Reproduction Clocks

Wonderful Pair of Antique
Reproduction Clocks
Current bid: **US $102.50**

Time left: **3 days 6 hours**

5-day listing
Ends Dec-07-04 19:30:00 PST
Start time: Dec-02-04 19:30:00 PST
History: 14 bids (US $59.99 starting bid)
High bidder: marvin (233)

Description

This is a pair of wonderful reproduction mantle clocks in excellent working order. They are both quartz operated and keep great time with no winding. I hate to part with them, but I'm selling these with no reserve to the highest bidder because I need the money for my College tuition

---

Well, he was the sort of person who wanted to help a College student in need, and it looked like a great deal, too. He used an online sniping program to place a bid at the last minute of the action and won these great clocks for only $176.00.

When he received the package he was very surprised at the small size of the box. His surprise turned to displeasure when he unwrapped his new toys. Here is a photo of the "mantle clocks" that turned out to be less than three inches tall.

Needless to say, he was quite indignant at being taken by his greed at getting such a great deal and his sympathy for the College student. Upon re-reading the item description, it accurately described the items. Technically, he was at fault for not asking about the size of the clocks. Since no actionable deception had taken place, he was unable to complain or get a refund and learned an important lesson that day.

In eCommerce it is important to note the fine print and actively look for omissions such as missing size information and quality guarantees. Some of the most common pseudo-scams involve these practices:

- **As-is** – Deceptive vendors will offer damaged goods in online actions with a "no refund" disclaimer. They often deliberately obfuscate their photographs to hide defects in their merchandise.

- **Inflated Handling Charges** – Many online auctions cover their downside risk by offering "No Reserve" auctions, playing on bidder's greed to get a great deal. For example, some people offer thousands of music CDs in online auctions, with the bids starting at only a penny! The winner may succeed in bidding for the CD for a penny, only to discover that when the bid was placed he or she agreed to pay a flat-rate $19.95 for shipping and handling.

- **Acts of Omission** – As in the example described earlier, always check to see that every aspect of an item is fully described.

These problems have become so widespread in online auctions that third-party escrow services are often used to ensure that the goods are delivered in the condition that they were offered. However, in real life, dissatisfaction with online purchases is at a record high. Every day, buyers issue thousands of negative feedback ratings for online purchases, and it is not always the fault of the seller. This dissatisfaction may be due to several factors:

- **Buyers Remorse** – In the heat of the bidding, the buyer may later regret paying the price. The purchasers will look for every opportunity to return the item, sometimes even damaging the item themselves in order to get a refund.

- **Not what they expected** – Many times the customer does not get an accurate concept of the product from the limited photographs in the online auction. This is a major issue with eCommerce and web developers are working on 3 dimensional interfaces to allow customer to examine goods from every possible angle.

To deter the fear of eCommerce, major companies are working to build trust among their customers, offering such features as super-fast delivery and no-hassle refunds. The next section examines what major eCommerce retailers are doing to improve consumer confidence.

The Upside of eCommerce

With billions of dollars at stake, Internet Retailers, also known as eTailers, will exert an exceptional effort to make their online shopping experience safe, fun and pleasurable. Some of these techniques include:

- **Price Guarantees** – A common complaint from online shoppers is buyer's remorse if they find the item somewhere else at a lower price. Many eCommerce vendors offer a lowest price guarantee.

- **Privacy Guarantees** – To alleviate fears of identity theft and credit card fraud, many eTailers are careful not to store any confidential customer data on their sites. Instead they entrust third-party specialty portals to handle the funds transfer and shipping.

- **Free Shipping** – The boom of eCommerce has been a bonus for shipping companies such as UPS, FedEx, and the US Postal Service. Often, large eCommerce retailers have enough shipping volume to negotiate discounted rates, which they pass on to their customers.

- **Convenience** – The web is a boom for anyone who wants or needs to scan thousands of items when making a purchasing decision. This is most evident in the antiques market. Prior to the Internet, antique collectors would have to spend years traveling around the globe to complete a collection. Today, specialized notification software can alert buyers to someone selling a super-rare item.

Retailers are finding that their online sales are growing rapidly and a web portal has some very appealing features for eTailers:

- **No Rebounders** - One plague of the Brick-and-Mortar (B&M) stores are the pseudo-customers who use the store as a rental facility. Because there is no penalty for returning an item, rebounders purchase expensive goods, use them, and then return them for a full refund. These practices have become such a problem that major chains now have computerized blacklists and refuse to sell to customers with a history of high return rates. This problem is now creeping into the online market as well since many eTailers offer "free shipping" both ways. In eCommerce situations where the customer pays shipping costs both ways, rebounders are less common on the web.

- **Creative Incentives** – With an online shopping cart, intelligent routines can be used to entice the customer into buying more goods. For example:

Your purchase total is $73.95.

Spend $6.05 more and you will receive a Free Gift!

Advanced data warehouse technology is also utilized in eCommerce databases. This is an amazing web-only technology that can be used to target specific types of customers with additional goods. Dubbed "recommendation engines," these powerful tools pay for themselves in a matter of months, and the customers love them because they present goods that customers are likely to want or need. The next section examines how this works.

Intelligent eCommerce

The melding of very large database technology with artificial intelligence has created some wonderful recommendation engines that benefit both eTailers

---

and customer alike. The process starts with a Point-Of-Sale (POS) data warehouse system that feeds all transactions into the web database. The information captured by the POS system includes line item details about all of a customer's purchases. To complete the cycle, the eTailer will entice the customer with an incentive to obtain demographic information:

Take our Quick Survey and receive a 10% discount!

Your gender: _____

Your education level: _____

Your age: _____

Your occupation: _____

Your yearly income: _____

Number of members in your household: _____

Using this basic demographic data, customers are lumped into general categories. Here are some over-simplified examples:

- **Yuppies** – Young professionals, college graduates under 40 years of age, with a disposable income greater than $100,000/year.

- **Dinks** – Double Income, No Kids – This is a special demographic that has a very high propensity to purchase luxury goods.

- **Archie Bunkers** – These are lower income, blue collar customers whose disposable income is focused on purchasing basic necessities.

- **Urban Princesses** – These are college educated females under 30 years of age who live in a city and have an income of over $100,000 per year.

Once the customer profiles have been created, the eTailer can perform sophisticated multivariate correlation algorithms against the data to find exactly those types of goods that people "just like you" want to buy. It should come as no surprise that the wants and desires of different groups are predictable.

Recommendation engines are amazing. In the 1980's, Sony Corporation developed the marketing concept of "need creation." By creating brand new products based on very specific consumer demographics, Sony discovered that customers would say "Yes, I need that." The Walkman is a prime example. The same principle applies to eTailing where the recommendation engine offers additional products that the customer is highly likely to covet. For example:

Your Rolex President watch totals	$23,947.63
Customers like you also purchased:	
Ninety day around-the-world cruise package	$128,000
Beluga Caviar – ten gallon bottle	$83,000
Burberry Raincoat	$1,200
Coach Luggage set	$4,200
Cartier diamond broach	$37,000
Napoleon Cognac – One gallon travel size	$13,500

In sum, eCommerce has fundamentally changed the way that people purchase goods and services. It has also opened a Pandora's box of fraud opportunities. Internet auctions have created a whole new world of eCommerce and this new worldwide marketplace has revenues greater than the entire Gross Domestic Product of many developing nations.

The next section examines the most common type of Internet scam, online auction fraud. eBay is one auction site that comes to mind almost immediately. By some estimates, eBay sales comprise more than 70% of all worldwide auction sales.

All about eBay

Self-proclaimed as *"the world's largest online marketplace,"* eBay is also one of the world's largest sources of online fraud. According to some estimates, eBay fraud costs Americans millions of dollars every year and the problem appears to be growing.

eBay offers some resources for buyer protection, but ultimately it falls on the purchaser to obtain as much information as possible about their potential purchase to protect themselves during the auction process. eBay also offers forums for dispute resolution when a purchaser has been unsuccessful in their attempt to resolve a complaint on their own. However, in the end, since eBay is not actually involved in the transaction beyond providing the venue where the transaction takes place there is very little they can do.

There are several common schemes used by web criminals on auction sites such as eBay including shill bidding, the cut-and-run scam, and buyer fraud.

Shilling Scams

Shilling is the act of bidding on ones own goods. In some states it is a perfectly legal act. In some states a seller may bid on their own goods when they have a legitimate intent to buy it back because of a low going price. In North Carolina, the auctioneer may bid on the item that they are selling so long as they announce it to the audience and it is not advertised as an "absolute" auction.

There have been auctions where an auctioneer says that he reserves the right to bid up to his reserve price. However, he does it in such as way that the audience is unclear of the meaning. Once immunized by the statement, what may happen is the auctioneer then bids himself. Unscrupulous auctioneers can start bidding wars by bidding for an item themselves whenever they sense that a bidder simply must have the item, at any cost. This type of zealous bidder can often be spotted constantly holding up their bidder card.

Often shilling is done using a team of "shill bidders." They will all have fake bidder cards and attempt to run up the prices and buy back any items that might sell at a low price. Obviously, bidders do not like auctions with a reserve, or minimum, price because they want to get the best deal. The shill bidders appeal to the greed of the actual bidder, often enticing them to pay a price far above the going rate.

On eBay shilling is against the rules but may not be a criminal act. The most famous incident of eBay shilling was conducted by a California attorney who was part of a conspiracy to sell fake modern art.

Real World Case: The Crooked Lawyer

Attorney Kenneth Fetterman received a 46 month prison sentence after being a fugitive for almost two years from an eBay scam that netted him a fortune from trusting bidders. Fetterman was the ringleader in a brilliant scam that preyed on the greed of art collectors.

Fetterman started by offering a fake painting that looked just like works of Richard Diebenkorn, an abstract artist whose paintings are now worth millions of dollars. He and his accomplices forged the initials "RD 52," a signature designed to make bidders believe that it was a valuable Diebenkorn original.

They offered the phony painting with an extremely low reserve price and said that they knew nothing about the work. Art enthusiasts, in their excitement over seeing the painting with the "RD 52" signature, bid the price of the painting to over $10,000. Fetterman was not satisfied, and he and his accomplices started a bidding war for the fake painting using names that looked suspiciously like those of fellow art dealers. They eventually lured a greedy art lover into cashing out his 401(k) retirement fund to pay over $100,000 for the painting.

Ultimately, in addition to his prison term, Fetterman was ordered to pay restitution to the eBay bidders who were taken in the swindle.

The Cut-and-run scam

Some online auction sellers will establish a reputation via the auction site's feedback mechanism through hundreds of honest transactions. Then they will offer hundreds of thousands of dollars worth of expensive and highly desirable good such as laptop personal computers at unbelievably low rates. Once they receive payment for this merchandise, the seller disappears.

Scammers are not just preying on auction buyers. Sophisticated scams have been developed to scam auction sellers as well.

Buyer fraud

Auction fraud works both ways. Bidders can commit online fraud as easily as sellers. The most common buyer fraud is the switch technique. In rare

---

glassware and pottery, a tiny chip called a flea bite may mean the difference between a $500 item and a $30 item. An online auction seller may be taken by this scam when they have mailed a pristine item to a buyer, who then claims it is damaged. The seller then offers a full refund to the buyer. However, instead of receiving the item that was originally sold, they receive a different item that is clearly damaged.

One way to a seller can protect him or herself from this sort of fraud is to carefully photograph every angle of an item and also employed an invisible pen to mark their goods.

Let's regulate that thar Internet thang

In an attempt to establish accountability for online sellers, the State of North Carolina in 1999 attempted to expand their interpretation of existing laws to encompass the web and require auctioneering licenses from anyone who sells on Internet auction sites. This excerpt is from CNN:

> North Carolina will soon crack down on auctioneers in the state who put items up for bid on the Internet without a license.
>
> By year's end, the North Carolina Auctioneer Licensing Board in Raleigh will distribute pamphlets to auction sites and the public, making them aware of a long-standing state law that requires auctioneers to be licensed or face misdemeanor charges and a $2,000 fine. The board earlier this month revisited the law to determine that it also applied to the Internet.
>
> North Carolina was not the first state to attempt to reduce online auction fraud. The New Hampshire Board of Auctioneers is requiring online auctioneers to be licensed. The Tennessee auctioneer commission's board is also considering expanding the scope of its license requirements.

Jeffrey Grey, Legal Counsel to the North Carolina Auctioneer Licensing Board, published this statement asserting the right of the State to regulate Internet auctions as it relates to North Carolina:

> Internet auctions, therefore, are no different than any other non-traditional auction. If the bids are solicited, received, or awarded in North Carolina, a North Carolina license is required. Period.

Becoming a licensed auctioneer in North Carolina is not trivial and requires that applicants attend a multi-hour class, pass a challenging exam, and pay an initial enrollment fee the first year and an annual fee each year thereafter.

In less than a week, the North Carolina Auctioneer Licensing Board's office was deluged with telephone calls from as far away as Japan in reference to the Board's "new law." . . . The Law that defines what an auction is and who needs a license was written in 1973. The Board had not changed its interpretation, but had merely restated it.

Source: North Carolina Auctioneering Licensing Board

Internet auction sites are often a haven for unusual items. At any point there may be anything to bid on from a submarine to an 80 acre ranch in Colorado. The following section describes some examples.

"The Gov' Mint"

For a short while on eBay, a person could bid on the chance to own a piece of the Ter-mint-ator himself. In one noted eBay case, a collector advertised a used cough drop that was discarded by Arnold Schwarzenegger. eBay pulled the original auction because it does not allow "body parts" to be sold.

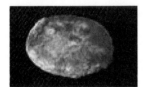

The famous used mint.

Since the original E-Bay listing on May 14 2004, publicity and controversy abound and "The Gov' Mint" has generated worldwide media attention.

At the recent 2004 Peace Officer Memorial in Sacramento on May 7, Governor Arnold Schwarzenegger was observed removing a cough drop from his mouth and discarding it prior to speaking to the thousands of attendees.

The cough drop, dubbed, "The Gov' Mint" was retrieved from the grassy knoll area near the podium, sealed in plastic and transported to an unknown location in Clovis, California.

There are often fun and frivolous auctions on eBay, posted more for their humor value than to scam a potential buyer.

Fuel efficient riding lawn mower

eBay is also a portal for funny auctions, and the low cost of listing an auction has made it a favorite of web jokers. Some eBay auctions are very entertaining as was this auction for a fuel-efficient riding lawn mower.

Wow! Holistic Riding Lawn Mower

Current bid: US $83.23

Time left: 2 days 1 hours
5-day listing

Ends Dec-07-04 19:30:00 PST

Start time: Dec-17-04 13:350:00 PST

History: 22 bids (US $59.99 starting bid)

High bidder: moped (3423)

DESCRIPTION

If you want to help foster a clean environment, this is the riding lawnmower for you. Extremely fuel efficient and environmentally friendly, this wonderful riding lawnmower is sure to be a favorite.

The following examples move away from auction fraud and examine how anyone who offers goods for sale on the Internet can become a victim.

Real-world case: Online sales fraud

After years of fun and enjoyment, Fred had decided to sell his "sand rail" off-road vehicle.

He advertised his sand rail in the online version of his local newspaper's classifieds hoping to attract a wide audience. He soon had an offer, but there was something very, very strange about the offer. It was for several thousand dollars over his asking price, and the buyer asked if Fred could send the difference to the company that would be shipping the sand rail to the buyers' home in another country.

---

sandrailfred@notmail.net · Printed: Wednesday, July 14, 2004 10:33 AM

From : balla mohammed <ballamohammed01@yohoo.com>
Sent : Tuesday, February 11, 2003 3:05 AM
To : sandrailfred@notmail.net
Subject : Machine..

Dear Sir/Ma,

I saw your ads online so i decided to write you. i am interested in buying your (SANDRAIL) for $2450.

pls kindly respond as soon as possible if my offer is acceptable because i need this so urgently..

Balla-Mohammed

While the check had still not arrived, the buyer was pressuring Fred to send the overage for the shipping costs. Fred was suspicious, but when the check arrived, he determined it looked legitimate. He decided that since it was drawn on a bank that had a local branch in his area, he would go there and cash it rather than wait for the check to clear in his own account. "It looked absolutely perfect", he said. When Fred presented the check at the bank, the teller alerted the police who detained and interviewed Fred, nearly arresting him check fraud:

"The entire time this deal was taking place, I was skeptical. The check looked good enough to pass me, and I was fairly skeptical. I took the check straight to the bank and that's when I knew it was a fraud"

The Upside of eCommerce

The police thought that Fred might be part of a scam involving the phony check and treated him as a criminal suspect. Only after Fred told his story and showed them the e-mail trail did they believe him. They then referred the matter to the FBI. The FBI told Fred to blow the whistle and tell the buyer that the FBI had been engaged in an investigation of the transaction. Of course, that e-mail message stopped all communication from the scammer.

Fred learned a valuable lesson. He was interrogated and demeaned and all of his co-workers were shocked to see the local police escorting him to work so they could see the e-mails. Despite the humiliation and degradation, Fred considered himself very lucky.

The next section explores some common charity scams.

Web Charity Scams

Many people are happy to donate to good causes and in this regard, the Internet has been both a blessing and a curse. On the positive side, altruists can locate and donate directly to a charity without a middleman, ensuring the maximum benefit for their funds.

Americans donate more than $200 billion every year and three-fourths of these donations come from private persons. Because those who donate to charities tend to be a trusting sort of person, they have become easy targets for web scammers.

Charities have also discovered that the Internet is a great way to reduce their solicitation costs. Instead of spending hundreds of thousands of dollars on a traditional mail campaign, charities can use e-mail to reduce their costs and leave more money to help their cause. Unfortunately, this movement toward electronic solicitation has also fostered a large rise in web charity scams.

Evaluating Charities on the Web

The explosion of online charity fraud has created the need for a self-policing system. Before donating to a charity, a potential contributor should verify that the charity is a valid 501(c) charity. This IRS designation allows the contributor to deduct their donations from their income taxes. Some organizations list themselves as non-profit or not-for-profit and others as tax-exempt. According to the Internal Revenue Service web page, www.irs.gov, the difference between these classifications is that the term "not-for-profit" is a state designation while the term "tax-exempt" is a federal designation. Most organizations that are designated as tax-exempt will also qualify as a state non-profit. Conversely, an organization that receives not-for-profit status from a state may not qualify for tax-exempt status at the federal level.

There are many online services to aid people in choosing a safe charity:

- The Journal of Philanthropy publishes lists of 501(c) charities and offers suggestions about the best charities.

- The GuideStar web site (www.guidestar.org) also provides information for donors including a "how to choose a charity" checklist and a specialized search engine that allow donors to locate local charities.

- The Better Business Bureau (BBB) has been known for many years as a good way to check the track record of a charity. In 2001, the BBB joined forces with the National Charities Information Bureau to form the BBB Wise Giving Alliance. Their website (www.give.org) provides information on organizations that solicit donations nationally in the United States. Local charities that solicit locally or regionally might be found on the local BBB web pages. The BBB Wise Giving Alliance also contains many useful links to information on charity topics.

Some of the most common web charity scams and hoaxes will be examined next.

The Auto Donation scam

One of the most popular charity hoaxes is the "donate your car" scam. This is very appealing to donors because they are allowed to take a generous tax deduction when they donate their vehicle to valid charity.

Before donating a vehicle, it would be a good idea see verify that the charity has an IRS 501(c) designation. Also check to see if the charity uses a third-party paid broker to accept car donations. Depending on how the charity receives funds from the broker (percent of sale, fixed amount per vehicle or per month), the amount that can be claimed for a tax deduction may be reduced or eliminated.

The next section explores online banking scams.

All about Online Banking

Before exploring online financial scams, the following are some reasons why online financial transactions and eCommerce have become so popular.

Societal Pressure - Many employers now require their employees to accept compensation payments by depositing employee paychecks directly into their checking or savings accounts. Consequently, many consumers feel comfortable using the web to perform financial transactions.

Fast Access - Retirement accounts can now be instantly accessed via services such as Schwab (www.eschwab.com). Investors can managed the stocks in their 401(k) retirement accounts via the Internet and instantly check the current value of their investments.

Lower Fees – The job of a stock broker has been largely displaced by web services (e.g. eTrade, AmeriTrade, eSchwab) since the investor can access and analyze historical stock prices themselves online.

But how does the consumer public choose a safe and secure financial institution? There are several common sense guidelines:

FDIC

Most people will want to make certain that their bank is insured by the Federal Deposit Insurance Corporation (FDIC). These banks usually carry the slogan "Member FDIC" or "FDIC Insured".

FEDERAL DEPOSIT
INSURANCE CORPORATION
INSURING AMERICA'S FUTURE

The FDIC provides a brochure with information for consumers. The brochure titled Safe Internet Banking is available at www.fdic.gov/bank/individual/online/safe.html.

Consumers should verify the legitimacy of the prospective institution by visiting well respected financial web sites and searching for information about the institution. For banks covered by the FDIC, an easy way to do this is to surf to www.fdic.gov/deposit/index.html and click on the "Is My Bank Insured?" link.

Banks that have chosen not to be covered by the FDIC are risky. If the decision is made to use an overseas-based bank, it is also important to realize that the FDIC may not insure those deposits either.

National Credit Union Share Insurance Fund (NCUSIF)

The National Credit Union Association (NCUA) is covered by the NCUSIF, and like FDIC, the NCUSIF provides financial insurance for credit unions.

Your savings federally insured to $100,000

NCUA

National Credit Union Administration, a U. S. Government Agency

In sum, the guiding principle on the Internet is "caveat emptor" or let the buyer beware. What follows is an example of a real-world online financial scam.

Real-world case: PayPal Scam

On July 20, 2000, a scam artist created an exact replica of <u>PayPal.com</u> and used the fake site to attempt to pilfer user names and passwords from customers of the online payment system. Named <u>PayPai.com</u>, the phony site was a convincing duplicate of the real thing and duped many consumers.

It is not uncommon for criminals to create a Trojan Horse web site and then direct victims to the site, usually with the promise of fast money. The greed appeal of the "come get your money" scam has been used successfully to bilk people and is widely employed by police departments to entice criminals into capture. Police send letters to those with outstanding warrants telling them that they must appear in-person to collect some valuable prose. When they show-up they are arrested.

```
Michael Swenson just sent you money with PayPal.

Amount: $827.46

Click here to get you new account bonus!

www.PayPaI.com/bonus.

Did you know you can earn money with the PayPal Refer-a-Friend
program? Go to www.Pay-Pal.com/specialoffers for more details.

To view your PayPal balance or other account information, log in at

www.PayPaI.com/login
```

Upon closer inspection of the e-mail, it can be noted that the "l" in PayPal was actually a capital "I". Hundreds of unsuspecting users went to this site, found what turned out to be an exact copy of the PayPal web site, and dutifully entered their user ID and password. The scammers then cleaned out the victims' accounts. Even though PayPal responded immediately to the threat, it took several hours to have InterNIC locate the domain in Russia and shut down the fake site.

The next section reviews some other common web sales scams.

Web Sales Scams

Ever since Ronald Popeil created the Veg-O-Matic, marketers have strived to expand their sales into a wider market. The next section explores the "Get Rich Quick" scheme.

The Nigerian 419 Scams

The original advance fee fraud was the Nigerian 419 scam, so named from the 419 section of the Criminal Code of Nigeria. Almost a cliché now, when this scan first originated it enticed many people into parting with their life's savings. Here is an example of one of the original scam letters, targeted at upper middle-income businessmen:

```
Lagos, Nigeria.
Attention: The President/CEO

Dear Sir,

Confidential Business Proposal

Having consulted with my colleagues and based on the information
gathered from the Nigerian Chambers Of Commerce And Industry, I have
the privilege to request your assistance to transfer the sum of
$47,500,000.00 (forty seven million, five hundred thousand United
States dollars) into your accounts. The above sum resulted from an
over-invoiced contract, executed, commissioned and paid for about
five years (5) ago by a foreign contractor. This action was however
intentional and since then the fund has been in a suspense account
at The Central Bank Of Nigeria Apex Bank.

We are now ready to transfer the fund overseas and that is where you
come in. It is important to inform you that as civil servants, we
are forbidden to operate a foreign account; that is why we require
your assistance. The total sum will be shared as follows: 70% for
us, 25% for you and 5% for local and international expenses
incidental to the transfer.

The transfer is risk free on both sides. I am an accountant with the
Nigerian National Petroleum Corporation (NNPC). If you find this
proposal acceptable, we shall require the following documents:

(a) your banker's name, telephone, account and fax numbers.

(b) your private telephone and fax numbers — for confidentiality and
easy communication.

(c) your letter-headed paper stamped and signed.
```

```
Alternatively we will furnish you with the text of what to type into
your letter-headed paper, along with a breakdown explaining,
comprehensively what we require of you. The business will take us
thirty (30) working days to accomplish.

Please reply urgently.

Best regards

Howgul Abul Arhu
```

It is estimated that the perpetrators of this scam received upwards of five
billion dollars since its inception in the mid 1980's when it was sent via fax
and traditional mail. The scam hit the Internet in the mid 1990's and has
been so successful that dozens of variants have been circulating.

Real-World case: The Nigerian Scam Murder

When innocent people are bilked out of hard-earned savings, it's not
surprising that the victims might react in unorthodox and unpredictable ways.

In 2003, an unidentified man took the law into his own hands and murdered
a Nigerian diplomat in retaliation for losing his life's savings to the 419 scam.
The suspect, a frail 72-year old retiree, was furious at having lost his life's
savings and visited the Nigerian embassy numerous times in a vain attempt to
recover his money. He was especially distressed that the Nigerian police were
unable to bring the crooks to justice and recover his money. Eventually he
lost patience and took his revenge with a gun. According to Dubem Onyia,
Nigeria's minister of state for foreign affairs:

> "This is the first time such a thing has happened to Nigeria in any of our embassies
> abroad.... The Czech ambassador to Nigeria has been summoned,"

While this is an extreme example, it helps demonstrate the harsh reality that
exists for the victims of these types of web scams.

Get Rich Quick Scams

These pitches include everything from the legendary Nigerian royalty scam to
schemes such as selling knives door-to-door. These cons prey on individuals
who feel society owes them a comfortable living. These individuals are

especially vulnerable to the come-ons of "Get the cash that you deserve" scams.

Help Me Steal Scams

In this variation on the Nigerian scam called the Advance Fee fraud, the criminal tells the victim that there is a lot of money and insinuates that money is of somewhat suspicious origin, such as over-billing a big company. When the victim participates, they think they are providing help to criminals to get dirty money out of their country.

Once the victim realizes the scam, the scammer reminds them that they are an accessory to a felony act. Even though no crime was ever committed, these victims are hesitant to contact authorities for fear of having done something unlawful.

The Overpayment Scam

In this scam, a foreign buyer appears and offers to purchase an item from an online seller. Because many online sellers do not understand international finance, they are easy marks when the phony buyer sends them an official looking cashiers check. The check is written for thousands of dollars more than the purchase amount and the scammer tells the victim to send them the balance and keep $1,000 for their trouble.

This scam has become so pervasive that many people are starting a new hobby called "scamming the scammers." The following section explores some of these scams.

Real World Case: Scamming the Scammers

Scamming the scammers has become very popular as web sellers engage the scammers and force them to pay exorbitant fees to mail them the fake cashier's checks.

Dubbed "Scambaiters," these people relish in wasting the time and money of the scammers, often stringing them on and making them waste huge amounts of time. Some of the most popular Scambaiter sites include www.bustedupcowgirl.com, www.419eater.com and www.dumbentia.com.

The owner of www.bustedupcowgirl.com, Ms. Danielle Goweler, is considered a master Scambaiter as she puts the scammers through a grueling email discourse, all while making them pay exorbitant postage charges to send her the fake cashier checks.

Danielle relishes in publishing the communications between her and the scammers and they are often hilarious, especially when Danielle shares a plan and one can see it unfold via the e-mails.

In the exchange below, Danielle has some fun and offers the scammer some beachfront property in Arizona! The scammer, obviously oblivious to being toyed with, continues their scam pitch:

> Too bad that I can't sell you the horse, but I have some oceanfront property in Arizona that I would like to sell you.
> _____
> hello
> let me see the pix of the oceanfrnt ok mat be i will be intreseted and why u did not want to sale me the horse give me reason ok and let me no the last price
> philip.........
> thanks nice doing bussins.....

As a competitive hobby, scambaiting has a scoring system, and all scambaiters keep a running total of how much money the scammer has wasted on postage and Danielle is nearing the $1,000 mark.

Here is a sample of one of her e-mails, telling the scammer that they have been scammed:

> My Dearest William Lewis,
>
> I regret to tell you I have sold the Mules....over 2 months before you first contacted me that is.
>
> I had a wonderful time with you. See, not all people are as foolish as you might think. There are plenty of us that know your type of scams. I do appreciate you sending me the money order and phoning me and spending some of that hard earned cash you have scammed off of other unsuspecting people.
>
> The money order was phoned into the bank on which it was drawn off of the minute it was received and then it was turned into the local police department.
>
> From your first email I have been posting this on my web site for people everywhere to laugh at. Myself and others will continue to waste your time and have you guys send us your fake money orders and spend your cash until you get so tired of it and find a real job.

Ms. Goweler also proudly displays her collection of fake cashier's checks,
whose total value is approaching $200,000. Here is an actual example of a
scammers check.

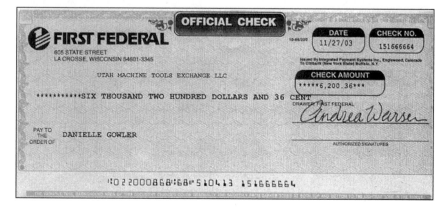

The quality of these fake checks is amazing, and they look very convincing, right down to the smallest detail.

Conning the con-artists can be risky, and Ms. Goweler is a very brave woman. There is always the concern that a scammer may determine where she lives. In one hilarious message, the scammer threatened to report Ms. Goweler to the FBI:

```
Brian,

Thank you for your condolences. It was very quick and unexpected. I
have been drinking my sorrows away all day. I think I have drank all
of the booze in the house by now. I guess I will have to go to town
after a bit and buy some more. A good thing did come out of all this
though, we learned a valuable lesson. Never stick a fork in the
toaster no matter how bad you want that last Pop Tart.

Anyway, I have attached the copy of the Western Union receipt for
you. I hope I have done it right. After all I am very drunk and
don't know much about computers. Please tell me if it doesn't come
through ok. Click Here for the copy of the receipt.

Talk soon,

Danielle


I figured by now all of you know about the "You Are An Idiot" thing.
If not, then you can read my first scam letter.

After he sees this more than likely he will be done with me. I can
only hope he will come back for more :-)


Yep, he was a mad boy! I really feel bad...NOT :-)



brian chadwick wrote:

Hello dani,

Thanks for the game.i realy enjoying it.but less i forget you will
hear from my lawer and from the FBI too.i promise you.
```

Another common scam is that of phishing and it has cost victims millions of dollars.

Phishing Scams

Phishing is a contact sport. The phisher contacts a potential victim via an e-mail message that presents as a legitimate message from common online sales portal. The victim is then directed to a fake imitation of the portal web page where they enter their private information.

According to eWeek Magazine, phishing has become one of the webs most popular scams:

> Since its emergence onto the Internet crime scene about 18 months ago, phishing quickly has become one of the more widespread and profitable forms of online fraud.
>
> In December 2003 there were 116 unique phishing attacks reported to the APWG. In July 2004, there were 1,974 unique attacks—nearly 20 times as many as just seven months earlier.
>
> Experts estimate that somewhere between five and 10 percent of people who receive a phishing e-mail will eventually fall victim to the scam.

A related deception called the mouse-trap will be explored next.

Mouse Trapping

A mouse trap is a web page that does not respond to the traditional browser exit command. Once the domain has been entered by the unsuspecting user, the back button on the browser does not function and the user is stuck inside the web site.

According to eWeek Magazine, phishing has been combined with mouse trapping to ensure that victims are taken in by the scam:

> "They used about a thousand lines of JavaScript code to make sure that no matter what the user did, the window came back up," said Bill Franklin, president of Zero Spam Network Corp. in Coral Gables, Fla., and a member of the Anti-Phishing Working Group, which works to identify and take down phishing-related sites.

> "Any time that window lost focus, it always came back to the front. It was a really good piece of social engineering. We could see traffic going to the site and could just imagine the losses mounting."

Hoaxes

Since it is very easy to believe something once it is written down, the web is a great place to start rumors and incite panic. For scammers, Internet hoaxes are also a great way to spread spyware and viruses. Here is an example of someone's poor idea of a joke.

Internet Pranksters Can Kill You Instantly in Your Own Home

By Bud Weiser

The department of Homeland security announced today that prankster hackers have developed a technology that can invade your computer and cause it to explode. Dubbed the "Joe Mamma" virus, the computer hardware is invaded by small electrical pulses that stimulate the cathode rays in the monitor, causing a huge explosion. According to Bud Weiser,

spokesperson for the National Virus Immunization Center, the viruses enter the PC with the e-mail subject lines such as "Cheap online Viagra" or "Grow your Penis". Once opened, the virus stimulates the circuits in the cathode Ray tube, redirecting powerful cathode rays directly into the computer's power supply. The resulting explosion can kill anyone within a six foot radius on the PC!

There are ways to protect yourself and your

loved ones from such a tragedy occurring. One way is to never open an email that appears to originate from colleges and universities.

These may include email addresses ending in .edu, .sch, .us and of course .fr

and other suspicious-sounding names. If you happen to receive a message you believe to contain the Joe Mamma virus, call the ATF immediately at one of the following phone numbers:
1-888-ATF-BOMB.

The resulting explosion can kill anyone within a six foot radius on the PC!
Bud Weiser

Internet Pranksters can turn your home computer into a bomb!

Sometimes Internet hoaxes can have criminal undertones such as the one that was targeted at African American taxpayers. The hoax letter went something like this:

Greetings,

As a proud African American I need to ensure that everyone is aware of the Slavery Compensation Act of 2003.

> Enacted into Law by Congress, the SCA provides for compensation of up to $30,000 for anyone whose ancestor was enslaved within the United States.
>
> Collection is easy, and our tax advisor will show you how to claim your compensation by filling-out a simple form. For a small administrative fee of only $200 we take care of all of the paperwork and get your money on its way to you
>
> Don't wait. Get the money you deserve.

In this hoax/scam combination, victims were lured into paying $200 in cash to learn how to claim their money from the Federal government. In a very sad ending, the scammers added insult to injury by telling the victims that their slavery compensation money could be deducted from their income taxes. Hundreds of misinformed taxpayers spent their tax withholding, believing that they were receiving a windfall. The IRS was sympathetic, but still required them to pay their taxes, along with the required penalties and interest.

The following is an example of how anyone can fall victim to e-mail scams. A noted Oracle DBA decided to pull a prank with an April Fools Day hoax using his database newsletter that reaches an audience of several thousand computer professionals. Here is a copy of the email:

> The Computer Incident Advisory Delegation (CIAD) has just issued a Severity-One virus alert for a security vulnerability for Oracle Databases on Linux and UNIX platforms. This virus affects Oracle RDBMS Releases 8.1.0 through 9.2.0.4 and may result in a complete loss of service. This virus may be serious and requires IMMEDIATE attention to neutralize the threat.
>
> Problem: The virus exploits a vulnerability in a Windows Oracle SQL*Net or Oracle*Net client, allowing an unauthorized Oracle user to gain root privileges on the UNIX Oracle database server. The virus then places a malicious Trojan executable on the server.
>
> CVR References: 41-20374, 75-28365.
>
> Platforms Impacted: Sun Solaris, Red Hat Linux, SuSE Linux, AIX and HP UNIX.
>
> Vulnerability Assessment: The risk is HIGH. The virus software allows the Oracle SYSDBA user to gain unauthorized root privileges and can cause serious loss of production service.

The virus spreads between Oracle servers using the UNIX e-mail gateway. These messages can be detected by their distinctive subject lines 'GENERIC VIAGRA', and 'GROW YOUR THINGY'.

Hallmarks of the Oracle virus include:

- It will rewrite your RMAN Oracle backup files, changing all active verbs to a passive voice and introducing undetectable misspellings into all text.

- You may see a variation on the "Oprah Winfrey" virus where your SYSTEM tablespace suddenly shrinks to 20 Meg, and then slowly expands-out to over 500 Meg.

- The daemon process will attack all PeopleSoft software on the server, in an attempt to take-over control of the application.

- The virus may also manifest as a variation of the "Monica Lewinsky" virus, sucking the entire RAM out of your SGA and then sends e-mails to all users, telling them about it.

- It will de-magnetize the strips on all of your credit cards and re-program your ATM access code.

- It will program your telephone to auto-dial 1-900 talk-dirty-to-me phone lines.

- It will re-calibrate your refrigerator's coolness settings so that all your ice cream melts.

- It will leave the toilet seat up and leave your hair dryer plugged in dangerously close to a full bathtub.

Many of the members of this email distribution forwarded this note to their management, and then found themselves trying to explain how this virus would open the refrigerator door. This goes to show that anyone can be taken by an email scam. It is especially troublesome when it comes from someone the recipient is accustomed to receiving email from and someone whom they consider to be reputable.

The next section examines a real world consumer scam.

Real World Case: Internet Consumer Scams

In early 2004 Mr. Smith, the owner of a software training company hired a computer consulting company to develop an extensive set of training courseware. The staff went to work full-time creating Mr. Smith's courseware and it was not long before Mr. Smith owed them a large bill for the courseware.

About that time, the consulting company started receiving dozens of telephone calls from people who wanted refunds for non-shipment of products they had ordered from Mr. Smith. Stunned, the owner of the consulting company explained that his company was not affiliated with Mr. Smith and that his company was just a subcontractor providing Mr. Smith with training material. Later, he learned that this Mr. Smith had advertised that his company was Mr. Smith's partner! Using the Internet to get more information, he discovered many new complaints about Mr. Smith taking money from customers and not delivering the products. Shockingly, this fellow appeared to be attempting consumer fraud.

Over the next several months, Mr. Smith continued to attempt to sell his products, using phony names and fake computer experts. Here are some comments about Mr. Smith's Internet operations that were found on the web. The names have been changed.

"Be warned. If you get an email from a certain Mr. Smith of Oraclexxxxxx.com about specially priced Oracle CD ROM training, do not make the mistake of purchasing these CDs or attending a training seminar. This is a scam. Phone calls and emails are never returned.

Their website (www.Oraclexxxxxx.com) provides contact numbers and email addresses but you never get to actually speak to any person."

"I signed up (www.Oraclexxxxxx.com) for the Oracle boot camp in Nov.2003. The camp was canceled and I was promised a refund check. Then the communication stopped. I never received any money and Mr. Smith did not return mails or calls. In Feb. 2004 I filed a claim with the better business bureau of NJ and this week I receive a letter

---

Hoaxes

saying they regret they are unable to mediate an adjustment and then refer me to the Ocean County Consumer Affairs Office."

"Yes, I also was victimized by this and every phone call to Mr. Smith or his assistant was ignored. The only support phone call inquiry which was returned to me was their ISP for the conference server which allegedly "hosts" their oracle certification lectures. At this point I am going to dispute the charge with my card issuer AND demand a refund via certified mail to lay the groundwork for a small claims court suit."

"In 2002 we signed up for the 8i boot camp which was supposed to include the 9i upgrade course for free. It has been 18 months and many, many, many emails and promises not met. Mr. Smith and Oraclexxxxxx are a total fraud."

"I got tired of waiting for Mr. Smith promises so I sued him. I won my case. What do I do next? Does anyone know?"

"I to have been caught out. I authored an ebook @ www.chrisxxx.com, I entered into an agreement for Oraclexxxxxx.com to resell but low and behold, he is doing his utmost not to pay me (dragging on for over 8 months to date). I am taking legal action in a few weeks. If you have purchased my ebooks from Mr. Smith from June 2004 onwards, please email me."

He immediately stopped producing courseware for this fellow and found that Mr. Smith did not intend to pay for the products that were delivered to him. He went to court and won a judgment against Mr. Smith and is still waiting for compensation from this judgment.

The next example is a continuation of this story and one of a more subtle form of consumer scam, the deceptive advertising angle.

The DBLearning Site Scam

Alerted to a web site by a fellow professional, the business owner was asked if he had ever heard of an individual named on the site. The website was flashy and advertised a database expert that he had never heard of. It all sounded very convincing. He did some quick checking and discovered:

- This alleged database expert had no industry articles or contact information and the photo appears to be a stock photo of a model.

- The address on the site was a phony suite mail forwarding service.

- The web site administrative contact was the same person who owed the business owner money from a previous judgment.

There was also more information on the web about people claiming to have been scammed:

I signed up with Mr. Smith for his boot camp. The camp had 2 of the promised 6 online sessions. Then everything mysteriously stopped.

Mr. Smith has refused all phone calls and emails. I filed a claim with the better business bureau and after 2 months they said the total of what they can do is to not list his company as a member any more and then referred me to the Ocean county consumer affairs office.

Mr. Smith is now offering CD ROMS of his "training." Don't buy them! Search the internet for others who have been duped by this scammer. And yet he is still offering this boot camp to unsuspecting people! And he has the gall to say that he offers a money-back guarantee.

Mr. Smith swindled me out of $1000, don't you be next!

The Web Site

A spam email recently appeared that reads as follows:

```
From: Robert Allen - Oracle Security Consultant
<reply@orasecure.com>
Subject: I recorded it incase you missed it
Date: Thu, 28 Oct 2004 16:40:28 +0000

Hi. I just wanted to send you a quick note to inform you that my
"Hack-Proofing the Oracle Database" online class sold out in less
than 48 hours.

Many of you have been calling my office to ask when the next course
will be offered, but unfortunately I'm booked for security
consulting assignments straight through March, 2005.

But I do have some good news however...
```

```
I recorded my entire "Hack-Proofing the Oracle Database" onto 5
digital video CD-ROMs; and I even had the course workbook printed
up.

I have 100 copies of this package available if you're interested.
You can get all the info on this package here:

www.orasecure.com/hackproof/hackproof_cdrom.html

Thanks for your time,
Robert Allen
Senior Oracle Security Consultant
OraSecure, Inc.
```

The following bio was found for Robert Allen:

My name is Robert Allen, and I'm the Founder of OraSecure, Inc.

With over 9 years of trial and error from painstaking research, I'm now acknowledged
as a promising top expert in the field of Oracle database security.

For the past 7 years, I've consulted dozens of Fortune 1000 companies on all areas of
Oracle Database Administration.

The areas I've focused my most attention to are Oracle Security Features and Security
Audits. I've personally audited over 400 Oracle instances over the years, as well as
taught and mentored more than 80 DBAs to do the same.

Would the Real Robert Allen Please Stand?

The following is an excerpt that is purported to have come from his website
prior to its demise:

```
Hello again. I'm glad you decided to get more information.
```

```
If you're a DBA with Oracle9i experience, we may be able to help
each other out. Let me explain...

During the past 14 months, I've been working with both Beta and
Production versions of the new Oracle Database 10g. I've recently
compiled all my testing into our new training curriculum:

Oracle Database 10g: New Features for DBAs

Our larger Corporate clients have been anxiously awaiting us to roll
out this new course. But before we do, we need to hold a couple
"Beta runs" of the course to ensure everything flows just right.

That's where you come in. We're offering a win-win solution that
will give you the opportunity to learn all the great new features of
Oracle 10g...including all the tricks and traps I've learned
throughout my 14 months of working with the product. In return,
you'll simply answer some questions and provide feedback.

In order for you to have the opportunity to participate in the beta
course, we need to make sure you really know your stuff when it
comes to Oracle9i. That's why we created a 10 question Qualification
Assessment.

Simply fill in your name and email address below and we'll take you
right to the assessment. If you qualify, we'll fill you in on all
the details of the program.

So go ahead, the assessment should take you only 5 to 10 minutes to
complete.
```

Media Attention on Fraud

A reporter from eWeek magazine did a story on consumer fraud:

> "Oraclexxxxxx.com recently became defunct and is now the subject of multiple Better
> Business Bureau complaints filed in Mr. Smith's home state, New Jersey. The portion
> of the BBB file that's publicly available states that the company has "an unsatisfactory
> record with the bureau due to unanswered complaint(s)." The complaints concern
> delivery issues and refund practices, according to the BBB."

To my great shock, he admitted that he was enticing consumers into buying his
products using a fake personality:

> "Mr. Smith admitted that Allen, represented as having "over nine years of trial-and-error
> from painstaking research" and now acknowledged as "a promising top expert in the
> field of Oracle database security," is in fact a figment of his imagination. "There is no
> Robert Allen," he said. "It's a marketing figure. Is it ethical? No. Is it used in business

often? Absolutely. Plenty of people utilize fictitious people in marketing their circumstances."

Why hadn't the authorities from his home state charged him with any crimes? According to eWeek, these types of activities rarely get the attention of the prosecutors because of the relatively small amounts of money involved.

"Mr. Smith's activities are clearly illegal, though, according to Andrew August, a business attorney and principal partner of San Francisco-based Pinnacle Law Group LLP."

"What he's doing is clearly illegal under a potpourri of federal and state statutory schemes," August said. That includes laws such as the CAN-SPAM Act, the Computer Fraud and Abuse Act, and the California Uniform Trade Secrets Act.

But the likelihood of Mr. Smith being brought to justice is small, August said, given the comparatively negligible amounts he owes his customers. "The amounts are so small," he said. "What capable consumer rights lawyer is going to take him on?"

The next section reviews some resources that can be used by victims of Internet scams.

Web Resources for Scam Victims

Depending on the statistics reviewed, auction fraud is either an epidemic or a minor problem, but the sheer number of fraud reports is mind-boggling.

Web scammers prey on unsuspecting web users. The sad part is that there are no real avenues through which one can obtain active investigation and prosecution unless the losses exceed $10,000. Even then, it can be very difficult to get any recourse against the scammer.

There are now independent watchdog groups such as World Wide Scam (www.worldwidescam.com) which attempt to expose Internet scams. Here are some other possible avenues:

- **The Attorney General (AG)** - The state's AG will usually be interested in taking a report of criminal activity that is targeting residents of their state. If there are enough reports, they may investigate and, if possible, pursue criminal charges against the perpetrators of the scam.

- **The Federal Trade Commission (FTC)** - The FTC accepts fraud complaints when users register them via the link marked "File a Complaint" from their main page at www.ftc.gov. Nearly 90% of reported online scams are related to web auctions and the FTC has created a special web site called "Consumer Sentinel" (www.consumer.gov/sentinel) to address this growing problem. Consumer Sentinel offers buying tips and guidelines but has little to offer in the way of investigation.

- **IRS** - To report suspected tax fraud to the IRS, call 800-829-0433 or address a letter to the Criminal Investigation Branch at the same address where taxes are filed.

- **Quatloos.com** is a web site with the goal of educating people about the financial and tax fraud scams that surface on the Internet.

- **TruthOrFiction.com and snopes.com** are also good sources to confirm or deny a possible scam story.

Using the Wayback Machine

Scammers who use web sites to entrap their victims are often caught through the use of the "Wayback Machine." Since web scammers quickly create and destroy web pages, victims can use www.archive.org, also known as the "Wayback Machine" to view the content of web pages long after they have been deleted. The Wayback Machine is the creation of the altruistic Internet billionaire Brewster Kahle, who has generously donated this wonderful forensic tool so that everyone can see the web at any time in the past.

INTERNET ARCHIVE
WayBackMachine

http://

Take Me Back

Advanced Search

Take The Wayback Machine With You

Put the Wayback Machine right in your browser!

The Wayback Machine Bookmarklet

Drag this link to your browser's toolbar: Wayback

When you visit a page that you want to find an old version of, just click the toolbar link.
You will be transported to any historic versions at the Wayback Machine.

Thanks to gyford.com

Named after the cartoon machine of the popular "Peabody" cartoons of the 1950's, the Wayback Machine is a great tool for gathering evidence of web scams. The Wayback Machine indexes everything on a web page, including images and chat room discussions. As of 2004, the Wayback Machine had archived over 10 billion web pages dating back to 1996. It has an amazing search function that permits searching of their massive historical database to find exactly what is needed:

	Other Advanced Search Options
URL Matching	◉ Retrieve page that most closely matches search criteria
	○ List all pages that match search criteria
Aliases	◉ Merge aliases (search results for yahoo.com, www.yahoo.com and yahoo.com/index.html will be merged together)
	○ Show aliases separately (a search for yahoo.com will list www.yahoo.com separately)
	○ Don't show aliases (a search for yahoo.com will not show www.yahoo.com)
Redirects	◉ Hide redirects (on the search results, we will not display pages that redirect to other pages)
	○ Flag redirects (on the search results, we will mark all pages that redirect to another page with an 'r')
	○ Show redirects (on the search results, we will display pages that redirect)
File Types All types ▾	Will only display files of the type you specify
Duplicates	☐ Show duplicates (if we have 20 identical versions of a page on the same day, we will show them all)
Comparison	☐ Show checkboxes to allow comparison of 2 versions of a page. Comparison technology provided by Docucomp.
Convert to PDF	☐ **(BETA)** Provide links to a service that will convert a version of a web page to PDF format. Conversion technology provided by 2Convert.

The Wayback Machine provides complete indexing services and shows the actual state of most web pages, organized by time:

Search Results for Jan 01, 1996 - Dec 07, 2004						
1998	1999	2000	2001	2002	2003	2004
0 pages	0 pages	4 pages	8 pages	9 pages	23 pages	1 pages
		Oct 02, 2000 *	Feb 01, 2001	Feb 20, 2002 *	Feb 07, 2003 *	Feb 24, 2004
		Oct 17, 2000	Feb 09, 2001	Jun 01, 2002 *	Feb 09, 2003	
		Nov 01, 2000 *	Apr 01, 2001 *	Jun 03, 2002	Feb 19, 2003	
		Dec 06, 2000 *	Apr 20, 2001 *	Aug 02, 2002 *	Mar 24, 2003 *	
			May 16, 2001	Sep 26, 2002 *	Mar 26, 2003	
			Jul 20, 2001 *	Sep 27, 2002	Apr 08, 2003 *	
			Sep 22, 2001 *	Nov 25, 2002 *	Apr 21, 2003	
			Dec 01, 2001 *	Nov 26, 2002	Apr 24, 2003 *	
				Nov 27, 2002	May 24, 2003 *	
					May 30, 2003	
					Jun 23, 2003 *	
					Jul 20, 2003 *	
					Jul 21, 2003	
					Sep 29, 2003 *	
					Oct 13, 2003 *	
					Oct 17, 2003 *	
					Oct 29, 2003	
					Nov 24, 2003 *	

The Wayback Machine Archive (www.archive.org)

The Wayback Machine is also used by attorneys and law enforcement agencies and has proven itself to be an invaluable tool for tracking changes to web scammer web sites.

Conclusion

It is impossible to cover all of the intuitive angles used by web scammers in this chapter. This information has been offered as a high level overview of the tools, techniques and types of victims that are targeted by web scammers. The main points of this chapter include:

- eCommerce is a multi-billion dollar industry and it is growing every year.

- Cheap connectivity and inexpensive computers are allowing more and more people onto the Internet.

- Web scammers take advantage of loose international laws to prey with impunity upon victims in the USA.

- Small third-world nations are a major origin of web scams

- Unless the loss exceeds $10,000, law enforcement agencies will rarely actively pursue the criminals.

- Online auction fraud is one of the most common scams and both buyers and sellers can become victims.

The next Chapter will examine identity theft and see how it has become a major problem on the Internet.

Identity Theft

Identity Theft

Identity theft is the impersonation of another for the purpose of obtaining or using that person's credit or other funds. Often, financial institutions find the deception an embarrassment. Unfortunately, identity theft has become a common practice, and the financial institutions tend to absorb the losses rather than suffer the publicity of having these breaches exposed.

To reduce identity theft, banks are undertaking a consumer safety campaign. For example, Citibank has run a series of advertisements to inform consumers about the danger of identity theft. These advertisements portray the victims of identity theft with a voice over by someone of the opposite gender or a markedly different age group bragging about their shopping spree and how it was free – for them.

Arizona Sen. John McCain and his wife, Cindy, went unnoticed on a recent shopping spree at clothing and grocery stores across the East Valley. They were shopping in name only. A Peoria couple was arrested this week on suspicion of stealing their identities.

-- East Valley Tribune July 17, 2004

The rate of identity theft crimes is growing. Some criminals consider it a victimless crime, since the credit card companies often absorb the losses. The criminal and victim may live many miles apart, so the criminal feels safe committing this type of crime.

Identity thieves do not discriminate based on wealth.

Identify theft is not always about draining the victim's bank account. Sometimes, when accused of a crime or simply receiving a traffic ticket, the identity thief poses as the person from whom they stole an identity to law enforcement personnel. This deception may remain undetected until the victim is arrested for failure to appear in court or their vehicle's insurance premium goes up due to a traffic ticket of which they had no knowledge.

Many people do not consider themselves wealthy, and they are, in fact, living paycheck-to-paycheck. It is a common misconception that low or moderate income exempts one from identity theft. Sadly, many criminals could take a meager credit score and use it to finance a new automobile at an exorbitant interest rate, drive it off the lot and never make a single payment. Everyone needs to be cautious with his or her personal data.

Physical Identity Theft

Recently, there have been more stories in the media about identity theft, but it is nothing new, nor does the Internet cause it. Criminals have invented many ways to steal from working people since the very first checking account was opened. This section presents some ways that low-tech criminals can still steal an individual's identity or resources.

Lost ID Cards

A stolen purse or wallet can be a gold mine for an identity thief. Not only can the thief use the credit cards for purchases, driver's licenses in some states use a person's social security number for the license number. Many people have their social security number printed on their checks for convenience. With a social security number and current address, a thief can obtain credit in many places.

Dumpster Diving

When someone finishes balancing their checkbook, their next action might be to file the bank statement or simply toss it in the trash. Even if the individual files it, at some point they will decide to discard old paperwork, perhaps as part of a house cleaning in preparation for a move. Whenever financial records like bank statements, phone bills, and credit card bills are disposed, there is an inherent risk.

Many criminals have no compunctions about digging through garbage and taking credit card statements, which normally contain the name, address, card number and available credit of the cardholder. This information can then be used to place orders online.

> A basic shredder for home use can be purchased for a reasonable price. Shredding all documents before discarding anything that contains private information is a smart way to protect oneself from dumpster diving criminals seeking to separate people from their hard-earned money.

Social Engineering Techniques for Identity Theft

Most people have been approached at one time or another by someone taking a survey. This person may offer a gift certificate redeemable at a local store in return for an opinion on a given topic. Many of these surveys are legitimate and are a valuable means of gathering public opinion. However, far too many are some form of fraud.

For example, an individual's personal information and demographics could be gathered to target them for new credit card offers. While annoying, there is nothing criminal about this particular activity. More troubling, these offers might invalidate one's registration with state or federal "Do Not Call" registries. The pollster could actually be a front for a business that has a telemarketing division. By innocently granting permission to use personal information, the fine print on the approval form might give permission to sell the individual's name and number to other companies.

Most troubling, this gathering of information could be an attempt to steal a person's identity. When a criminal, while executing such a scam, hands over the incentive gift for participating in the survey, they ask the person to fill out a form this is allegedly for tax purposes. The form may be a simple name and address disclosure acknowledging receipt of a gift card. It may have a space for Social Security Number.

If the company responsible for the survey is actually legitimate, they will most likely keep personal information safe and secure. It is still possible, however, for those forms to be lost, stolen or copied. Whoever obtains them has the power to cause many people a lot of headaches.

Another way criminals use social engineering to gather information about an individual is through casual conversation. What about that seemingly nice person in the coffee shop that was so friendly and interested in the job of the person casually sitting next to them? They may have just been a friendly person; however, they may have been learning about that individual in order to get one step closer to stealing their identity.

Phony ATMs and Identity Theft

WIXOM, MI -- U.S. Secret Service agents and Wixom police have arrested a man accused of stealing more than $3.5 million by installing ATM machines across the country and stealing customers' account numbers (The *Detroit News*, December 5, 2003)

The criminal in the news story actually purchased ATM machines and set them up as if they were legitimate ATMs. He then used card numbers and PIN codes of unsuspecting ATM users to steal from their bank accounts. Although the specifics are not mentioned in this news item, it is not a unique story. Sometimes, as in this case, the entire machine is a fake.

Other times, criminals will attach a duplicate card reader to the front of the machine along with a small digital video camera, which allows them to witness a user entering their PIN, all from the comfort of the criminal's laptop that can be up to 200 meters away.

Computer-Assisted Identity Theft

The growth of portable technology and home computers has provided a major access and convenience advantage to users all over the world. Unfortunately, it is yet another tool criminals use to gather information about individuals in order to steal their identity.

A lost Personal Digital Assistant (PDA) or a laptop is a major headache. Prudent users will have current backups of all of their information, but they will still need to access another computer to reinstall their programs and data. If they do not have current backups, some information will certainly be lost. That might include information from the user's checking account, updated resume, email, appointments and many other important items.

While the loss of all of this information can make life miserable until the lost computer can be replaced and rebuilt, it can be a treasure trove for the person who ended up with the equipment. They can view checking account balances, use personal information to apply for credit and run up a huge balance on a credit card in the victim's name that they do not even know about until it's too late!

All the above methods of gathering information have one thing in common aside from the fact that criminals are involved: they are physical. The person setting up the fake ATM machine or sifting through the trash must be geographically close to the victim. However, with the explosion of the Internet, identity theft has been given an entirely new realm in which to flourish.

Virtual Identity Theft

In contrast to the previously mentioned information gathering methods, electronic-based theft does not require physical proximity to the victim. The Internet has made the world smaller, thus criminals can now reach their victims without leaving their state, much less their house.

Network Sniffing Tools

Network sniffing is a process by which a device can monitor the communication on a given network; much like a dog sniffing the trees to determine whom else has been there.

Legitimate reasons for network sniffing would include technicians troubleshooting a network problem. There are a large number of tools available to do this, including *tcpdump*, ethereal and others. Unfortunately, the use of these tools for network sniffing is not just limited to authorized technicians. The identity thief can use these tools to copy all communication that comes and goes from a PC. With a little technical know-how, from these packets of information they can extract details about the web pages visited by the user.

```
22:03:09.991818 192.168.8.2.1407 > phx-dns-01.inet.qwest.net.domain:  7499+ A? www.azdiamondbacks.com. (40) (DF)
22:03:10.046016 phx-dns-01.inet.qwest.net.domain > 192.168.8.2.1407:  7499 1/2/2 A[|domain]
22:03:10.047341 192.168.8.2.4157 > 216.74.142.14.http: S 3944484967:3944484967(0) win 5840 <mss 1460,sackOK,timestamp 104706
403 0,nop,wscale 0> (DF)
22:03:10.048743 192.168.8.2.1407 > phx-dns-01.inet.qwest.net.domain:  17923+ PTR? 14.142.74.216.in-addr.arpa. (44) (DF)
22:03:10.098277 192.168.8.101.1667 > 192.168.8.2.telnet: . ack 130949 win 17126 (DF)
22:03:10.098399 192.168.8.2.telnet > 192.168.8.101.1667: P 130949:131353(404) ack 1 win 5840 (DF) [tos 0x10]
22:03:10.154046 phx-dns-01.inet.qwest.net.domain > 192.168.8.2.1407:  17923 NXDomain 0/1/0 (115)
```

Figure 8.1 - *An example of Network Sniffer logs*

Figure 8.1 shows raw data gathered by a network or packet sniffer such as *tcpdump*. While this may be uninteresting data to most people, to the identity thief this small snippet of the log file generated tells them that their future victim is probably an Arizona Diamondbacks baseball fan.

When this information is combined with the fact that Qwest provides the DNS services, it narrows down the possible geography of the user. Finally, the IP addresses contained in this log file tell the interested observer what network addresses are in use at the target site.

All of these components become a part of making a profile of the target. Of course, the more information thieves learn about their intended victim, the more damage they can inflict. Potentially, even usernames and passwords could be available to a sniffer, but encryption is becoming more and more common. Encryption is a process through which data is encoded so as not to be understandable to anyone but the recipient. Using encryption makes the data that is gathered more difficult to analyze since the encryption must first be deciphered before any readable text is found.

Using a network sniffer becomes less useful for a hacker when the network is switched or segmented into virtual LANs (VLAN). This is because of the way a network transmits information between machines. A non-switched network transmits all information to all of the machines on that network and leaves each machine to ignore any unintended messages.

In comparison, a switched network only sends the information to the intended recipient machine. A switched network is still at risk if a hacker is able to compromise or break into the switch, but that is usually more difficult than just compromising any workstation on the network. A hacker can also use other tools like DSNIFF to steal or borrow network packets and read private information.

E-mail Scams for Identity Theft

As mentioned previously, email scams are commonplace on the web. As a public service, the Federal Trade Commission (FTC) issues a consumer alert listing the 12 most common scams likely to arrive in a user's mailbox. Some of the more common ones are listed as follows:

- Business opportunities including work-at-home jobs - With the ease of electronic communication, there are increasingly more opportunities to work at home or "be your own boss". However, most of these are either an outright fraud or simply an offer to purchase a business that one could get a better deal on elsewhere.

- Health and diet supplements - These supplements include the "enlargement" advertisements most Internet users receive from time to time. These products usually either do not work or else they would be available in the local pharmacy. They also may not have been reviewed by the Food and Drug Administration and may pose a health risk.

- Investment advice - There are excellent sources of financial information on the Internet. Sadly, there are even more sources for financial misinformation on the Internet. Charlatans publicize stock that they own as a "must buy" and "guaranteed winner." They then sell their stock as soon as enough people have started buying it and they can make a profit. The rest of the investors in the company, frequently a small company in financial trouble, are left holding stock that is worthless.

- Credit repair - An individual's credit score is designed to track how well, or poorly, they have used credit. The credit fixer services can only fix credit by instructing users to violate federal law. Unless there are genuine

---

errors in an individual's credit file, only time and a consistent repayment of credit can help a credit score improve. If there are errors, they can be corrected at no cost to the individual by following the instructions of the reporting agency.

Many e-mail scams will contain a link saying something like "click here to be removed from our list". **Don't do it!** Most of them result in more e-mail since they have confirmed that someone is reading that particular e-mail account.

For a look at the many various types of e-mail scams, please refer to the previous chapter, *Internet Scams*. The next section provides information on more ways a thief can access an individual's personal information.

Web Searches for Identity Theft

Back in the days when UseNet was the bastion of academia and harmless people, web users were far more open about themselves. Old UseNet postings are commonly used by identity thieves, especially those that were posted in the mid 1990's.

The following is an example UseNet group posting that could be used to steal identity:

```
Hi Marge,

Yes, Jack and I are very excited about our new addition.  We named
him John Jacob Astor after his Dad and he was born on the same day,
March 25 of this year, exactly 25 years after Dad's birthday!

We are having a shower next week and I would invite you to stop by
if you can:

Marge Astor
14 Lovely Place
Bellaire, CA
```

Back in the mid 1990's nobody envisioned that the UseNet newsgroups would be made available for instant worldwide search. A web thief can combine Google Groups (UseNet) searches with Wayback Machine (www.archive.org) searches, and it is amazing how much can be revealed about a person. The Wayback Machine is especially useful for finding out about people since comments made in a forum back in 1999 can now be quickly resurrected. The Wayback Machine has complete archives of forums and they can be read today just as they existed back in 1999.

One can dig up details about people's interests, hobbies and family members with astonishing ease. Many web crooks use these techniques to impersonate an old friend:

```
Hi Jack,

It's been such a long time!  I remember that good old days when we
raced our 56 Chevy's down on Colorado Boulevard and I'll always
remember that time that Cindy got mad at you about the prom.

I've been meaning to stop-over for a visit and catch up!  I lost
track of you when you moved from Burbank, and I'd love to see you
again.  Send me your contact info, and let's get together!

Randy Maars
```

The next section examines information on how fake websites can be used to steal an individual's identity.

Fake Websites and Identity Theft

A fake web site exists when someone creates a web page that imitates another legitimate one. For example, www.citibank.com is the official web page for the Citigroup family of companies. If someone were to setup a web page at www.citibank.org and were to make it look like it was the official page for the Citigroup family of companies; that would be a fake website. It would also be a violation of many copyright and trademark laws and would likely be shut down very quickly.

However, before being shut down, if an innocent victim happened across it and did not realize that this was not the legitimate Citigroup website, they might enter private information like their account number and PIN. This information, when collected by the creator of the fake site could be used to start a shopping spree using the victim's credit card.

Double Check URL's - When conducting business online, always verify the address in the browser to make sure the name matches the company.

Phishing for Identity

When people say something smells fishy, they mean that it might not be good. Phishing is another way for identity thieves to harvest private information, and there is definitely nothing good about that. The basic scam involves receiving an e-mail from a nonexistent company. The messages usually warn that something bad will happen if one does not follow the instructions, or the message provides some other reasonable reason for the user to go to the bogus website.

The "from" address in these email messages will often make the message appear to be from the company in question. They usually have a link that the recipient is instructed to click on. The link will appear to be part of the same company. Figure 8.2 shows a typical email message used in this type of scam.

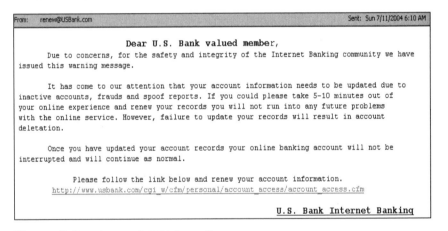

Figure 8.2 - *A sample Phish-mail*

The first item to note is that this is a pretty good email message. Several of the usual cues that the message is a fake are not present. There is neither the horrible grammar nor the poor spelling that is common with this type of swindle. Additionally, the message plays on fear by stating that this message is to prevent the user from having future problems. Rather ironic, isn't it?

Finally, the air of legitimacy is supported by the link that not only appears to be part of the US Bank website, but if one were to manually type it in to their web browser, it would take them to the genuine US Bank Account Access web page. Unfortunately, the link in the e-mail does not take the user to a website belonging to any part of the US Bank. In fact, it directs the user to a scammer's home page that is cunningly made to resemble the genuine article.

If that link in the email is clicked, the user will be prompted to enter more information like their address, account number, Personal Identification Number (PIN), mother's maiden name and other privileged information. This falsely obtained data could be used to steal that individual's identity by taking over accounts or obtaining new ones in that individual's name.

The best protection is common sense and a telephone. For starters do not click on any such link from within an e-mail message regardless of how realistic it appears. If going to the company's website is the objective, then open a separate browser window and type in the URL manually. If the message is purportedly from a bank with which the individual normally does business, take out the credit card or most recent financial statement and call the number found there. American Express, Citibank and US Bank are all common targets in this type of scam. Do NOT call any number found in the e-mail message. Once the legitimate company has been contacted, the individual should inquire there as to the legitimacy of the email. The company can then direct the individual on how to proceed.

War-Driving and Identity Theft

War dialing was the name given to the process of having a computer call thousands of phone numbers to find any that had a modem attached. Once a modem was found, the hackers would try to gain access to that system. The term "war dialing" gained recognition from the 1983 movie War Games where this process was used.

War-driving is the next generation of this method of attack. Instead of looking for computers equipped with modems, the war-driving hacker drives around neighborhoods in an automobile with a sniffing laptop looking for wireless networks.

Wireless networks are dropping in price, and thus, becoming more common. Every system comes complete with default settings. One of these defaults is called the SSID or the Service Set IDentifier. The SSID is the name of the wireless network and is usually something simple for a hacker to guess like WLAN (Wireless LAN). This should be changed to something different but without any personal identifiers.

If one wants to make their WLAN SSID include their name, the person war-driving through the neighborhood can easily use a phone book and find the individual's house as well as steal their wireless network. This SSID is also one of the pieces of information that is usually broadcast by a wireless network system. Some configuration utilities will let users configure the wireless router to not broadcast the name.

Another setting that can be overlooked is encryption. By default, many times encryption is disabled, which means that any communication between that computer and the wireless access point can be sniffed by anyone within range of the system. Additionally, anyone close enough to the wireless system is capable of using that individual's Internet connection to cause trouble. This could land the victim in a heap of trouble when a crime is investigated and the evidence points to that individual's system.

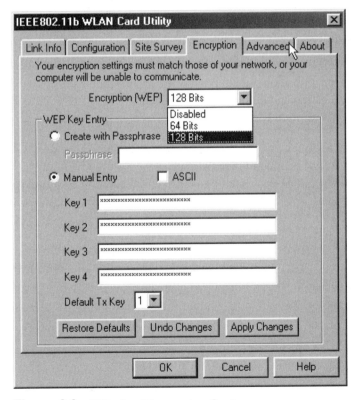

Figure 8.3 - *Wireless Encryption Settings*

Figure 8.3 above shows a configuration screen where the encryption setting is made. This example shows that for this system, the choices are: Disabled; 64 bits; and 128 bits. Disabled offers no protection against hackers, 64 bits provides medium protection and 128 bits is the highest level of protection.

There is, however, a performance impact involved with higher levels of protection. This is because encryption requires the computer do a bit of additional work to code the transmissions before sending them over the network. This performance impact is generally fairly minor, but if performance is critical, one may prefer to use physical network cables or a lower level of encryption.

In spite of these warnings, many wireless networks are left without encryption. These are the targets of the hacker who is war-driving and the less encryption they find, the happier they are. There are also some operating system settings that make an unsecured wireless network even more dangerous. If properly configured, file and print sharing can let all of the computers in a house share printers and files. If not properly configured, it can give anyone access to all the files with no control or security.

If neither the operating system nor the wireless network is set up in a secure manner, the system is vulnerable to be compromised by any criminal who drives past the house. Police and insurance companies have long said that a determined thief can steal any car, regardless of anti-theft devices and alarms present. Nonetheless, a good reason for using these devices is to encourage the less-determined thief to pick an easier target. Similarly, even with encryption enabled, there are programs that will allow a hacker to monitor the encrypted traffic on a network and quickly determine the encryption key. However, the savvy user can make it more trouble than it is worth. This will be covered in more detail in a later chapter.

Preventing Identity Theft

The saying, "An ounce of prevention is better than a pound of cure" certainly holds true in the case of identity theft. Many of the recommendations below are free or low-cost and are certainly less stressful than dealing with a case of identity theft:

- Shred documents with personal information before putting them into the trash. This includes credit card offers received in the mail and even some of the reply envelopes that have personal information on them. This will deter the identity thief from easily obtaining information about someone from their trash.

- Avoid carrying unneeded credit cards on a daily basis. This makes a lost or stolen wallet less trouble when contacting creditors to report the loss and obtaining new cards and account numbers.

- Make a photocopy of both sides of everything in a wallet or purse. Include driver's license, credit and debit cards, health and automobile insurance cards. Libraries, grocery stores or copy centers all have copy machines available for public use for a small fee. Keep this copy somewhere safe, other than the wallet or purse, like a file at home.

- Be careful about giving information over the phone or Internet. If the call was received rather than initiated, be especially wary of a request for a credit card number or other personal information even if there is a special limited time offer for a desired product. This is a common ploy by identity thieves and is very dangerous.

- Request to not receive the pre-screened credit card offers through the mail by calling 1-888-5-OPTOUT (1-888-567- 8688). They require the cardholder's Social Security Number so the account can be flagged. Even if someone opts out, some offers may still be sent because some credit grantors use other sources than the credit bureaus for their lists. Reducing these offers in the mail reduces the chance that someone else could steal them and accept the cards in place of the intended recipient.

Recognizing Identity Theft

There are many ways to find out if one's identity has been stolen. The following list is a compilation from several credit card companies, credit-reporting agencies, and the Federal Trade Commission:

- An individual might get bills for a credit card account they never opened.

- An individual's credit report may include debts they never knew they had.

- An individual's credit report shows addresses where they have not lived.

- An individual might miss a credit card or bank statement that they were expecting.

- An individual may see charges on their credit card bills that they do not recognize.

- An individual's financial account balances are lower than expected and have unexplained withdrawals.

- An individual receives a credit denial when they have not applied for credit.

- An individual receives calls from creditors for accounts they do not have.

Vigilance is important to prevent identity theft

Recovering a Stolen Identity

If an individual's identity is stolen, their credit and possibly criminal history will contain inaccurate information. No one has a more vested interest in setting those records straight than that individual does. One could pay someone else to handle the cleanup operation, but it is likely that the individual needs to be involved regardless. When searching for assistance in reclaiming one's identity, an individual also needs to be cautious, as there are scam artists that will claim to repair credit and will do nothing but further victimize that individual.

When opting to pay someone to help recover an identity, it is a good idea to check with the Better Business Bureau and the Chamber of Commerce for the city in which they are located. In addition, one should get a contract, in writing, stating what they will do and the expected outcome. The idea is to avoid having them claim that they tried, and yet, there is still an arrest on one's record that was committed by the identify thief.

The most effective and safest approach is to take on identity recovery as a personal project. There are resources available from the Federal Trade Commission's ID Theft resource web page (www.consumer.gov/idtheft) and The National Center for Victims of Crime (www.ncvc.org) that can help anyone organize the required documentation and develop an action plan.

One thing that an individual needs to do once they discover that their identity has been stolen is to file a police report. This will likely be needed for some creditors as proof of the crime.

The following are some steps that an individual will need to take to start working on recovering their identity:

- Call and write the fraud units of the three main credit bureaus and ask for a fraud alert to be placed in their file.

- Check credit reports. Contact the creditors that opened the fraudulent accounts and have them remove those accounts from their record. This should be done in writing and copies maintained.

- Seek support from family members and/or close friends. They may also want to speak to a counselor or victim advocate. Besides being time consuming, dealing with identity theft is emotionally exhausting.

- Find out what their state's identity theft laws are and what their rights as a victim are.

- Contact their local bar association or legal aid office, especially if they have been left with a criminal record due to the identity theft.

Legal Protection Against Identity Theft

July 15 2004 (Bloomberg) -- President George W. Bush signed legislation increasing the punishment when fake identification cards are used to commit crimes, including domestic or international terrorist acts.

In addition to the Federal laws, there are laws on the books in most states that make identity theft illegal. Even where identity theft is not specifically named, there are usually laws against the actions that are part of identity theft. For example, North Carolina defines identity theft in §14-113.20-23 as:

Financial identity fraud.

(a)A person who knowingly obtains, possesses, or uses identifying information of another person, living or dead, with the intent to fraudulently represent that the person is the other person for the purposes of making financial or credit transactions in the other person's name, to obtain anything of value, benefit, or advantage, or for the purpose of avoiding legal consequences is guilty of a felony.

The statute goes on to define identifying information. This definition encompasses social security numbers and credit card numbers, but also includes any other numbers or information that can be used to access a person's financial resources.

Check www.consumer.gov/idtheft/federallaws.html#criminalstate for the laws for each state. This is the website of the Federal Trade Commission and provides links to the laws available for each state. For more information on Laws relating to Web Stalkers, see Chapter 4.

Each state's Attorney General is the person responsible for enforcement of the state statutes. If the case warrants, the U.S. Secret Service, the FBI, U.S. Postal Inspection Service, and the Social Security Administration's Office of the Inspector General can investigate violations of federal law. These cases would be prosecuted by the U.S. Department of Justice.

Conclusion

This chapter has introduced the crime of identity theft. Hopefully the information here will help increase awareness of the many ways that criminals can collect and use an individual's information. Some ways are high-tech and others are low-tech. Throughout this chapter, a number of suggestions on how one can protect oneself against some of these attacks.

Criminals can steal an identity in a variety of ways. Some suggestions for making their job harder and reducing the risks of identity theft are:

- Buy a crosscut shredder.

- Use a shredder before discarding anything with personal information, especially credit card and bank statements.

- Closely review credit card and bank statements.

- Closely review credit reports on a regular basis.

Identity theft is a crime that causes pain to its victims. Not physical pain but mental anguish. The Identity Theft Resource Center concluded that victims of identity theft spend an average of 600 hours recovering from this crime, sometimes over a period of years. Many resources for victims of identity theft are available on their website at www.idtheftcenter.org.

"The crime of identity theft undermines the basic trust upon which our economy depends."

-- President George W. Bush

Self Protection on the Web

Online Security Measures

The proliferation of portable computer and wireless technologies has increased the challenge of the individual to protect themselves from cybercrimes. The freedom afforded by the new wireless systems can lull users into a false sense of security. The good news is that there are measures that anyone can take to protect their wireless systems from criminals; however, forgetting to also protect one's hardwired system at home or work could be a large mistake.

The two high school students were out for a drive. This was not just any drive; they were not headed for a party or the mall. Their goal was to see how many wireless networks they could access. They had a laptop with a wireless card and a couple of freely available programs that would help them identify and access any wireless cards they happened across.

Taking turns driving, they discovered several of their neighbors had wireless networks with no protection in place. They also found businesses with wireless networks that gave them full access to corporate systems with confidential data. Even most of the networks they found that were protected fell quickly to the software they were using.

"I've just decided to go wireless"

The Appeal of Wireless

The beauty of the wireless network is that it is just as the name implies: wireless. It is not hard to imagine that it is a simple matter to sell anyone on the benefit of a system that provides all of the services of the old desktop PC without all the bothersome wires. Wireless networks are now available at many electronic and computer stores for fairly reasonable prices. As the costs drop, the use of wireless is becoming more common. Many people who are buying equipment to setup a wireless network do not have enough knowledge to implement adequate security.

The story at the beginning of this chapter describes a new hobby called wardriving. While this book is written to help non-computer experts, the subject covered in this chapter is a bit more technical. If there is a wireless network in the house or the plan is to acquire one, press on even if the subject is challenging. Each user owes it to himself or herself and their safety to know what the danger is and how to protect themselves and their loved ones.

When discussing wireless access, this chapter is referring to the technology that is called 802.11. There are a couple flavors of this technology currently available. 802.11b is the older version and has a lower capacity and speed than 802.11g. Besides the increased performance that is possible from

802.11g, there are security enhancements that make it the better choice if a user is buying or upgrading equipment.

There are other methods of wireless access, including "air cards" that use the cellular phone networks to provide Internet access. However, these methods will not be covered in detail in this book.

Risks of Wireless Communications

Wireless technology brings convenience and danger. Know what the risks are and protect against them.

One of the vulnerabilities that comes with the use of wireless technology is the Service Set Identifier (SSID). Simply stated, the SSID is the name of the wireless network. The default or factory setting is a piece of information that is simple for a hacker to acquire or guess. For example, WLAN, short for Wireless LAN, is a common name that is easy to guess.

Depending on where the wireless network is purchased, some basic instruction should be included on changing default or factory settings during initial setup and use of the computer. The SSID name should be changed to something that would be as difficult as possible for a hacker to guess or determine easily through the use of programs designed to discover such information. Although it's easy to remember a last name, it's a bad idea to use it in the identification of a wireless network.

Assuming that the person war-driving in the neighborhood is able to get the SSID of the family wireless network and it includes the family's last name. It is then a simple matter of checking the telephone book or doing a quick online search to determine the family's address. To add insult to injury, they can do this while logged into the family's own wireless network. With name and address information in hand, the hacker is now completely armed to steal the identity of any member of the house. Some configuration utilities allow users to configure the wireless router to not broadcast the name. This will make it a bit harder for the drive-by hacker to gain access to a user's network.

With public wireless access, anyone can see anything that the computer sends or receives. If a user is accessing a secure website, the information the computer is sending is reasonably secure. If personal e-mail messages with most web pages or applications are being sent, the user id and password, along with the text of the messages, are available to anyone who cares to look.

There is a risk when using wireless connections. Users should always be aware that they are on a wireless network and pay extra attention to the information that they are sending and receiving. The lack of encryption probably presents the biggest security risk when using a wireless network.

Encryption

Another setting that can provide an additional level of protection that frequently gets overlooked is encryption. There are many ways to implement encryption. The most common use is to take regular communications such as email or chat sessions and change them into a coded message. Without the appropriate encryption code, that coded message would appear to be gibberish to any other person or program.

"An encrypted message appears to be nonsense without the code."

Users should be aware that many times encryption is disabled in wireless networks by default. This means that any communication between that computer and the wireless access point can be sniffed by anyone within range of the system. Additionally, anyone that is close enough to the wireless system is capable of using its Internet connection. Once hackers tap into that wireless network, they can commit a variety of cybercrimes. This could land the computer owner in a heap of trouble when a crime is investigated and the evidence points to their system.

Rewards of Wireless Communications

The benefits of wireless are seen regularly in advertisements that tout the benefits of mobility. The ability to work using a laptop and wireless card wherever a computer is needed is the scenario that is promised. The reality is that a person can still be more productive in their office than they are in the airport waiting for a flight, if there is no wireless access at the airport. The places with wireless connections available are generally places where people congregate like coffee shops, bus or train terminals, and airports. Some are paid services and some are free.

Corporations that enjoy name recognition often sponsor free services. In some cases, a company provides free access in certain places to gain name recognition. As an example of this, hotZona, LLC, a company in Arizona provides free wireless access to the Arizona State Legislature. This coverage is free, even for visitors to the facility. It is provided with Cox Communications and Intel.

The Albuquerque, New Mexico airport is another publicly accessible wireless access point. Free connection locations are available in many areas and help to deliver some of the promised benefits of wireless Internet access.

Paid services usually share the revenue with the hosting location such as the coffee shop. For many busy people, the opportunity to catch up on email while having their morning coffee or latte is worth the cost of the access.

"No, I don't have a firewall. Why?"

Wireless has arrived in many homes and businesses. It is important to balance the risks against the benefits it provides when deciding whether or not to use it. If the decision is made to go wireless, careful consideration should then be given to where it is used.

The benefits of wireless:

- The ability to work anywhere, even in the backyard or by the pool.

- Increased productivity.

- Increased accessibility.

The possible risks are:

- Loss of personal information.

- Security vulnerability.

- Costs.

Next, the concept of firewalls will be introduced. The following sections will present details on why they are important to individuals and take a look at some of the different types of firewalls.

"Don't get burned online by not having a reliable firewall"

What is a Firewall?

When many buildings are designed, they are built with certain walls more durable than others. In concert with specially designed doors, these walls make it more difficult for a fire to spread. By slowing down or stopping the spread of the fire, it allows more people to be evacuated safely. These safeguards are called firewalls.

Positioning valuable assets so that they are protected by firewalls also provides more security for important documents and equipment. In computer security, a firewall slows down or stops an attacker before they gain access to the information that should be kept private. Figure 9.1 shows how a basic home network would look with a firewall.

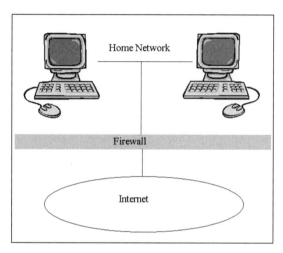

Figure 9.1 - *A simple diagram of a home network with a firewall*

In the corporate world, organizations will sometimes use multiple firewalls to separate different parts of the organization for security reasons in addition to protecting its resources from unauthorized outside access.

There are different types of firewalls that provide different benefits. Hardware and software firewalls each have strengths and weaknesses.

Types of Firewalls

All firewalls consist of both hardware and software. The dividing line between what is classified as a hardware firewall is whether or not the hardware is used primarily as a firewall. If the hardware is primarily a firewall, it will be called a firewall router. Multi-purpose devices such as a wireless router fall into this category. Otherwise, it will be considered a software firewall as it involves software being installed on a computer or network system.

Hardware Firewalls

A hardware firewall is a separate piece of equipment. This type of firewall is sometimes integrated into a wireless hub or access point. Other times it is a self-contained unit, much like a DSL or cable modem. It will generally be installed between the DSL or cable modem and the computer, hub, or wireless gateway.

"You want hardware? I've got hardware..."

Technically adept folks can use an older computer and install a second network card and free software to create a robust firewall. One of the advantages of hardware firewalls is that one can be properly positioned to protect multiple computers. This can be advantageous for a home user with more than one computer.

A downside to hardware firewalls is that there is a new piece of computer equipment for the user to deal with. That means another product competing for an electrical connection in the already crowded computer area.

Software Firewalls

A software firewall is simply a program that runs on a computer that performs the same functions as a hardware firewall. It takes advantage of the computer's ability to do more than one job at a time. This is called multitasking. The software firewall process causes the computer to work more than it is usually required to as it simply keeps up with the human's limited requirements.

The danger with using a software-based firewall comes when the computer it is protecting is using more resources than usual. This is common when users are playing certain modern games with advanced graphics. When this happens, performance can become noticeably worse. When playing video games, the result will be that the action within the game becomes choppy. Someone listening to digital music will hear it skip or stall. This is one of the biggest drawbacks to software firewalls.

One of the strengths of software firewalls is that with laptops, when using the laptop somewhere outside the home, they remain protected by the firewall. This is especially important when using wireless connections, whether inside or outside the home.

Recommendations for Firewall Safety

First and foremost, it is important to use a firewall. Do not fall into the trap of thinking that company or personal information is not valuable enough to bother protecting. If a user has any "always on" Internet access like DSL or digital cable, they are at risk and should have a firewall. Cleaning up after someone has stolen an individual's identity is not a fun experience. A firewall can make that a less likely problem.

Sometimes it will make sense to use a hardware firewall for home use and a software firewall for use on a mobile computer. To increase performance, users might want to adjust the settings for the mobile computer when using it at home to run a lower degree of protection.

If a door in a physical firewall is left open, it reduces the effectiveness of the firewall. This is necessary at times to move equipment in or out. In a computer firewall, there are times when certain people outside the firewall need to legitimately gain access to resources inside the firewall. This might be employees that travel, work from home or are business partners. There are technical solutions to this requirement, but sometimes the easiest solution is to open a virtual door. This is dangerous as hackers are very adept at finding open doors. Whether a firewall is protecting home or business, it is crucial to avoid leaving any doors open.

Once a firewall solution appropriate for any particular set of circumstances has been implemented, it is important to make sure it is working. An easy way to perform that check is by using a reputable firewall evaluation website. It is important that the site be carefully evaluated prior to starting a check. Hackers could operate a website that would evaluate a computer or network system's security, notify the user that everything is secure when it is not, and then use any security weaknesses they find to hack the computer system.

"Hackers try to defeat firewalls with multiple different methods"

Users should bear in mind that any evaluation done by a firewall vendor might have a hidden agenda such as trying to sell their product. Use the methods discussed here to evaluate a web page that provides an evaluation of a computer's firewall.

Most computers are not capable of being turned on remotely. If a computer is not going to be used for an extended period, it should be turned off. This length of time may vary from situation to situation. Some people turn off their computers only when they are going out of town for a couple days. Others turn the computer off if they are not planning on using it for more than a couple of hours. For security purposes, users should remember that leaving the computer on subjects it to a greater risk of intrusion than turning it off.

An Internet Protocol address (IP address) is how computers find and communicate with each other. IP addresses are similar to street addresses. They are unique which allows mail and emergency services to be able to locate them. There are public IP addresses and private ones. Public IP addresses are how web browsers can find the computers that run websites.

The current addressing methodology limits the number of available addresses.

The Internet Assigned Numbers Authority (IANA) is the group that controls the assignment of IP addresses by blocks. These blocks of addresses are grouped geographically, so an IP address frequently will indicate where in the world a particular computer is located.

If a user wants to know what their IP address is, two web-based resources are available. They are:

- www2.simflex.com/ip.shtml

- www.whatsmyipaddress.com

These resources will reveal the public IP address the ISP has given the user. This is usually dynamic so it may change from time to time. This IP address may be different from the one used by your computer depending on how the network is set up.

Private IP addresses are generally used either for computers that do not need to access the Internet or for ones that access the Internet through an intermediate server that serves as a relay station. For home Internet users, either their DSL or cable modem or their ISP serves as a relay station. This means that they are able to use private addresses.

Private addresses are a good idea because they cannot directly access the Internet. This enhances security because a virus or hacker cannot as easily force a computer with a private address into performing illegal activities.

The Internet Assigned Numbers Authority (IANA) has reserved the following three blocks of the IP address space for private internets:

- 10.0.0.0   - 10.255.255.255

- 172.16.0.0 - 172.31.255.255

- 192.168.0.0 - 192.168.255.255

Generally the IP address that is assigned to a computer is obtained automatically by using predefined network settings. In setting up home networks, if specific instructions are not provided with the networking hardware, it is best to consult a networking professional.

Conclusion

It may seem that the only way to make a computer completely secure is to turn it off and take it off the Internet. While this is one way to avoid an intrusion, there are ways to make computers less accessible to hackers. The following are some of the tips for firewall safety that were discussed in this chapter:

- Use at least one firewall.

- Regularly test firewall integrity.

- Do not leave a computer on when it is not needed.

It is not possible to secure a computer from all threats any more than it is possible to guarantee that an automobile is theft proof. If someone wants to break into a computer system badly enough, it is likely that they will be able to one way or another.

The goal of this chapter, and indeed this whole book, is to make users aware of the different risks. Additional information is provided on how to take sufficient measures to make it difficult for someone to break into computer systems with the overall goal being to get the hacker to move on to easier prey.

Protecting Children on the Web

COLORADO SPRINGS, Colorado. -- A soldier committed suicide after being arrested on suspicion of arranging a sexual encounter with a 13-year-old girl over the Internet.

Source: AP Wire September 03, 2004.

Introduction

In today's world, the media inundates the public with reports of children becoming the victims of crime. Stories of child molestations, abductions and worse are in the newspaper headlines, on the nightly news and posted on the public notice boards at local grocery stores.

When these crimes occur, they gain the public's attention. It is an alarming fact that the groundwork for these appalling acts has often been prepared well in advance. The perpetrators have been working silently, steadily maneuvering past parental defenses and invading homes day after day, through the Internet.

The proliferation of these crimes has required that new and tougher laws be passed to deal with them. Some of these laws came in the form of a new piece of legislation known as the *Protection of Children from Sexual Predators Act of 1998*. The goal of this law is to make the job of law enforcement less difficult while increasing the penalties for those who perpetrate crimes against children.

One measure enacted by this new law specifically increases penalties for those who use interstate facilities for communicating information about children if it can be determined that there is criminal intent. Since there is no better facility of interstate or foreign commerce than a computer connected to the Internet, this significant piece of legislation hit the nail on the head with regard to computer crimes against children.

Real-World Case - The Death of Christina

Christina Long was an ordinary 6th grade child who died at the hands of a web stalker. Enthralled by the Internet, Christina morphed into a different person and paid the ultimate price.

While on the Internet, Christina developed a new persona, using provocative screen names like "Hot es300". She also pretended to be beyond her tender years. In a deadly turn of events, Christina agreed to a real life meeting with a 25 year old man with whom she had become acquainted in an Internet chat room. She met him in a seemingly safe public place, a shopping mall; however, he was able to lure her away and eventually raped and strangled her.

Christina paid the ultimate price. In a shocking turn, her murderer was only charged with two counts of interstate travel to engage in unlawful sexual activity and received a mere 25 year sentence, and is eligible for parole in a little more than a decade.

Danger of Online Relationships

Sadly, Christina's story is not unique, and children are not the only ones at risk for being misled by their online "friends." Web stalkers prey on the weaknesses of people and take advantage of their vulnerability. In one case, a pedophile used the web to pretend to be a girl. He then enticed a lonely college student to his death.

In this unfortunate case, Kerry Kujawa, the web stalker told his victim that "she" was stuck in a destructive relationship and lured Kerry to come to "her" aid. "She" was actually, Kenny Wayne Lockwood, a 31 year old man who brutally murdered the vulnerable and altruistic college student.

The following section contains information on the serious threat posed by meeting people online and endeavors to present details to help one understand the mindset of the killers that haunt the web.

The Dangers of Chat Rooms

How much fun would it be to have a conversation about a favorite hobby with people in 21 different states all at once? A networking arrangement known as a chat room may be just the ticket. Chat rooms allow people of common interests to exchange information in real time, very much as they would if they were all sitting together and chatting in the same room. This is how chat rooms got their name.

"...and I found a lovely teapot on e-bay..."

Most chat rooms have a theme or a topic around which discussion revolves. There are virtually no limits to the variations of available themes, ranging from the ludicrous to the life saving. A doctor for example, in a remote area, may be able to log into a discussion among physicians and gain insight on a problem he has been facing. People who work in technology can network with others facing similar challenges; collectors of all kinds get the chance to tout their latest find; and children can be tutored or just catch up with the latest from their friends.

Chat room interactions can occur through various technologies. At one time, text messages posted to a common message board that could be read by anyone logged into the chat room was the only option. Some still work this way.

Others have introduced voice and graphics into the mix. While this advance in technological capability is laudable, it also creates an environment that lends itself to an entirely new range of subversive activity aimed at accessing children.

For anyone interacting in a chat room environment, a key point to remember that things, especially people, may not always be what they appear. A grown man with a predatory bent will not announce the truth about himself when he logs into the room. To become a 16 year old boy with a dog and a baseball mitt who wants to talk to a nice girl, he need only introduce himself as exactly that. There is no verification process. There are no identity police, and children are especially vulnerable to this sort of deception. They have yet to learn skepticism through the school of hard knocks from which most people graduate at some point. Children are naturally trusting; therefore, they are easily deceived. Once the deception has begun, it is frighteningly easy to convince children to behave in ways that may be dangerous or deadly.

Once con artists gain the confidence of their chat room mates, they can then begin to introduce material into the room that suits their particular perversion. In a chat room that is graphics enabled, a pedophile may post mild, sexy images to pique interest. The pedophile then steadily graduates to child pornography, gaining tacit acceptance step-by-step along the way.

A pedophile may introduce themselves into a chat room as an adult who can be trusted. If this deception is successful, he may then begin to share images of child pornography. It is conceivable the child may be left with the impression that such activity permissible.

These deviants are persuasive, deceptive and know how to achieve their desired end result. Chances are good they have done this before. Their ultimate goal is to move the interaction off the web and into real life. If they can achieve that transition, the threat level skyrockets.

"Time for a talk, kids..."

Children must be warned of such dangers in language that makes sense to them. They must be made to understand that not all adults are good and not all adults are their friend. Parents must take responsibility for ensuring that each child understands the specific types of behaviors that are never acceptable from anyone, and what to do if they encounter it.

Responsible adults must be proactive and anticipate the lies that sexual predators may use to lure children online and counteract them ahead of time. The online predator will try to drive a wedge between a parent and their child, actually persuading the child that they, the predator, have the child's best interest at heart and that their parents do not. They may attempt to get the child to believe that a parent is unreasonable or mean to deny them a new friendship. If the child had participated in any questionable activity, such as being shown pornographic images, they may be told that they have done something wrong, and that to tell anyone about it will only get them into trouble.

Open communication between parents and children is vital to help kids stay safe online. Parents should talk often to children with online access and make sure they understand the dangers and assure them that it is not their fault if they are approached. Parents must not let the bad guy fool their child. Responsible adults must bear the ensuring that each child understands that parents and guardians are their friends and that the stranger is not.

Once a child has been made aware of the dangers in an age appropriate manner, their participation in a chat room can be a fun and exciting activity. As an added layer of protection, some chat rooms are monitored by adult staff members or through software programs. The monitor acts as a chaperone and keeps a watchful eye out for the wolf that is intent on entering the sheep's pen.

While monitoring does provide an additional level protection, it is far from perfect. Chat rooms monitored by software filters can be bypassed by tech savvy intruders. Even chat rooms monitored by staff members cannot protect children who are approached outside the chat room. A predator may meet a child in a chat room and do nothing inappropriate that would alert the monitors; however, they can then contact the child directly through other means, such as e-mail or instant messaging, which do not use the chat room network to communicate. Allowing the use of monitored chat rooms is a good precaution, but adults must still be vigilant. Children must be prepared to protect themselves and parents and guardians cannot let their guard down.

Games Children Play

There are computer games available for just about anybody, regardless of age, gender or interests. There are games that help pre-school children learn how to read and advanced first person military games that may tap the abilities of even the best strategists.

Chess is one familiar and traditional game that is ordinarily played by opponents who sit on either side of a game board. As a means of engaging players in geographically distant locations, many players historically used the postal service to mail their moves to each other between states or even foreign countries. Needless to say, these games took time.

"Come play with me!"

The telephone helped facilitate this sort of distance gaming, but there was only marginal improvement in game quality. It was not until the advent and wide availability of Internet e-mail that the concept of remote play caught on with many people. Games can now be played from start to finish in a matter of days, or hours rather than months, even if opponents are stationed in opposite corners of the globe. For the gaming aficionado, the world is their oyster, so to speak, with a pool of challengers that is both talented and virtually limitless.

The continuing advance of technology has not only made it possible to play traditional games in new ways, but has changed our whole concept of what games are and how they are played. Games abound for every conceivable demographic and can be played in a wide variety of configurations and scenarios.

The gaming world has also changed the way many people think about computers. Children, especially, tend to regard them simply as a way to have fun; and why not? A young child who has just mastered the intricacies of tic-tac-toe is likely to wear down anyone within ear-shot with endless requests of "One more time!" A computer that plays tic-tac-toe without tiring or wanting to quit will be more than a diversion, it will be a playmate.

"I'll win no matter how long it takes!"

With advancements in technology have come improvements in the overall quality of computer games. The graphics, realism and user interfaces are leagues beyond what could have been imagined a short time ago. The themes and premise of these games, however, are other issues entirely. Market forces have allied with technology and made many games too intense for young players. Adult oriented material and excessive graphic violence have mandated the passing of still more new laws. Games are now labeled according to a standardized rating system. As with movie ratings, they are designed to help parents protect their children from inappropriate material.

The popularity of the Internet has given rise to games with new and different structures. With some online games, it is possible for two players from different locations to team up and play against the computer rather than against each other. Sometimes multiple players engage each other and the computer acts as the game master and referee.

Many changes in the world of gaming have had a positive impact on those who play them. Children have found new avenues for making friends, and have even been exposed to elements of foreign cultures.

Other aspects of the changing world of Internet and computer games have not been so positive. A major area of concern for many people is computer game addiction. People of all ages are susceptible to this problem, and details on the problem will be presented in a subsequent chapter.

There are a number of reasons why computer game addictions can be harmful. Not the least among these is that time spent in front of the computer is time not spent engaging in other important activities. While one may argue about the merits or shortcomings of computer games, it stands to reason that no single obsession should dominate a child's life. Children who sit at their computer monitors for hours on end, day after day without being able to tear themselves away are neglecting the other activities that go into helping them develop into well-rounded adults.

Psychological Effects of Computer Games

As previously mentioned, another cause for concern is the nature of the computer games children are playing. Many of the most popular games today incorporate scenarios in which graphic violence is central to the theme of the game and in which the player participates. One game of particular infamy allows a player's character to have sex with a prostitute. If the player opts to kill the prostitute afterward, they will score extra points. It is hard to imagine how this sort of game could not have a negative impact on the player, regardless of age.

Psychologists have identified certain elements of the learning process that are particularly important. Two of the most prominent are rewards for desired behaviors and repetition. Most computer games, by their very nature, incorporate these two factors. The players are in the game, interacting as part of the events, often inflicting damage and injury and being rewarded for it.

Studies have shown that game players involved in visually realistic and interactive games experience emotions and physiological responses similar to real life situations. Increased heart rate and blood pressure, rapid breathing and body chemistry changes have all been measured while players battle their opponents during computer games.

In addition to the psychiatric assessments of the effects of computer games, other childhood experts agree that excessive amounts of time spent in a physically sedentary way can be harmful. Healthy development and overall well-being require a rounded program including lots of physical activity. Less physical activities like computer games can play a part but should not dominate. Most kids find sports and other outdoor events an exciting and fun way to spend the day, even if it doesn't involve blasting the enemy with a mega-death ray.

Now that some of the dangers present on the web have been introduced, the next logical step is to move on to other areas that can cause problems. A search engine is a great tool for finding good things on the internet. The following section will illustrate how it can also be a high-speed route to some places no child should ever go.

Appropriate Use of Search Engines

In earlier chapters, there were introductions to examples of how search engines can be used to gather personal information. The ability to find music and go shopping online also requires the use of Internet searching.

Internet search engines provide information, and lots of it. The quality of that information varies widely. It can be helpful or not, and sometimes it can be dangerous. Learning to use a search engine correctly is the single most effective way to minimize inappropriate search results. Teaching children the proper techniques for conducting Internet searches is not difficult and can mean the difference between a child finding what they are looking for, and something menacing finding them.

One problem with Internet search engines is that they cast a very wide net when gathering information. This can lead to many unintended consequences. For example, if a student searches the Internet for breast cancer, they may find what they are looking for; however, they are also likely to find a whole lot more that will not be of much use in their research. There are ways of formatting an inquiry to help overcome this problem, but the better solution may be to make use of a searching tool that is dedicated to a narrower range of topics. In the example above, the student could have used WebMD (www.webmd.com) or the Mayo Clinic website (www.mayohealth.org) and located volumes of useful information without having to wade through hundreds of less helpful sites. Additional sites available through the government are www.medlineplus.gov for health topics and www.cdc.gov for disease control and the like.

There are other topic-centered search engines and websites dedicated to specific fields. These sites have done some of the research work in advance and have assembled quality information on their particular topic for easy access. Using these tools and websites can save time and reduce the likelihood of a child being inadvertently exposed to potentially damaging material.

Another good approach that has the added benefit of helping parents stay in tune with their kids is for parents to do the preliminary searching of the Internet for their child. Once a number of legitimate, non-threatening websites that meet the needs of the child are located, the parents can create shortcuts to those locations on the desktop. The child is then free to explore those areas that have been pre-screened by their parents. This approach will probably be most helpful with young children.

Another useful technique is to incorporate a filter into the search engine. This filter can be set to return search results at varying levels of protection. Amazon.com operates a search engine at www.a9.com that makes use of this method. In providing this feature, Amazon allows their customers to search their extensive database, as a family, without having to cringe.

Understanding how search engines work and how to refine and configure their operation can take a user a long way in the right direction towards avoiding common Internet problems. It is, however, only one tool in the Internet security toolbox.

Protecting Kids with Monitoring and Filtering Software

Another way of promoting safe Internet usage can be found in the form of monitoring software. This type of software can be configured to monitor everything that is done on a computer. It also has the ability to make copies of emails and chat room postings, and automatically send them to a parent's account. SpectorSoft Corp. has a number of products along this line for both home and business use available at www.spectorsoft.com. Some critics have raised an eyebrow at this tactic, considering it an invasion of privacy. One must weigh a child's right to privacy with a parent's right to keep them alive and unmolested.

The fact is that monitoring software does work in amazingly similar ways to illegal spyware. The difference, and this is a big difference, is that monitoring software is purchased knowingly and voluntarily by the owner of the computer, installed on their own machine and configured according to their own preferences. Monitoring software only serves to add to the user's knowledge of what is happening on their own equipment, as is their right. Spyware, on the other hand, is a clandestine product, operating illegally, without the knowledge of the owners of the system on which it is running.

Monitoring and filtering software is an absolute requirement.

Other programs designed to increase safety through filtering and monitoring are Cyber Patrol, CyberSitter, Norton Internet Security, Net Nanny and Cyber Snoop. Some of these programs feature configuration options that allow parents to regulate when the computer is allowed to be connected to the Internet. The owner of the program pre-sets times during the day that Internet access is allowed. With the exception of these pre-set times, the computers ability to access the web is completely disabled. This can be a great benefit for families with slightly older children who might be home alone at times.

Guidance and more information about these and other products as well as additional safety tips and tools can be found at www.getnetwise.org and www.safekids.com.

Another tool that can be used for monitoring Internet usage is built into the browser itself. Every web browser contains a history file, documenting websites to which the browser has been directed for a set time period. Viewing the history file provides a detailed account of websites the user has visited. This method of monitoring is easily defeated, however, as the history file is not difficult to erase and older children may know how to do it.

Performing a search of a computer's hard drive may yield some additional clues about the browsing habits of computer users. When a website is visited, files associated with that site are stored on the hard drive to facilitate quick loading of the site the next time it is visited. Files are also sometimes manually saved by the user into other directories for easy access later.

A file name can provide clues about its content. If a search returns results including a file named cool_girl.doc, it could be an indicator that something is going on, or it might mean nothing at all. Parents should not jump to conclusions. It is likely that a quick peek at the file will give the adult clear insight into their child's particular activities online. File extensions contain information about the type of content of the file. File names ending in .gif, .jpg, .bmp or .tif indicate files that are images. Babe_1.jpg could be a strong indicator that the computer is being used to view inappropriate material; however, a responsible adult should view the content of the file and discuss any inappropriate content with their child.

Using ISP Filters

Occasionally, software system requirements can be a limiting factor when installing filtering programs on home computers. In cases where two different operating systems are used in one household, for example, one program version may not work on both machines. An ISP filter might be the better choice.

Internet Service Providers (ISPs) are companies that act as a kind of portal through which personal computer users are able to access the Internet. Once connected, the portal allows a free flow of information between a user's computer and the Internet.

As the gatekeepers of the Internet, ISPs are keenly aware of the magnitude of the problems caused by online abuse. In response, some ISPs have set up filtering systems that selectively limit the nature of the information permitted to pass through their particular portal. In most cases, these filters are built into the ISP and cannot be disabled by the user. Other filtered ISPs, however, allow for a password protected bypass of this safety feature.

Among the ISPs providing filtered Internet access are pkFamily.com, Integrity Online, PAXWAY and Safe Access. These companies and others are working to create an online environment in which the web can be accessed both safely and productively.

As with any safeguard, filtering by ISPs or programs installed on individual computers have drawbacks that should at least be mentioned. The primary disadvantage of any filtering process is that its pass-through selection criteria will not be infallible. Programmers aspire to design filters in as watertight a manner as possible, but the sheer variety of the types of objects that must be encountered, evaluated and either passed along or blocked, make it impossible to succeed in every case. The approach then, is to err on the side of caution.

For example, if a computer running filtering software attempts to download information from a website containing the word "nudity," it will probably be blocked. Possibly, the website features pornography or otherwise objectionable material. It is also feasible that the web page is dedicated to art history and describes a painter known for beautiful landscapes who rarely painted the human form or "nudity."

There are numerous examples that easily come to mind where the word "nudity" or a host of other words that might trigger a filter block could be used in non-offensive context.

The challenge, and it is a large and complex one, is to gather as much useful information as possible for any given search, while filtering out the objectionable material that also meets the search criteria. The weight of each opposing interest needs to be measured against the other. For the purposes of this chapter, the protection of children, most would likely conclude that the potential blocking of a few legitimate websites is a small price to pay for the safety of a child.

Knowing When a Child Is at Risk

Educating children in an age appropriate manner is the first and best line of defense against the dangers of the net. Help them to understand that just as in life, there is good and bad everywhere, and everyone has to keep their eyes open in order to stay out of trouble.

Parents need to be in touch with what their kids are doing and the dangers to which they are susceptible. Young children are very vulnerable to becoming the wide-eyed victims of all sorts of deceptions.

Older children may go looking for trouble on their own as part of a natural desire to express independence. In these cases, a software monitor could be utilized to track their online activities.

It is vital for parents and other responsible adults to know what kids are looking for online, as well as what's looking for the kids. One helpful guide that can help parents assess their child's risk of danger related to Internet usage comes in the form of a pamphlet put together by the FBI called, *A Parents Guide to Internet Safety*. The pamphlet lists some of the warning for which parents and guardians should be aware. As with physical disease, early detection is an important factor in helping children stay safe on the Internet. Some behavioral indicators identified in the pamphlet to be aware of listed below. Parents should actively pursue any of the following indicators that manifest in their child:

- Spending large amounts of time online.

- Finding any pornography on a computer to which the child has access.

- Making or receiving phone calls to or from people who are unknown to the parent.

- Receiving mail or gifts from people who are unknown to the parent.

- Sudden screen change when an adult walks into the room.

- Becoming withdrawn from other family members.

Warning signs can indicate a problem even if there is not a computer in the home. A child may have Internet access at a friend's house or at the public library. Parents and guardians must be watchful, investigative, and vigilant. After all, a child's safety is on the line.

Conclusion

Many law enforcement agencies are taking a multi-faceted approach to making children safer on the web. These approaches are educational as well as investigative.

The educational approach is a proactive methodology where law enforcement representatives visit schools or other youth organizations and talk about the things of which children need to be aware and the specific reasons why it is important for children to be very careful online.

Everyone accepts risks when they access the web, but for children the stakes are higher. Quite literally, their life can be on the line, but neither they nor their parents or guardians are helpless. Parents and others responsible for children must make the effort to recognize the threat and take action to counteract it.

In this chapter, some of those threats and steps that can be taken to help protect children have been presented in detail. Listed below are some of the main points that are important for parents and other responsible adults to know:

- They should carefully evaluate computer games for content and rating.

- They should limit the amount of time the child spends playing computer games.

- They should educate children about the potential hazards associated with the Internet in a clear, effective manner that does not intimidate, but equips them to protect themselves.

- They should use computer filters to help protect children from unwanted exposure to objectionable material.

- They should actively monitor a child's online activity. It is important to take the time and effort to know what is going on.

While there are no measures that can guarantee safety in every situation, the safeguards covered in this section can help a child become a difficult target to hit. Awareness and vigilance on the part of responsible adults can never be replaced. Ignorance or apathy should never become contributing factors in a crime against a child.

"Children are curious and are risk takers. They have lots of courage. They venture out into a world that is immense and dangerous. A child initially trusts life and the processes of life."

-- John Bradshaw, US philosopher, lecturer, author

Now is an appropriate time to examine the concept of spies on the web and learn about the dangers of spyware and intrusive measures that are used to violate privacy and security.

Internet Spies

"You can't see us, but we can see you."

Spying and Marketing, Who is in Their Sights

Donnie could not believe it. He had just purchased a new computer and only connected to the Internet a few times. Donnie thought the friend who had convinced him to buy a Spyware detection program was being a little paranoid. Now, he was shocked to find a rogue piece of software, secretly running behind the scenes, recording his every keystroke.

Every password, username, e-mail and website he had visited had all been recorded. This record, in all likelihood, was to be sent via a secret email to the owner of the Spyware. Donnie thought about some of the emails he had written recently. If his boss found out about the new business he was trying to start, he was sure he would be fired on the spot.

Spyware is a special kind of software that runs on a system without the user's knowledge. These kinds of programs are able to monitor a computer by collecting data and recording information about the habits of the unsuspecting user. As Donnie's story illustrates, Spyware is capable of going as far as recording every keystroke performed on a machine, and emailing that information back to the owner of the Spyware.

Adware is similar to Spyware in that it can trick users into supplying valuable information to unscrupulous operators. Adware is also capable of recording and tracking user activity for the purposes of targeted marketing. This makes Adware an invasive, unwelcome program.

In this chapter both types of programs will be presented in detail as well as ideas on how they can be countered.

Discovering the Secrets of Spyware

The use of the term Spyware might invoke images of secret agents on dangerous missions. In fact, Spyware is not quite as exotic as that, but the danger can be just as real. The use of Spyware is controversial since it involves gathering data about a person or their habits without their knowledge. When employed properly, however, it can lead to better security systems for legitimate computer users. Of course, in the wrong hands, it can be devastating.

There are a number of sources on the Internet that provide information about Spyware itself as well as programs that function to detect it. Two popular websites on the subject are www.firewallguide.com/spyware.htm, and www.spywareguide.com. www.spywareguide.com makes available a resource that rates Spyware programs on a danger scale of 1 to 10, with 10 being the most dangerous.

When a Spyware detection program scans for Spyware, it may sometimes incorrectly identify anti-virus utilities or even other Spyware detection programs as Spyware. It is important to know what software is legitimately installed on the computer system.

More detail about anti-Spyware programs will be provided later in this chapter.

The Upside of Spyware

Spyware was originally designed to be used as a security tool by legitimate programmers to help protect against the emerging threat presented by hackers. Some have called the usefulness of Spyware into question, citing the dangers of its abuse; however, the software itself is neither intrinsically good nor bad. It is the user and their intent that makes this software either beneficial or harmful.

One benefit of Spyware is that it has become a powerful tool in the hands of vigilant parents as they fight to keep their kids safe on the Internet. Knowing what a child is doing on the Internet is vital. Using Spyware, a parent can closely monitor their child's online activities and step in to protect them should the need arise. As discussed earlier, some Spyware programs designed for use on home computers can be configured to monitor how the computer is being used and send that information to another email account without the user knowing that it is happening.

Other parents may wish to discourage unsuitable use of the Internet by informing their children that the computer is keeping track of what they do. If they choose to disclose that information to their child, it may be wise for them to configure the program in such a way that the Spyware will be impossible to disable without a password.

While this might seem like a drastic measure, these are desperate times for some families. The list of threats kids face on the Internet range from exposure to sexually explicit material to being targeted by predatory deviants. Families need tools that can help them counteract these threats. Chapter 10 covers the dangers children face on the Internet in more detail.

Employers have also been known to install Spyware on their computer systems. A review of company policies related to the use of the Internet is in order before setting up a Spyware-monitoring program on a company system.

While it is considered appropriate for employers to inform their employees when they are being monitored, it is the law in some locations. The failure to inform employees that monitoring software is running on their system could potentially expose the employer to liability if charges of privacy invasion are brought.

Notifying employees that Spyware is running their system does not necessarily detract from the effectiveness of the Spyware. After all, the company's goal when installing the software is to make sure employees make good use of company resources. Informing them that they are being monitored closely while using the computer is certainly a good way of doing that.

The Downside of Spyware

Of course, there are risks involved with the use of Spyware, even when it is installed with the best of intentions. Imagine that an employee violates company policy and uses company resources on company time to conduct personal business. Suppose the employee does online banking and transfers funds between accounts, then logs off and returns to work. The Spyware does its job, reports the activity, and a wayward employee has been identified, right? Maybe.

Yes, the Spyware flagged personal business being conducted on company time, but now the employer is in possession of some very sensitive information. The company will have the employee's personal username and password. They will very probably have his bank account numbers and perhaps even balances.

Could the possession of this sort of information present a liability risk for the company? Yes, it could. Once in possession of the information, the company is responsible for its security. If unauthorized access and subsequent misuse results in financial loss for the employee, the company can be held liable for damages. Even if no financial loss occurs, just the act of allowing access to this sort of personal information is in violation of privacy protection laws and could result in legal problems for the company.

Spyware is a leading cause of poor PC performance

Another downside to Spyware is that it can seriously affect the performance of the computer on which it is running. For a company trying to increase efficiency and productivity by keeping people focused on their work, an office full of bogged down machines is a bad thing.

One possible solution to this problem is to adjust the level of monitoring performed. In some cases, the amount of data collected and computer operations stored by the Spyware can be configured. It may not be necessary to know every single keystroke that is performed on every machine in the office. If there are areas of the company's operations that can be monitored less intensively, then that alternative should be considered.

The most significant downside, however, is its deliberate misuse. If Spyware is secretly installed on a machine by an individual with malicious intent, a very dangerous situation can develop. Spyware in stealth mode will work quietly and steadily, gathering up large amounts of personal or business information. This information is then sent to someone who will use it for their own benefit.

The Spyware in the Middle

Some programs that might not seem like Spyware are in fact just that. For instance, Comet Cursor is a harmless little utility that is supposed to make web browsing more fun. With Comet Cursor installed, the user's cursor changes from an arrow into a cartoon character or some other unusual graphic.

Though it sounds innocent enough, there are a few problems with this program. The program was installed on users' systems without their consent or participation. They were not asked if they wanted it, nor did policy mandate that they approve of its use. It was just set up for them by web designers who thought it would be amusing.

The second and more serious problem is the information the program needs in order to run. In truth, the program tracks IP addresses, websites visited by the browser, system settings and so on. This program was not malicious, and it was intended only to give the Internet surfer a little smile when their mouse pointer unexpectedly transformed into Mighty Mouse.

While the writers of the program may have been above board, the hard fact remains that a program the user did not ask for is running on their system and tracking what they do. This presents a problem. Unauthorized access to any computer and the use of the information gathered from that computer is a genuine risk.

Detecting Spyware

An article titled *Poor Defenders* in *PC World* magazine found that many Spyware detection programs are lacking. Even more frightening, many of the web-based Spyware detectors will actually infect the PC with Spyware:

"Even more remarkable, two other programs we tested installed spyware applications on our system. SpyAssault left a file called FavoriteMan, a browser hijacker listed in online spyware databases such as SpywareGuide.com. MyNetProtector installed a whopping 57 files, including 19 that attempted to make connections to the Internet, in some cases within seconds of installation."

The following comprehensive article rates each spyware removal tool by their ability to locate and remove Spyware in both the PC files and the MS-Windows registry:

PROGRAM	Spyware applications and related files removed[1]	Spyware Registry keys removed[1]	Comments
MyNetProtector $40 www.mynetprotector.com	0	0	Program added 57 spyware files to the test computer, and then detected (and removed) only a cookie from DoubleClick.
NoAdware $30 www.noadware.net	0	2	Could delete only a few Registry keys associated with two of our six test spyware applications.
PAL Spyware Remover $30 www.palsol.com	0	0	Claimed that a legitimate component of the Trend Micro antivirus program was spyware.
SpyAssault $20 www.spyassault.com	3	0	Multiple false positives; free and paid scanners gave inconsistent results. Added and later removed a spyware app.
SpyBlocs 2 $40 www.eblocs.com	0	0	Identified Microsoft Windows' signed driver folder as "Severe" spyware and deleted it during the cleanup.
Spyware Stormer $30 www.spywarestormer.com	3	2	Labeled cookies as "high-risk"; misidentified a standard Windows Registry key as a browser hijacker.
XoftSpy $30 www.paretologic.com	4	1	Removes most files but leaves many Registry keys behind; exaggerates the risk of tracking cookies.
REFERENCE APP			
Spybot Search & Destroy 1.3 *Free* find.pcworld.com/42052	5	4	*Could not remove one particular browser "toolbar" hijacker; real-time TeaTimer tool prevented some infections.*

Source: PC World

Figure 11.1 – *Spyware detection software*

Free Can be Better

The results of the PC World article clearly noted that the freeware tool *Spybot Search & Destroy* product was the best tool in their tests, beating all of the extra-cost products. The Spybot vendor asks for a small donation and provides semi-weekly updates to their vast array of spyware definitions.

This author installed Spybot and found that it detected spyware that other products had missed. Spybot has an easy-to-use interface and was very simple to configure and execute. Figure 11.2 depicts the main screen setup for the Spybot utility.

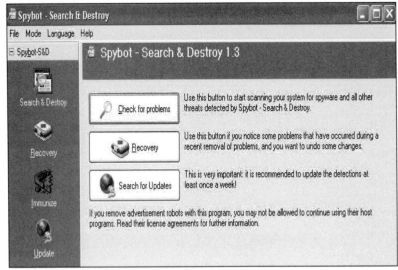

Source: Spybot

Figure 11.2 - *The Spybot main screen*

Removing Spyware

There are many free and low-cost products that remove Spyware from computers. Removal should be a goal as it is clear that some Spyware is malicious and is planted by criminals to capture confidential information about the computer's users.

The best prevention is to use a web browser that does not accept Spyware infections. Some of the most popular include:

- Apple Safari browser (www.apple.com/safari)

- Open-source Firefox browser (www.mozilla.org/products/firefox)

If a computer does become infected, most of the spyware can be quickly removed using a removal product. Most of the best Spyware products include software program leaders such as the *Ad Aware* product by Lavasoft (www.lavasoftusa.com/software/adaware). The *AdAware* product keeps master definition files on the web and the product will download the most recent definitions prior to starting the PC scan. Figure 11.3 shows the Ad

Aware setup screen. Figure 11.4 shows the available options for system scan mode.

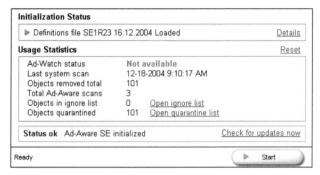

Figure 11.3 – *Ad Aware Initialization Status*

Because the definitions know where to look, an entire PC can be scanned in less than a minute using a "smart scan" utility:

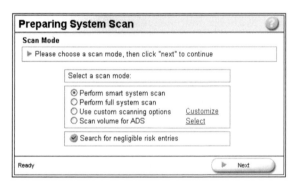

Figure 11.4 – *Ad Aware System Scan Mode*

After the spyware scan, the product will display a list of all of the adware and spyware cookies and give the option of keeping them in a quarantine area or deleting them.

Spyware and the Law

As noted in Chapter 5, *All about Cybercrime*, many laws are ineffective in a global arena. The good news is that this is not stopping the U.S. Congress from making the introduction of spyware a criminal offense.

The Internet Spyware Prevention Act, dubbed "I-SPY", introduces criminal penalties ranging from substantial fines up to five years in prison for parties who cause spyware to be downloaded or copied onto a computer without authorization. This law applies to spyware that is introduced with the intent to either to compromise the computer's security or to use the information gained to defraud or injure a person. As of 2004, this Bill is awaiting approval from the U.S. Senate.

Privacy Breeches on the PC

Particularly tech savvy cyber criminals with a knack for hacking may prefer a different method for gaining access to information. Rather than placing a spy program on a machine and letting it do all the work, they will attempt to access information directly, while a computer is online. The challenge of accomplishing this may not be as daunting as it first appears.

Personal and business computers can be outfitted and configured in such a way that makes them very difficult to hack into. The problem is that computers are often preconfigured and sold with their security settings at an absolute minimum. These security configurations provide an inadequate measure of protection, at best. At worst, it makes the computer a sitting duck for anyone with malicious intent who happens along.

Some of the ineffective default settings are:

Web browsers that allow Active-X controls – Some web browsers will be default configured to allow for automatic execution of programs with Active-X controls. This means that if a web page is encountered with an Active-X control at the site, the browser will automatically execute them. A hacker can anonymously email a link to a web page with an Active-X control programmed to transfer Spyware. If the e-mail recipient clicks on the link and their Active-X enabled web browser goes to the site, they will become the proud owner of a shiny new piece of Spyware. Many of the more recently released browsers such as Firefox and the Apple Macintosh browser have disabled the Active-X controls.

E-mail allows automatic execution of script – Another preferred method of gaining access to private information is to send anonymous emails with scripts contained within them. When the email is opened, the script will run. If the script is a Spyware program, the computer has just been opened up like a book to whoever sent the email.

"Is your computer safe?"

There is virtually no limit to the type or amount of information that can be retrieved from a computer. Some machines are considered particularly easy to hack or plant Spyware on. A Windows XP machine running the default security settings and connected to the Internet has been dubbed a "honeypot" by the bad guys.

Apple computers on the other hand are regarded as very difficult to break into and are immune to many common hacking methods.

Spyware and advertising may not seem to have a lot in common on the surface, but, as the next section will show, in some ways they are very similar.

Discovering the Secrets of Adware

Businesses advertise because it works. Billions of dollars are spent in the U.S. every year by companies trying to get their product in front of the American people. It didn't take long for businesses and advertisers to realize that the Internet is one of the most effective ways to get a message out. With this realization, came the birth of Adware. Adware is software that is designed to display or deliver advertising messages. The name itself is a commingling of the words advertising and software.

As with Spyware , Adware can be good or bad depending on the user.

The Upside of Adware

While everyone loves to hate advertisements, the ads do, of course, have a legitimate function. Most people have, at one time or another, had the experience of encountering an advertisement about a product or service that turned out to be just the thing they needed.

Ads can also alert people to problems they did not even know they had. One ad aired in a local market instructs potential patrons to inspect their doors for fit and theirs walls for cracks as a sign of problems with shifting foundations. A person may do just that, discover they have a problem and get the problem fixed, all because of an advertisement.

And, of course, ads can also direct people to great bargains when they come along, making sure they do not miss out on the big deals.

The Downside of Adware

Of course, it goes without saying; there are downsides to advertising as well. Online and off, people everywhere are adrift in a sea of advertisements. Apparently the Madison Avenue retail market is very concerned that consumers will not be adequately be apprised of their shopping options, and may make poor buying decisions for lack of information. While their concern is admirable, everyone is now bombarded through television, radio, newspaper, magazines, billboards and now computers by an endless stream of marketing messages.

In this age of computer advertising, just staying abreast of the promotional emails that overflow inboxes day after day can become a project in itself.

Pop Up Windows

One popular form of Internet Adware is known as the "pop-up window" advertisement. Pop-up windows look like a small version of a web browser screen. Typically, they actually pop-up unexpectedly and are displayed on top of the current view. This is how they got their name. The only way to get rid of the pop-up is to either close the window manually by clicking the 'X' in the top right corner or by clicking inside the window on the ad itself. This can sometimes be more difficult or risky than it sounds.

"Got Pop-ups?"

The writers of Adware know that they are a nuisance and try to make it difficult for their ads to be easily ignored. One trick is to make the closing of a pop-up window a trigger for launching one or more new pop-ups. As each of those new pop-ups is closed, they will trigger the opening of another new pop-up, and on it goes. Some users have reported having to reboot a system just to get out of the pop-up window loop. Needless to say, this sort of interruption in work can cause a great deal of frustration.

Another scheme commonly used by pop-up window advertisers is to write the advertisement in such a way that it looks like an official warning, possibly generated by the operating system. A message may read, "Your computer is infected by a virus. Click here for help!" Another misleading message may read, "Your computer is not running at top speed, and is in need of an upgrade."

These messages will provide hyperlinks that will direct the unsuspecting user to the website where products are available for purchase to fix the problem. Of course, there is no problem. These messages insinuate that the computer has been evaluated and is in need of their product to perform more reliably or remove a virus. In fact, the pop-up has gone out to millions of users, blindly seeking those that will believe the message and buy the product.

Pop-up advertisements or marketing surveys are sometimes camouflaged as games. One trick displays a window with a cartoon monkey moving slowly around inside. At the top of the window a message reads "Click on the monkey and win $50!"

The advertisement masquerades as a game of skill. The monkey is a moving target, inviting the unsuspecting web surfer to click it and win. Of course, the monkey is moving very slowly, and makes an easy target. Sure enough, it is; however, the game is actually a hyperlink for the advertiser.

Some variations of this idea inform the person that they are indeed a winner and to collect their $50, they must provide name, address, phone number, SSN and so on. While it is highly doubtful they will ever see the $50, they almost certainly will see a marked increase in the amount of advertising they receive. Depending on the amount and type of information divulged, they may also find that someone has stolen their identity and is out in the world doing all the fun things identity thieves like to do.

One last note here; if a person knowingly supplies their phone number to a marketer, it can effectively remove them from the "Do Not Call List" and open them up to still more advertising.

Protection from Web Spies

Fortunately, there are tools available that can be used in the fight against Spyware and Adware.

"Fighting Spyware is a constant battle."

A product called Spy Sweeper has been developed by Webroot Software Inc. Spy Sweeper, as the name implies, will go through a system looking for Spyware and Adware. Spy Sweeper is available as a free trial on Webroot's website at www.webroot.com/products/spysweeper.

Another company producing these sorts of products is Lavasoft Inc. Lavasoft is the maker of Ad-Aware, which is capable of detecting and eliminating Adware and Spyware. Different versions of the Ad-Aware program are available to meet the needs of different users. Basic versions of the software are available for free, while a more full featured product can be purchased.

Spyware and Adware detection programs all have the same goal, but they work in different ways. Some are easier to use than others and costs will vary. It is important for each user to know their specific needs and evaluate program options carefully to get the product that is right for them.

It is highly recommended that a third party verification of the effectiveness of any detection program be obtained before installing even a free trail version. This is because some programs presenting themselves as free trial anti-Spyware software are themselves in fact, Spyware. For a list of supposed anti-Spyware programs that have not performed as promised see www.spywarewarrior.com/rogue_anti-spyware.htm.

To learn more about what works and what doesn't, visit these informative websites. Useful resources can be identified that will help evaluate which Spyware and Adware detection programs are best suited to each individual's needs.

- www.spywarewarrior.com/rogue_anti-spyware.htm#trustworthy

- www.firewallguide.com/spyware.htm

- www.pcpitstop.com/spycheck/top25.asp

In addition to the software tools presented in this chapter, there are other steps that can be taken to reduce the risk of exposure to malicious and dangerous Spy and Adware programs. These steps include:

- Exercise caution in all computer related activities. Don't get paranoid, but all users must keep their eyes open and be aware of what's going on with their computer.

- Never respond to pop-up ads by clicking on them or following their instructions. Just shut them down by closing the windows manually.

- Make use of on-line resources to learn about the threats posed by Spyware and how to counter them.

- Never install any program of any kind that is not from a recognized and reputable source.

Conclusion

While there are legitimate applications for both Spyware and Adware, less altruistically motivated variations of these programs clearly pose a threat to unsuspecting computer users.

A computer user's best defense is knowledge. Understanding the threat, how it works and what can be done to counter it will go a long way toward keeping personal information safe and private things private.

Listed here are just a few of the benefits of staying on top of the security issues that affect computing:

- Reduce fear and uncertainty about the security of the personal computer.

- Understand the threat that spy and Adware pose and how to counter it.

- Being well versed in the anti-Spyware/Adware world, and knowing how to locate and use the best product for the user's needs.

In the next chapter, information will be presented on viruses and the Internet. Spyware and viruses have some things in common, but there are important differences. Some of those differences will be presented in detail.

"What we call 'progress' is the exchange of one nuisance for another nuisance."

-- Havelock Ellis (1859 - 1939) English psychologist

Virus Attacks

*Viruses are more contagious than influenza
and more common than the cold.*

Exposure to Viruses

Tom was exhausted. The extended business trip had done its work, and drained him completely. He knew this would happen; these trips always had that effect on him, but he had learned to live with it. This time, however, it was more. His flight had been delayed, and the airport was now his one star hotel for the night. He tried to call home and let his wife know that he would be late, but his cell phone went on the blink as he tried and it did not recover. Stranded and frustrated, Tom decided to get some cash from the ATM machine for dinner at a vendor's stand. No luck, his transaction was denied. This was getting weird. There was no way that account was empty; he knew this to be a fact. A day late, hungry and broke, Tom arrived at home and discovered he could thank a computer virus for his trouble. Now, Tom was angry.

The consequences of a virus attack can be dramatic, making headlines in the papers or leading off the evening newscast. Less dramatically but even more frustrating, virus attacks can wreak a wide range of havoc on individual computers and result in the loss of work, or worse.

"The attack came swiftly and without warning. At 12:30 a.m. eastern standard time, January 25th, a single packet of data containing the Slammer worm began spreading across the Internet. Within 10 minutes, the worm reached 90 percent of the Net and infected more than 75,000 machines. At its peak 30 minutes later, it disrupted one out of five data packets. The result: service blackouts, canceled flights, and disabled ATMs."

Excerpted from May 2003 issue of *PC World* magazine

It can be difficult for most people to imagine just how much disruption was caused by the Slammer worm described in the previous excerpt. A real world example might help put the severity of the attack in perspective. Imagine traveling along a major thoroughfare at the height of rush hour traffic. Now imagine that all at once, cars begin to be disabled, and within a very few minutes one out of every five cars on the road is either dead or dying. At this point, all bets are off, nobody is going anywhere. The four out of five cars that are running properly will be hopelessly entangled in a web of disabled vehicles and the whole system will grind to a speedy and ugly halt.

On the Internet, data packets are the cars, and the network is the highway. With one out of five data packets affected, it is impossible for the remainder of system to function properly. When a problem of this magnitude develops, there are consequences. The network administrators and IT professionals that might otherwise quash a problem before anyone else takes notice, are quickly overwhelmed.

The resultant back-up overflows out into the real world and things start to happen. Airline scheduling systems fail; telephone networks falter; financial and banking institutions shut down and no one gets their daily double raspberry cappuccino with their debit card.

While virus attacks are prolific; this chapter will present information on some other lesser known types of attacks that can be just as destructive. These include computer worms and the Trojan horse. The similarities and differences in those types of attacks will be examined and information about how computers can be protected from attack will be included.

What Is a Virus?

A computer virus is a piece of code, or perhaps a program that is capable of replicating itself and spreading throughout a computer network in a fashion similar to biological viruses. These viruses attach themselves to other files without detection and operate within the computer according to the instructions given to them by the virus' author. Like biological viruses, there are many variations of computer viruses, and they work and spread in different ways.

A virus does something. What exactly it does, its purpose, its function, is commonly referred to as the virus' payload. The payload is determined by the author of the virus at the time it is created, and it reflects a set of instructions given to the virus. The kinds of instructions given are limited only by the imaginations of their authors. They range from harmless to incredibly dangerous and all the points in between.

Some viruses will lie dormant on a machine until a trigger is tripped. The virus may be waiting for a certain date and time. Others will be looking for a particular kind of operation to occur on the computer, and then it executes its instructions at that point. One commonly used trigger is the opening of an email message to which the virus is attached.

"We typically see 800-900 new viruses every month".

Chris Kraft, Senior Security Analyst, Sophos Inc.

Not all viruses however are dependent on a trigger. Some are instructed to begin operating the instant they arrive at a machine. This type of virus will usually hit hard and spread fast. Viruses of this type can use email systems to send themselves without the user's knowledge.

What kinds of things will a virus do once it begins to execute? Amazingly, there are people who go to the trouble to write harmless viruses. One example is a virus that will generate an animated cartoon image with a funny message. People who write these viruses are sometimes motivated by curiosity. They may just want to see how far it will spread.

Other viruses are more malevolent and are written with the destructive intensions. One kind of virus, sometimes called Spyware, will gather

---

information and e-mail it off to whatever e-mail address is specified by the virus' author. This can all be done below the radar, and the computer user may never know it is happening.

"Eek! Where are my files?"

Other dangerous viruses will try to damage and delete files. Word processing, spreadsheet and database files, containing vital and sometimes irreplaceable information can be lost, with devastating results. The virus can also target files that are necessary for a machine to run properly. If these files are damaged, the computer might stop working altogether.

An example of a virus of this type is a variation of the well-known Melissa virus, also known as W97M/Assilem.A. This little gem was written specifically to target Word97 normal.dot files. Once the infection is established, any Word document that is opened will become infected and capable of transferring the virus to still more machines. Since Word documents are often sent as email attachments, the virus had a ready-made mobility.

However, there is a limiting factor to this scheme. The user must manually send the infected file in an e-mail. Of course, they will not know the file is infected when they send it. It is possible that the virus will have to wait a very long time for a file to which it is attached to be sent. It may, in fact, never be sent. In this case, the virus stays on the machine and is not spread to others. This makes such viruses much slower spreading, if not less damaging.

When Worms Attack

A worm is a program similar to a virus. Both are able to replicate themselves and move between machines; and both are potentially harmful.

Unlike a virus, a worm does not attach itself to a file. It is a free-floating entity in itself. This makes the worm much better at spreading itself quickly since it does not need to wait for infected files to be sent. Worms can use the networking capabilities and file sharing routines of any program to get itself from one place to another. Of course, the worm is able to use email as well, and it does not require the user to send it manually. It is able to send itself. This makes a worm extremely mobile and able to spread with unbelievable speed. A worm can quickly become a global threat.

"Worm Uses Webcams to Spy on Users", by Sharon Gaudin

"A new variant of the Rbot worm has the ability to take over users' webcams and use them to spy on people in their offices and homes."

August 24, 2004 www.esecurityplanet.com

When the Trojan Horse Rolls Through the Gate

Most people are familiar with the concept of the Trojan horse. In Greek legend, the Greeks were able to prevail over their ancient rival, Troy, by presenting a peace offering to the city in the form a huge wooden horse. The offering was received by the inhabitants of Troy and brought inside the city walls. Inside the horse, however, were Greek soldiers who were now inside the city and able to destroy from within and win the Trojan War.

A Trojan horse program works in the same way. It appears to be something harmless or fun. It may look like a game or a new screensaver, but these appearances are only a veneer, a thin coating for a destructive program.

The programs that Trojan horses use to disguise themselves may work only marginally or not at all. A game, for example, might not work or might work only for a couple of levels. But even if a program appears to be completely inoperative on the surface, rest assured that it is possible that it is working just as intended, and the damage is being done.

Viruses and Personal Safety

Howard Schmidt is an expert. His long list of qualifications includes serving as a Computer Crimes Detective in the Chandler AZ, Police Dept., Chief Security Officer for Microsoft and Cyber Security Advisor to the White House. In 2001, Mr. Schmidt testified before the Subcommittee on Commerce, Trade and Consumer Protection, and delivered a report entitled "Cyber Security & Consumer Data: What's at Risk for the Consumer". During that testimony Mr. Schmidt estimated that a single, particularly virulent virus, known as the ILOVEYOU virus, launched in 2000 had cost an estimated $8 billion to eradicate.

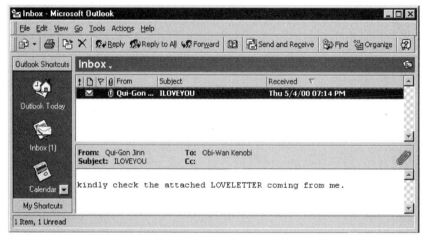

Image reproduced with permission from Sophos

Figure 12.1 - *The ILOVEYOU virus spread through e-mail*

The potential for more and even costlier attacks in the future is great. As society becomes increasingly dependent on technology to function from day to day, the risk factor associated with interference in that technology escalates.

The costs and disruptions caused by virus and worm attacks are incurred primarily in the following areas:

- The loss of business during periods of network failures.

- The loss of consumer confidence in businesses hit by viruses.

- Detection and removal of damaging viruses and worms.

- Restoration of lost or corrupted data.

Large companies, says Howard Smith, incur significant costs when there is a major outbreak of a virus. It takes time and money to go through large networks, finding and destroying viruses; not to mention the costs of recovering lost data and returning the system to its pre-infected state. While the up-front costs in dollars and cents may be higher for large companies, mid-sized and small businesses typically expend more funds as a percentage of total available revenue on the problem. Thus mid-sized and small businesses are less able to absorb these types of attacks.

Additionally, small and mid-sized businesses' reputations are more easily damaged by problems resulting from computer attacks. Very large, nationally known companies are not likely to actually lose customers due to a virus attack. They will lose orders during the time the network is inoperative, but people will continue to do business with them as soon as they are able.

A small, lesser-known company experiencing similar problems for similar reasons may, in fact, lose customers altogether. Consumers try new places, looking for good deals online. If a transaction does not go smoothly, an order is lost or cannot be placed due to technical problems; the customer may likely blame the company itself and conclude they are dealing with a shoddy operation. Possibly, they will look elsewhere for a good deal or go back to the nationally recognized company.

High profile virus and worm attacks make headlines and breaking news. Coverage of the ILOVEYOU virus or the Code Red worm may alert computer users to examine their own systems a little more closely. However, not all virus creators are interested in spectacular damage and headline coverage.

Some kinds of viruses do not want to be noticed at all; for these, secrecy is the key. They are designed to hum along quietly in the background, unnoticed. Quietly or not, they are doing damage; often gathering system data or personal information for use in any number of unpleasant ways.

Once the details of a user's email account have been compromised, whoever has the information can begin sending spam or otherwise objectionable email as if they were the user. They may even be able to log in as the user and access the email account directly. This sort of activity can cause the email account to be shut down completely. On occasion, the user may be denied Internet access through their ISP altogether. Chapter 13 will cover spam and the problems it can cause in more detail.

Businesses take note:

A successful virus attack can have devastating consequences for a business. It is imperative to cover every base where security is concerned. If a business has employees that work from home, or do company work on home computers, be careful. Make sure that any computer where company files are stored or used is protected. Home computers are often overlooked when a company devises its security policy.

In recognition of this fact, a major source of computer virus protection software, Sophos, provides licensing for home use to all employees of companies that use their products, free of charge.

For better or worse, companies that make extensive use of the Internet become dependent upon it. A problem with the Internet means a problem at the company. Any number of business functions can be affected; including planning, shipping and customer communications. Problems with any major area of operation are likely to negatively impact company performance, and a difficulty that continues for any length of time, can affect a businesses reputation.

While most people understand that attacks against their computers pose a real threat and that it is important to take precautionary steps, some do not. Not everyone is dependent on his or her computer for everything. These people may not run a business or even make extensive use of their computers for entertainment. People in this category sometimes believe that the worst that can happen is for them to be unable to access email for a couple days.

Senior Security Analyst, Chris Kraft of Sophos Inc. advises that the danger is more serious than that. An unprotected computer is an easy mark, and a successful virus attack could cause enough damage to require re-installation of the entire operating system.

If the user has not maintained thorough backups, everything would be lost. Email addresses, word processing documents, budget and financial data would be gone forever. Even if a methodical regimen for backup procedures had been followed, performing a low-level format from scratch can be difficult. For inexperienced users, it may be impossible to do this, and outside help will have to be called in. For those who know how to perform the format, it is a monotonous and time-consuming task, made all the more unpleasant because it was so unnecessary.

If enough of the right kind of information is compromised through a virus attack, it is possible for a computer to come under the control of a third party. If this happens, the computer can be used to conduct illegal activity, and chances are the owner of the computer would be unaware that it is occurring.

If an investigation of the illegal activity ensues, chances are detectives will follow the digital trail to the unwitting owner of the captive machine. This can be a bit embarrassing, to say the least. Nobody wants the Computer Crimes Investigations Dept. van parked in front of their house. It isn't likely that charges will be brought against an innocent person, but there are other repercussions. An investigation could be lengthy, and require a significant amount of time and effort on everybody's part. It may also be necessary to confiscate the computer as evidence, at least until the case has been closed.

It should be clear at this point, that it is important for everyone to protect themselves against virus attacks. How dependent someone is from day to day on his or her computer makes no difference. For those who rely heavily on their computers, the need for protection is self-evident. Businesses especially must consider both customers and employees who depend on their services and continued operation for their own well-being.

Viruses: Who's Behind Them

When discussing viruses or computer worms and the damage they are capable of, a natural question that arises is, "Who is doing this, and why?" In answer, some have speculated that the anti-virus and security companies are behind at least part of the problem, trying to ensure an active market for their product.

"The infamous virus writer revealed."

Chris Kraft of Sophos Inc. has a blunt response to those kinds of charges. "That is a myth. Antivirus software companies do not develop viruses." An antivirus company does work with the viruses that other people develop. They are dissected and analyzed in order to see how they work and how best to defend against them. Chris contends that antivirus companies will have no shortage of business in the foreseeable future. "There are enough malicious people out there," says Chris, to keep them in business for a long time.

So who is writing the virus software? Most of the people creating viruses remain anonymous, but enough of them have been discovered and investigated for an outline of certain personality types to develop.

At least a portion of those creating viruses are looking for notoriety among their hacking peers. The amount of damage they can do, how fast they can do it and whether they can get the attention of the popular media all contribute to their standing. Not unlike real world criminals where the size of a heist might grant them a kind of fame among other crooks, computer hackers focus on the number of machines they can hack and the problems they can cause.

Some virus authors are merely thieves, motivated by the lure of easy money. These types of crooks might hack directly into a system and steal money if they can. Alternatively, they may steal information from a site and sell it to others who will then use it to commit still more crimes.

For example, some online merchants have reported their online shopping carts stolen. These are the secure areas of a website where customers' information, including credit card numbers, are kept. A crook who absconds with such a shopping cart is in possession of a very valuable commodity. They will have no problem finding a buyer for the information.

Still others try to create viruses that defeat the security measures of as many computers as possible, making unauthorized access very easy. A listing of these compromised machines is then compiled, and sold to other crooks looking for easy targets.

The last category of virus creators covered in this chapter, are not really virus creators at all; at least, not intentionally. In fact, these kinds of viruses are better categorized as bugs. They are mistakes in the programming of legitimate software that may cause a program to behave in a virus-like manner. For example, suppose the author of a piece of software wants to be informed by email every time someone installs a copy of it on their machine; however, as the result of a programming error an e-mail is sent to everyone in a user's address book, informing them that they have installed this new piece of software. While there is no criminal intent, the results can be an inconvenience.

Regardless of the motive for creating viruses, it is good to know that there are effective defenses against them. In the next section of this chapter, guidance will be presented on what one can do to stay ahead of the bad guys.

Virus Prevention Software

A key factor in achieving effective protection against virus attacks is to make use of dependable and up-to-date antivirus software. There are a number of reputable, time-tested companies from which this sort of software can be purchased. The following is a list of some trusted companies producing antivirus software:

- Symantic™

- Proland Software

- McAfee, Inc.®

- Trend Micro, Inc. ™

- Sophos, Inc

There are a number of factors to consider when evaluating antivirus software products. Of course, there is price, but pricing should be a secondary concern. Solid protection from real threats is valuable. It is not easy to achieve and it's worth the price. No protection program will ever be as costly as one successful virus or hack job.

Buyers should consider the level of customer and technical support provided by the company. Virus protection is a technical business, and less experienced computer operators may need someone to help them configure their software to meet their needs.

Moreover, bear in mind the "cutting-edge" factor when choosing a vendor. New viruses are discovered daily. For any program to be effective there must be constant research and development. An update service needs to be a part of the license agreement, with new virus definitions available for automatic download on a daily basis. This is an absolute must. Due to the proliferation of new viruses, any antivirus program will be obsolete on the day it is purchased. Updates at installation and daily updates thereafter are the only way to be truly protected.

The illustration below, Fig. 12.2, shows the summary box utilized by Sophos Anti-Virus. In this example, two viruses have been located and information about each of them and the circumstances of their detection are displayed. The option of what to do with the viruses is provided, and a cleaning or purging utility is usually run to remove the viruses from the system. If there are damaged or infected files, the program can repair or purge them and restore them for use.

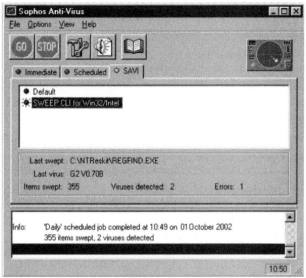

Image reproduced with permission from Sophos

Figure 12.2 - *The summary box utilized by Sophos Anti-Virus*

The importance of updating antivirus software regularly is stressed by Kraft, "Your antivirus software is only as good as your most recent update." This makes a straightforward and intuitive update process imperative. A program that allows for scheduling of automatic updates to be downloaded and installed without any input from the user is the best option for many people. A program with an ungainly update procedure will likely be neglected, with potentially disastrous results.

Software Best Practices

As previously mentioned, keeping antivirus software updated is vital. The updates however, are usually only available via a subscription service. When the program is purchased and registered at installation, the owner is automatically enrolled in the subscription service for a period of time, usually 12 months. During that period, the software can be updated at any time.

At the end of that period, however, updates will no longer be available. Attempting to update beyond that time will result in a message stating that the subscription service has expired. Usually, a link is provided to a website where the software can be renewed on the spot. Anyone tempted to save the cash and not renew the subscription should reconsider. An unprotected computer is an infected computer. It's just that simple.

In summary, antivirus best practices dictate the following:

- Installation of a trusted antivirus software program.

- Scheduling of automatic system scans.

- Upgrading to latest version of antivirus software available.

- Schedule automatic updates of virus definitions.

Protecting the Operating System

It is important to make sure that the operating system on the computer is completely updated or patched. Operating system manufacturers are made aware on occasion of security lapses in their systems. When an operating system is released, people immediately start trying to hack it. Eventually, someone will discover a weakness. When it becomes apparent that there is vulnerability in the system, manufacturers will devise a patch for the repair. As long as new breaches of security are located, new patches will be issued for their correction.

Microsoft and others makes their system updates and patches available on their websites. These updates and patches can be configured for automatic retrieval and installation. Retrieving these updates in a timely manner is important since they are made available to counter a weakness or deficiency in the program. The operating system itself will also notify the user when updates are available. In addition, Microsoft has utility called Windows Update that will help system users locate and install updates and patches that match the version of the system they are running.

Backups and Web Safety

A successful virus attack can damage or erase files that may or may not be recoverable by an antivirus program. If data is damaged or lost and cannot be repaired or restored, the only option remaining is the use of backup files. Backup files contain important data that has been copied ahead of time and stored outside of the computer. These files need to be thorough, current and represent all the important data that has just been lost to a virus. While backup files require time and effort to replace, they prevent data from being lost.

Having those backup files ready to go when they are needed means following a strict data back-up regimen. This is not as hard as it sounds because it can be scheduled to be performed automatically by the operating system.

There was a time when performing a full system backup on a regular basis was impractical for the home computer user. The storage medium available just made it too impractical and time consuming. Anyone remember being asked to insert backup disk number 65? That is not an issue today, and there is no excuse for not having thorough and recent backups of everything. The advent of the writable DVD and CD ROM drives has made storage of huge amounts of data relatively simple. If a computer is not equipped with either of these drives, it is likely they will have a USB port, which will support a USB flash drive able to hold up to 256 MB or more.

Common Sense

At last, there is a best practice that won't cost a penny. Common sense is a key asset in all of life's endeavors, and navigating the challenges of the Internet is no exception.

If an email appears in the inbox of a computer asking that an attachment be opened; the user should stop, think and consider the following things:

- Who is the e-mail from? This is a major consideration. Never open an e-mail attachment from an unidentified sender. There really are no exceptions to that rule. Think about it. Why would a total stranger send an attachment? If the email is from a friend and an attachment is about something of mutual interest, it may be legitimate.

- Internet email can be very easy to counterfeit. If anything seems suspicious about the message, confirm with the friend that they did indeed send something. If they are security conscious as well, it shouldn't surprise them to receive such a call.

- What if the message is from the president of the company wanting to share some great news with you in the attached file? Should it be opened? Be careful. If someone is sending malicious email attachments; they will try to motivate the recipients to open them. This tactic was partly responsible for the success of the ILOVEYOU virus. If an email

---

attachment is in question, a little research should be conducted to attempt to confirm whether it is legitimate before opening.

These common sense steps combined with regularly updated antivirus software, along with making regular backups and copies will go a long way toward keeping anyone's data safe from hackers.

Remedies for Virus Attacks

Regardless of all these efforts, it is conceivable that something could happen. Should that unfortunate event occur, repair and restoration will be necessary.

Watch for some of these indicators that a virus may have made it past a computer's defenses:

- The computer is running more slowly than normal.

- There seems to be activity on the hard drive, even when the computer is apparently idle.

- Other email users may give notification that they have received a strange or unusual email that appears to have been sent by a particular user.

- Receiving emails from others complaining they have been infected with a virus from a particular user's machine.

"Do viruses have you bugged?
It's time to face the crisis."

However, these kinds of occurrences do not necessarily mean a virus has infiltrated the system. An active hard drive could be the result of a pre-scheduled utility performing a routine of some kind. A computer running more slowly than usual may have other explanations as well. A new program could be bogging the system down and slowing the process, but if these explanations do not apply, or if multiple symptoms begin to occur at one time, the best course of action is outlined below.

- Make sure anti virus software is installed and running the latest version with the virus definitions updated.

- Make sure all security patches and updates for the operating system have been downloaded and installed.

- Check to see that the latest version of the web browser in use has been installed.

- Shut down the computer's ability to access the Internet whenever a connection is not needed.

- Power down the computer completely.

- Get in touch with antivirus software vendor support center for further instructions.

Conclusion

Unfortunately, the problems associated with virus attacks are an ongoing challenge. Computers must be secured today, but they will also need to be secured again tomorrow. In fact, they will need to be secured every day if the goal is to stay in front the evolving threat.

The growing presence of viruses and increasing hacker activity make it unlikely that any computer will ever completely escape an attempted attack by a virus or hacker. However, thanks to the variety of protective measures available today, many computer users will never even know the attempt was made. The defensive actions taken by the vigilant user will repel attacks and the virus will move on seeking a softer target.

Computer users who fail to keep their systems in a solid defensive posture, however, will inevitably find themselves dealing with the inconveniences associated with a successful virus strike.

In this chapter, the threats posed by computer viruses and other destructive programs were detailed. The keys to successfully protecting your system were covered. The key steps include:

- Install a trusted antivirus program from a reputable vendor.

- Ensure regular updates of antivirus software to protect against constantly evolving viruses.

- Make sure operating system and browsers are up to date, with the latest revisions and patches installed.

- Use common sense. Be aware of the danger.

- Know what is normal for each computer and be sensitive to changes in its operation.

While viruses, worms and hackers are a threat, unfortunately they are not the only threat. In the next chapter, the world of spam will be explored and tips on understanding how it is used to intrude on safety and privacy are included.

Spam, Spam, Spam, Spam

"Looks like we have too much spam again."

Where Spam Originated

The term "spam" was popularized back in the 1970's by Monty Python. The term was used in song and verse in a series of silly skits. People everywhere were singing "spam, spam, spam, spam," over and over, and the term became synonymous with a repeating message.

According to web guru Brad Templeton, one of the world's leading experts on spam, the term, as it applied to the Internet, was coined by early Internet user groups.

> "The term spamming was applied to a few different behaviors. One was to flood the computer with too much data in order to crash it. Another was to "spam the database" by having a program create a huge number of objects, rather then creating them by hand.

> And the term was sometimes used to mean simply flooding a chat session with a bunch of text inserted by a program (commonly called a "bot" today) or just by inserting a file instead of your own real time typing output."

Templeton also asserts that the world's first true Internet spam was sent by a marketer back in 1978:

> "The DEC marketer, Gary Thuerk, identified only as "THUERK at DEC-MARLBORO" (There were no dots or dot-coms in those days, and the "at" sign was often spelled out.) decided to send a notice to everybody on the ARPANET on the west coast.
>
> In those days there was a printed directory of everybody on the Arpanet, which they used as source for the list. The message trumpeted an open house to show off new models of the Dec-20 computer, a foray into larger, almost mainframe-sized systems."

Spam is in the Eye of the Beholder

Spam, also called Un-requested Commercial E-Mail (UCE), is usually defined as unwanted or unsolicited messages, most likely advertisements. If an e-mail message is received because a request has been made for more information regarding a product or service, the message is not considered spam. However, if a request has been made to be removed from the advertiser's e-mail list and the messages are still arriving, they must be categorized as spam.

"You will never get rid of SPAM!"

Although spam is universally despised, there is no universally accepted definition for it. One person's spam is another person's useful information.

Due to this diversity in personal tastes, filtering spam has become an extremely difficult task. If a filter is too aggressive, it might prevent important messages from getting through because some messages share spam-like characteristics. If the filter is not aggressive enough, spam will continue to arrive, though usually in reduced quantities.

"The "free" distribution of unwelcome or misleading messages to thousands of people is an annoying and sometimes destructive use of the Internet's unprecedented efficiency."

--Bill Gates, 1998

Why Does Spam Exist?

The technology to stop spam has existed for decades, but it is critical for any anti-spam software to be able to recognize unsolicited spam from a legitimate spam newsletter. For example, an expert programmer or program analyst might have a database tips newsletter that is distributed to 12,000 people every week, and this is quite different from a generic "You've been approved for a new home mortgage" message.

A legitimate spam newsletter is called an opt-in spam, where the enrollee must respond to an e-mail verification message in order to be enrolled. One popular delivery tool for opt-in spam is called Topica (www.topica.com).

Even with solicited spam, messages from legitimate opt-in spam sources, messages are often trapped inside server-side spam filtering software. In one notable case, a woman sent out a horse-related newsletter to her 1,000+ opt-in subscribers. The message was quarantined in spam filters. It was only after investigation that it was determined that the spam filter had quarantined her message because it contained the word "Sweetwater." In this case, the reason for the quarantine was not immediately apparent; however, careful scrutiny of the message revealed that the message was quarantined only because the word "Sweetwater" contains the text string "twat"!

With spam, just like telemarketers, it is widely accepted that "Nobody likes it". Of course, the telemarketers located a few people who actually claimed to enjoy unsolicited sales pitches and Americans are now forced to use the opt-out method with the national "Do Not Call" list. The same thing may happen with spam.

The spammers scoured the globe searching for a single person who actually likes spam. Once one was located, they used him as a justification that they are providing an important free service. The following is an example of what a pro-spam ad might look like:

Everybody loves spam!

"Spam is my life." Joe is a typical spam lover, and spam has changed his life! Joe now corresponds with new friends in foreign lands and learns about new cultures, all while finding cheap sources of online Viagra and fake Rolex watches.

Seriously, what can be done about spam? In the real world, there are several approaches. For some people, receiving the daily mail is met with much anticipation. In spite of the fact that most of it is junk mail, they enjoy the routine of sorting through their mail regardless of its content.

Likewise, some people truly enjoy reading e-mail even if it is for products or services they do not want or need. The truth is that most people do not like 99% of the e-mail they receive on a daily basis. For them, wading through spam is a waste of time and increases their risk of becoming the victim of a scam or being infected with a computer virus. The following section presents ideas on how the war against spam can be waged.

So, assuming a person considers themselves to be one who is among the vast majority of people who detest spam, then what can be done to prevent it? Some common spam fighting techniques are presented in the following section.

Fighting Spam

Many people have experienced the difficulty of wading through a deep quagmire of e-mail messages to find the one message that really matters. Unfortunately, the volume of spam alone has caused many to miss those few important messages. This has become a serious problem for the e-mail user. So what does one do to rectify this ever-growing problem?

Spamboy

Back in the ancient Internet days of the late 1980's, many computer users fought back. One user suffered considerable indignation when he received his first unsolicited message, and since most Internet users were technically savvy back then, he decided to retaliate.

There were no Internet laws back then, and this user would respond by fighting spam with spam. He developed a tiny script he called "spamboy." He would use this script to respond to unwanted spam. The script sent the message "The seeds of greed bear bitter fruit" one million times to the person who sent him the spam. This would clog their e-mail server and make their systems administrator very angry.

This old west form of spam justice is illegal now, but the following code is what the script looked like. It has deliberately been made non-functional, since distributing the actual script would likely result in a visit from law enforcement.

```ksh
#!/bin/ksh

counter = 1

do
    counter=`expr i+1`
    if [ $counter  -lt 1000000 ]
    then
       mailx -s "The seed of greed bear bitter fruit."\
          bill.gates@mircosoft.com
    fi
done
```

Reasons to Ignore Spam

There are many reasons to ignore spam and not take any proactive actions. Something as simple as opening a spam message can trigger a response message that will alert the spammer that the recipient's e-mail address is alive-and-well.

Spam Is a Waste of Time

Most computer users report that the vast majority of their inbox is spam and out of approximately 50 e-mail messages per day, only one or two of those messages were legitimate. The problem of spam is clearly out of control. The time it takes to open a message, read enough to determine that it is not wanted and then delete it, infringes on an already tight schedule for many.

In today's world, most people have so much to accomplish in a day that wasting even 30 minutes on junk e-mail consumes the precious few moments that could otherwise be used to play with their kids, catch up on reading, or simply relax.

Don't Risk Being a Victim

Besides being a time waster, another danger of manually reviewing all e-mail messages is the risk of becoming a victim of a scam. Chapter 7, *Internet Scams*, showed that many scams arrive via e-mail. If successful, these scams can cost time, money and even lives.

Reducing the quantity of e-mail messages in a user's inbox will allow them time for a more careful analysis of a suspicious message and can improve the chances for recognizing a con in a timely manner.

Don't Risk a Virus Attack

Still another possible danger that rears its ugly head in spam e-mail is the potential for virus attacks. Chapter 12, *Virus Attacks*, details the damage that viruses can bring to a computer system. Without adequate protection, viruses arrive unchallenged and an infection could result.

Spam Best Practices

Refusing to supply an e-mail address may reduce incidents of spam, but it also greatly limits the effectiveness of having e-mail. Some e-mail addresses are more likely to be targeted by spammers, especially those handled by large national service providers.

Though spam may never be completely eliminated, there are several ways to reduce the quantity.

- **Do not reply.** - Replying to a spam e-mail message verifies for the sender of the spam that the e-mail address is valid. The end result of that validation is more spam. Sometimes a link is included in the message that reads, "Click to be removed from the mailing list". Clicking on the link will also confirm that the target address is valid and will again result in more spam. The best response to spam is to simply delete the message.

- **Do not provide e-mail addresses to companies.** - When registering new purchases or submitting warranty information, do not supply an e-mail address. Provide a phone number and street address so that should a problem or recall arise, contact can be made via postal mail.

- **Hide addresses from computers.** - When posting to Internet forums, such as Usenets or Weblogs, make use of an alternate email address or make sure the primary address is not machine readable. Computer programs designed to scan web pages for e-mail addresses will not recognize an address written in a non-traditional format. For example, rather than providing the address webstalkers@gmail.com, use the alternate syntax, webstalkers AT gmail DOT com. This effectively communicates the e-mail address but will not be recognized as such by another machine.

Safely Peeking at Spam

The problem with spam is the increasingly sophisticated use of seemingly legitimate message headers. If one uses a mail program with Active X enabled, just opening one of these spam messages can cripple their computer with adware, spyware and maybe a malicious program. One such malicious program might send an embarrassing e-mail from the user to everyone in their address book with the message header, "Me Nude".

Savvy e-mail readers can peek inside a suspected spam message by using the "properties" function. This can be achieved by highlighting the suspected spam message and clicking the right-mouse button. Figure 13.1 shows how the "properties" option can then be selected:

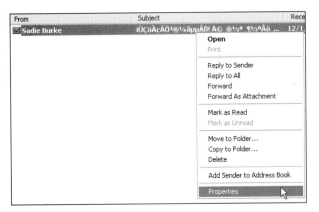

Figure 13.1 – *Peeking inside spam using "properties".*

This allows a user to peek inside the suspected spam without having to actually open it. From the properties option the "details" tab can be clicked so that the actual message header is visible. Figure 13.2 shows a sample header of a suspicious message.

Figure 13.2 – *Using the details tab to reveal the header*

The message header reveals the IP address of the sender and other important details about the message such as the web routing. Users should always be wary of unexpected messages from foreign domains.

When the "Message Source" button is clicked, the internal test of the message is visible. Figure 13.3 shows the message source.

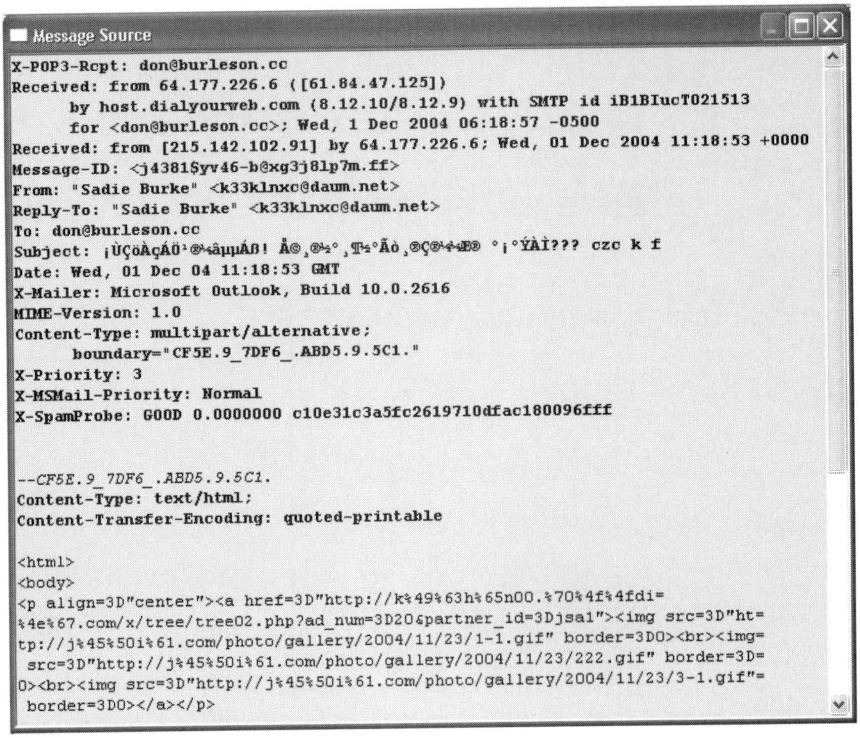

Figure 13.3 – *Message source*

The presence of HTML inside the body of the message is a normally a dead give away that the message is spam. Invocations of PHP Hypertext Protocol (PHP) or Active Server Pages (ASP) content can also be clear indicators that the message is spam. These can invoke malicious script to infect the computer.

The following section provides a closer look at tools that can be used to avoid spam.

Tools to Avoid Spam

There are several ways to reduce the quantity of spam messages received via e-mail. A good way to accomplish this reduction is to install a filter program or to create personal spam filter software. There are several types of spam filtering tools and techniques:

- **PC-side spam filters.** – These spam filters accept updated spam definitions from the web and apply the rules to incoming spam messages.

- **Server-side spam filters.** – These spam filters run off of the hosting server and stop spam before it hits the inbox. Some of the more sophisticated tools rely on user-reported spam and update the server definitions to quarantine them.

- **Approval-based spam.** – Using this technique, all messages are quarantined except those from individuals identified by the user as friends. The spam bucket should be reviewed periodically and approved e-mail addresses should be added to the list of friends.

- **Manual spam filtering.** – Tools such as Microsoft Outlook express allow the manual definition of spam filter conditions that can either quarantine or delete the messages.

The following section provides a favorite, cheap and easy manual method of spam filtering. For example, up to 50% of the spam delivered to the inbox can be eliminated in just a few minutes by quarantining messages with unusual characters, like this e-mail subject line:

```
¡ÙÇöÀçÅÖ¹®½áµµÁ̈ß!  Å©,®½°,¶½°Åò,®Ç®¼¼Æ®  °¡°ÝÀÌ
```

Let's use Microsoft Outlook Express as an example. First, the user must go to Tools → Message Rules → Mail option. Figure 13.4 shows the user screens for this operation:

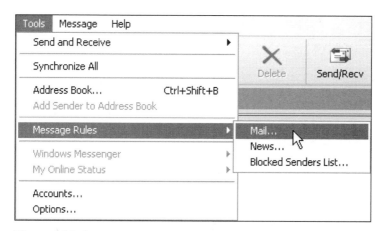

Figure 13.4 - *Outlook Express Message Options*

This lands the user in the correct location in which to create a set of generic spam filtering criteria. To be safe, everything should be moved into the "Deleted Items" folder without automatically deleting it, just in case a real message becomes trapped in the rule set.

In Figure 13.5, all of the cryptic non-English characters are listed one at a time into the filtering for the subject line. This takes a few minutes, but it will reduce overall spam by 50%.

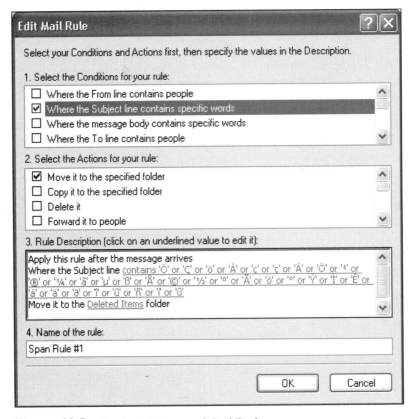

Figure 13.5 - *Outlook Express Mail Rules*

The next section will present an overview of the more common approaches, along with the advantages and disadvantages of each approach.

Using Spam Control Programs

There are programs designed to reduce the influx of spam. This section will present information on those programs that are commercially available and how they can aid in a user's efforts to reduce the amount of spam that makes it into their inbox.

Anti-spam programs are available for a wide range of prices, starting at no cost and growing up to more than $100.00. While price is a factor for many people, one should focus closely on functionality first. Saving money at the check-out counter will not be of much benefit if the program is confusing, or worse, does not work.

As might be expected, there are various techniques employed by anti-spam programs to achieve the goal of reducing spam. One method defines a list of words that are often used in spam messages and then scans the incoming e-mail for those words. If a message contains too many of the words on the list, the message will be identified as spam and then dealt with accordingly. A second method compiles a list of known spam senders and automatically deletes any message received from a target address.

Both methods have their limitations. The word list variation is particularly weak for two primary reasons. First, the word list rule is extremely easy for spammers to get around. All that is necessary to skirt the word list filter is to modify a word in any way that obscures the ability of the filter to identify it as a target word.

This is, in fact, the same method introduced earlier as a way to make an e-mail address non-machine-readable. For example, the sender of spam e-mail targeting dog owners may choose to use the representation "d0gs" when the word dog is intended. The meaning is clearly communicated, and the spam filter cannot pick up the target word because it is not present. There are thousands of variations on this theme that are used every day to defeat word list spam filters.

The second primary weakness of the word list filter method is that it is impossible to identify words that will appear exclusively in spam messages. A spam message highlighting a pornographic website may contain the word "breast." A word list spam filter configured to delete messages containing the target word would indeed deal with the incoming spam; yet, it would also delete a message regarding a local fundraising event for breast cancer research.

A spam filter that targets and rejects all e-mail from a list of known spammers also suffers from two major flaws. The first is that the list will never be complete. Spammers jump between ISPs and make hundreds of almost imperceptible changes to their e-mail addresses, effectively flooding a user's inbox with messages from the same spammer with a new address. The second way spammers thwart this type of filter is to actually break into another e-mail server and use that server to send their spam messages. If the hi-jacked server is identified by the system as a known spammer, it is possible that future legitimate e-mails from this server will not make it through.

In addition to the word list and address filters, there are other methods employed by commercially available anti-spam programs. These programs use various methods to determine what the user considers spam. One approach is to use a statistical analysis scheme known as Bayesian Statistics. The Bayesian approach is powerful because it promotes increasing accuracy based on historical data.

"Some anti-spam approaches are more confusing than others."

The user of the program identifies messages as spam and instructs the program to delete them. The program essentially learns what is spam based on this input from the user, and it automatically places subsequent messages with similar characteristics in a special folder. The user may view the contents of this special folder to ensure no legitimate e-mail has been mistakenly placed there.

Several anti-spam programs are listed below. Many of these programs use a variety of the approaches described above. Their inclusion is not an endorsement of accuracy, but merely a starting point for additional research.

- SpamBayes (spambayes.sourceforge.net)

- SpamInspector (www.giantcompany.com)

- SpamEater (www.hms.com)

- Qurb (www.qurb.com)

- Matador (www.mailfrontier.com/products_matador.html)

These are just a few of the tools at a user's disposal. Many of the anti-virus companies also have products in this category.

Using Spam Services

There are services available that offer to help reduce the influx of spam. These services are not programs installed on an individual computer. This section will review those services that can be purchased.

Web-based e-mail is very popular, in part because people can access their e-mail from any computer with an Internet connection and a web browser. This makes anti-spam programs in the previous category ineffective since they run only on a specific computer.

Fortunately, many of the web-based e-mail providers are actively addressing the spam problem. Some providers allow the user to determine the level of security. If the user chooses an aggressive strategy, they may inadvertently send some important messages into the spam or trash folder. If the mistake goes unnoticed and the messages are not removed from the spam or trash folder, they are automatically deleted within a specified number of days.

Another aggressive option is to allow only messages into the Inbox that are on the users list of contacts. The free web-based e-mail services sometimes limit the number of addresses on that contact list, but that limit is usually generous enough for most people.

Using the "no e-mail from strangers" filtering policy may sound good, especially if one is currently getting flooded by spam, but the risk of losing something important is high. Unless an e-mail address is specifically placed on the list of acceptable e-mail senders, it will be rejected. There are no exceptions to the rule with this method. While effective, it is clear there are many situations in which a legitimate e-mail message may be sent from an unfamiliar address. Unfortunately, the message will be routed to the spam folder. Overly aggressive tactics in dealing with spam can have negative consequences.

Other services offer less drastic filters and are compatible with many popular Internet e-mail sites including MailBlocks (www.mailblocks.com), Spam Arrest (www.spamarrest.com) and various others. When an e-mail is received from a sender not specified on the list of authorized addresses, an automatic reply is generated by the system, directing the sender to a special web page.

When the unauthorized sender links to the page, they will be required to enter data in response to queries provided at the website. When the sender successfully completes this task, their e-mail transaction will become authorized and their message will be placed in the Inbox. This requirement prevents bulk spam programs from successfully sending e-mail to the users of this type of service.

One of the downsides to this type of service is that it requires extra work on the part of the sender the first time they send an e-mail message. If this additional work causes the sender to decide the message is not worth the extra effort, the e-mail message will not be delivered.

An Alternative View of Spammers

While most people view bulk e-mail as spam, this is not always the case. There are many businesses, civic groups, charities, political organizations, and other groups which make use of bulk e-mail in order to communicate with their members.

Businesses in particular find the cost-benefit ratio of bulk e-mail to be very favorable, especially when generating sales leads. The cost of generating a similar number of leads through other means such as telemarketing or direct mail is many times higher.

A positive factor to consider, as the recipient of unsolicited advertising, is that it is quicker and easier to delete an e-mail than it is to wade through piles of actual junk-mail or convince persistent telemarketers that one is not interested in their product or service.

No Free Lunch

Some restaurants enter patrons in a prize drawing as an incentive for completing a survey on the quality of their experience. One person relayed their story about completing one of these surveys at an upscale restaurant.

This person later received an e-mail message with information regarding an upcoming special event at the restaurant. The message was sent to everyone who had completed the survey. Every participant in the survey was listed in the "To" field of the message header. The result was that more than 100 restaurant patrons now had access to every other e-mail address listed.

The loss of privacy was not part of the deal for those patrons who were kind enough to take the time to complete the survey in the first place. To make matters worse, the lack of response from the restaurant when the problem was brought to their attention showed a serious lack of concern for their patrons e-mail security. Despite repeated attempts to resolve the problem, it took several months of dealing with management before similar e-mails were stopped.

Learning More about Spam

It may help to know more about the way e-mail works in order to understand how spammers use it effectively. Figure 13.6 below is a representation of a popular e-mail scam. This category of fraudulent spam is known as a phish-scam. It is designed to convince the recipient that they have been contacted by a major financial institution with important business to conduct.

The sender of the message does not know anything about the recipient's actual financial status or where they have accounts. The scammer is playing a game based on percentages. They know from experience that a certain number of people will accept the message as legitimate and respond to the message accordingly. This will always have negative results for the unsuspecting victim, since the goal is to extract actual financial information from the target recipient.

Once information is released, such as bank account numbers or credit card information, the scammers will empty accounts or run up charges to the

---

limit. Users must be vigilant. This sort of information should never be exchanged via e-mail.

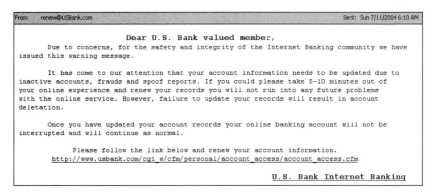

From: renew@USBank.com	Sent: Sun 7/11/2004 6:10 AM

Dear U.S. Bank valued member,
          Due to concerns, for the safety and integrity of the Internet Banking community we have
issued this warning message.

          It has come to our attention that your account information needs to be updated due to
inactive accounts, frauds and spoof reports. If you could please take 5-10 minutes out of
your online experience and renew your records you will not run into any future problems
with the online service. However, failure to update your records will result in account
deletion.

          Once you have updated your account records your online banking account will not be
interrupted and will continue as normal.

          Please follow the link below and renew your account information.
          http://www.usbank.com/cgi_w/cfm/personal/account_access/account_access.cfm

                                                                    U.S. Bank Internet Banking

Figure 13.6 - *Phishing scams will appear to come from a legitimate company.*

There is a program readily available over the Internet known as Sam Spade (www.samspade.org). This program is designed to help the user track e-mails received back through the route by which it came. By making use of information contained within an e-mail header as shown in Figure 13.7 below, the originating IP address can be identified. Of course, scammers are criminals, and they go to great lengths to cover their tracks. An e-mail's header contains all the information necessary to track the message, but reading a header can be a daunting task.

Internet headers:	X-Message-Info: 6s5XyD95QpUyhsXbTnL4z65u3oTweYU6
	Received: from unixhost5.thewebhostingpeople.com ([216.109.76.16]) by mc6-f13.hotmail.com with Microsoft SMTPSVC(5.0.2195.6713);
	Sun, 11 Jul 2004 05:38:39 -0700
	Received: (from root@localhost)
	by unixhost5.thewebhostingpeople.com (8.11.6/8.11.2) id
	i6BD9b712106;
	Sun, 11 Jul 2004 09:09:37 -0400

Figure 13.7 - *Sample e-mail header.*

Fortunately, Sam Spade can be of assistance here as well. Running the "Parse email headers" utility contained within the program allows the user to perform an analysis of an e-mail's header information and yields a report containing message routing details in a user friendly format.

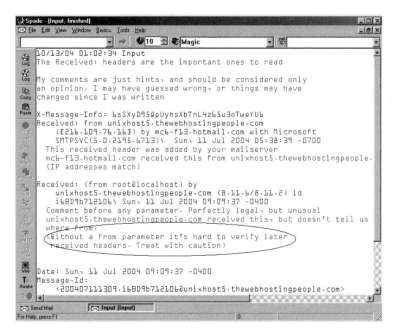

Figure 13.8 - *Results of parsing the headers in the spam message shown earlier.*

Notice the circled section in Figure 13.8. This warning indicates there is missing information. It does not automatically indicate a fraudulent source, but it should raise some warning flags. Users should proceed with caution at this point. Prior to linking to any of the sites indicated in the questionable message, it is advisable to make use of another helpful Sam Spade function. Rather than clicking on any link provided, the recipient should perform a right-click on the suspect link and select the "View Source" option. Doing so will display a line of text indicating the actual target of the link.

```
http://211.233.5.177/requestCmdId/USBank/InternetBanking/DisplayLogi
nPage/RequestRouter/
```

The "Decode URL" function can then be used to help identify the true source of this address. Figure 13.9 below shows the results of this function for both the link and its associated location. It is easy to see that the web page the user would be directed to is not part of the bank's website. In fact, it is not even registered with DNS.

Figure 13.9 - *DNS lookup can be used to validate and address.*

The main lesson to take from this example is that caution is advised when dealing with links associated with unsolicited e-mail. Researching before acting can save time and money in the end. Whether simply making a phone call to the customer service department of the company in question to verify their e-mail message, or using some of the sophisticated tools that have been presented, be sure to investigate.

A Case Study in Spam

Several weeks after taking a family vacation in San Diego, one person received the message shown in Figure 13.10 below:

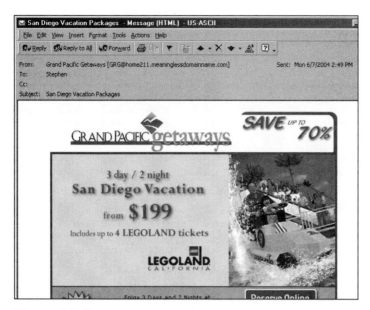

Figure 13.10 - *Spam sometimes contains offers that are too good to be true.*

The recipient of this message remembered that he had supplied his secondary e-mail address when checking into a hotel while on vacation. Whether his e-mail address was sold to a marketing company or the hotel system was hacked and his address stolen really makes no difference. He is now the target of a marketing campaign.

Is the offer legitimate? Consider carefully who the message is from; GRG@home211.meaninglessdomainname.com. This unusual address should make the recipient suspicious. If the message had been received from sdchamber.org, the recipient might have more confidence since this is the address for the San Diego Chamber of Commerce. Savvy users always research and investigate.

Conclusion

Spam e-mail is a part of life for Internet users, and can be the source of great frustration if a solution is not found and implemented. This chapter has presented ways to deal with the issue of spam. Some of the salient points are as follows:

- Suspected spam should be deleted.

- Suspected spam should never receive a reply.

- Internet Best Practices should be implemented.

- Spam filtering programs and services should be used to authenticate e-mail.

While there have been legislative efforts made to regulate the out of control world of spam, it is only legitimate bulk e-mailers that abide by new rules as they are passed. Many spammers operate below the radar screen and are already engaging in criminal practice. These types of spammers are not likely to adhere to additional regulations.

The more likely solution to the e-mail problem will come through the education of consumers. As the population becomes increasingly Internet savvy and learns to detect and avoid fraud and scams, the amount of money to be made by engaging in these activities will decrease. As profits fall, so will motivation to engage in the practice, and spammers may begin to consider other ways to spend their time.

Book Conclusion

The saying goes "knowledge is power." By publication of this book the hope was to arm the reader with knowledge of the perils that may exist while using the Internet as well as tools to use to avoid becoming a victim.

The Internet offers seemingly innumerable opportunities for learning, communication, and commerce. It is a shame that some unscrupulous individuals have taken a resource developed to improve communication and share information and turned it into an outlet for fraud, coercion, and corruption. By remaining cautious, using some of the tips and tricks provided in this book, and using common sense, the Internet user can safely navigate the Internet for its intended purpose and have an enjoyable experience. Happy surfing!

Index

About Stephen Andert

Stephen Andert has been a database administrator for many years and has worked with Oracle for 5 years. He has been working with various different relational databases for over 12 years. He has been a technical reviewer for several Oracle books from O'Reilly & Associates, authored an article on SQL*Loader tuning and has presented at local and international Oracle user group events.

Stephen is an Oracle8 and Oracle8i Oracle Certified Professional and is currently serving on the Board of AZORA, the Arizona Oracle User Group (www.azora.org).

About Don Burleson

Don Burleson is one of the world's top Oracle Database experts with more than 20 years of full-time DBA experience. He specializes in creating database architectures for very large online databases and he has worked with some of the world's most powerful and complex systems.

A former Adjunct Professor, Don Burleson has written 32 books, published more than 100 articles in National Magazines, and serves as Editor-in-Chief of Oracle Internals and Senior Consulting Editor for DBAZine and Series Editor for Rampant TechPress. Don is a popular lecturer and teacher and is a frequent speaker at OracleWorld and other international database conferences.

As a leading corporate database consultant, Don has worked with numerous Fortune 500 corporations creating robust database architectures for mission-critical systems. Don is also a noted expert on eCommerce systems, and has been instrumental in the development of numerous Web-based systems that support thousands of concurrent users.

In addition to his services as a consultant, Don also is active in charitable programs to aid visually impaired individuals. Don pioneered a technique for delivering tiny pigmy horses as guide animals for the blind and manages a non-profit corporation called the Guide Horse Foundation dedicated to providing Guide horses to blind people free-of-charge. The Web Site for The Guide Horse Foundation is www.guidehorse.org.

About Mike Reed

When he first started drawing, Mike Reed drew just to amuse himself. It wasn't long, though, before he knew he wanted to be an artist. Today he does illustrations for children's books, magazines, catalogs, and ads.

He also teaches illustration at the College of Visual Art in St. Paul, Minnesota. Mike Reed says, "Making pictures is like acting — you can paint yourself into the action." He often paints on the computer, but he also draws in pen and ink and paints in acrylics. He feels that learning to draw well is the key to being a successful artist.

Mike is regarded as one of the nation's premier illustrators and is the creator of the popular "Flame Warriors" illustrations at **www.flamewarriors.com**, a website devoted to Internet insults. "To enter his Flame Warriors site is sort of like entering a hellish Sesame Street populated by Oscar the Grouch and 83 of his relatives." – Los Angeles Times. (http://redwing.hutman.net/%7Emreed/warriorshtm/lat.htm)

Mike Reed has always enjoyed reading. As a young child, he liked the Dr. Seuss books. Later, he started reading biographies and war stories. One reason why he feels lucky to be an illustrator is because he can listen to books on tape while he works. Mike is available to provide custom illustrations for all manner of publications at reasonable prices. Mike can be reached at **www.mikereedillustration.com**.

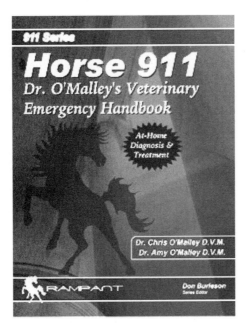

Horse 911

Dr. O'Malley's Veterinary Emergency Handbook

Dr. Amy O'Malley D.V.M.
Dr. Christian O'Malley D.V.M.

ISBN: 0-9759135-3-0
Retail Price $27.95 / £19.95

There is no worse feeling in the world than standing over your dead horse and being told that you could have saved its life if you had you only known what to do. In case after case, panicked horse owners fail to give their beloved friends the lifesaving treatment that they need to survive until the vet arrives.

Written by practicing Emergency Veterinarians with extensive experience, Drs. Amy and Chris O'Malley share their secrets for emergency at-home treatment. Written in plain English and packed with real-world examples, the Drs. O'Malley show you how to confidently provide life-saving first aid to any acutely-ill horse. You will also learn about those indispensable items that you need to keep inside your equine first-aid kit.

Join the ranks of competent horse owners and learn how to diagnose illness and perform life-saving medical procedures. When every minute counts, count-on this indispensable veterinary guide to save your horse's life.

http://www.rampant-books.com